THE
EVERYTHING®
THAI
COOKBOOK

From Pad Thai to Lemongrass Chicken Skewers—
300 tasty, tempting Thai dishes you can make at home

Jennifer Malott Kotylo

Adams Media Corporation
Avon, Massachusetts

EDITORIAL
Publishing Director: Gary M. Krebs
Managing Editor: Kate McBride
Copy Chief: Laura MacLaughlin
Acquisitions Editor: Bethany Brown
Development Editor: Michael Paydos
Production Editor: Khrysti Nazzaro

PRODUCTION
Production Director: Susan Beale
Production Manager: Michelle Roy Kelly
Series Designer: Daria Perreault, Colleen Cunningham
Cover Design: Paul Beatrice, Frank Rivera
Layout and Graphics: Colleen Cunningham,
Rachael Eiben, Michelle Roy Kelly, Daria Perreault

An Everything® Series Book.
Everything® and everything.com® are registered trademarks of F+W Media, Inc.

Published by Adams Media, a division of F+W Media, Inc.
57 Littlefield Street, Avon, MA 02322 U.S.A.
www.adamsmedia.com
ISBN 13: 978-1-58062-733-7
ISBN 10: 1-58062-733-1
Printed in the United States of America.

10 9

Library of Congress Cataloging-in-Publication Data
Kotylo, Jennifer Malott.
The everything Thai cookbook / Jennifer Malott Kotylo.
p.   cm. -- (An Everything series book)
ISBN 1-58062-733-1
1. Cookery, Thai. I. Title. II. Everything series.
TX724.5.T5 K68 2002
641.59593–dc21

2002009983

Many of the designations used by manufacturers and sellers to distinguish their products are claimed as trademarks. Where those designations appear in this book and Adams Media was aware of a trademark claim, the designations have been printed in initial capital letters.

This publication is designed to provide accurate and authoritative information with regard to the subject matter covered. It is sold with the understanding that the publisher is not engaged in rendering legal, accounting, or other professional advice. If legal advice or other expert assistance is required, the services of a competent professional person should be sought.

—From a *Declaration of Principles* jointly adopted by a Committee of the
American Bar Association and a Committee of Publishers and Associations

Illustrations by Barry Littmann.
This book is available at quantity discounts for bulk purchases.
For information, call 1-800-289-0963.

Visit the entire Everything® series at everything.com

Contents

INTRODUCTION V

CHAPTER 1 *Thai Curry Pastes, Marinades, and Other Concoctions* 1

CHAPTER 2 *Dipping Sauces, Salsas, and Vinaigrettes* 21

CHAPTER 3 *Appetizers* 31

CHAPTER 4 *Soups* 55

CHAPTER 5 *Salads* 67

CHAPTER 6 *Meat Dishes* 81

CHAPTER 7 *Chicken Dishes* 101

CHAPTER 8 *Fish and Seafood Dishes* 117

CHAPTER 9 *Vegetable Dishes* 133

CHAPTER 10 *Noodle Dishes* 149

CHAPTER 11 *Rice Dishes* 165

CHAPTER 12 *Desserts* 183

CHAPTER 13 *Drinks and Teas* 203

CHAPTER 14 *Thai-Inspired Cooking* 211

CHAPTER 15 *Regional Cuisines* 235

APPENDIX A *Glossary: Thai Flavors and Ingredients* 275

APPENDIX B *Thai Meals* 278

APPENDIX C *Thailand Resources* 280

INDEX 282

Introduction

THAILAND'S ROOTS can be traced back to the T'ai tribesmen who lived under the shadow of the Chinese in what are now the Chinese provinces of Yunnan and Sichuan, which lie along important east-west trading routes. The first true Thai kingdom was established in fourteenth century when the T'ai tribesmen created the Kingdom of Sukhothai, or "The Dawn of Happiness." During this era, the Thai adopted their first alphabet and the tenets of Buddhism.

According to depictions on the great Cambodian temple, Angor Wat, the Khmers, who have always been known as great warriors, used the Thai as mercenaries. They called the Thai Syams, meaning "golden skin color." It is believed that the Kingdom of Siam, as Thailand was known until 1939, derived its name from this word.

The thriving seaport city of Ayutthaya became the capital of Siam in 1350 and a monarchy was established. Portugal set up the first embassy there in 1511. By 1662, Holland, Denmark, England, and France all had embassies in the city.

The French began amassing troops in Siam beginning in 1675, intent on colonizing the area. But in 1688, the Siamese forcibly removed the farang (slang for "French" at the time, the word now means "foreigner") from the country and sealed its borders for 150 years. Strikingly, Thailand is the only Asian country never to have been colonized by a European power, although it has been occupied by the Khmer, the Burmese, and the Japanese.

During his reign from 1824 to 1851, King P'ra Nang Klao began developing trade with China and reopening the borders of the kingdom. The 1930s saw a wave of democracy surge over the country, and in 1932 a constitutional monarchy was formed. Soon after, the country was officially renamed Thailand, meaning "Land of the Free." Today, 75 percent of the population are ethnic Thais, roughly 11 percent are Chinese, and 3.5 percent are Malays. The rest is a combination of

Vietnamese, Khmer, and various others. There are only a very small number of non-Asian permanent immigrants.

Geography

The landmass of Thailand is approximately 197,400 square miles (a bit larger than the state of California) and is shaped like the head of an elephant. The "trunk" of the elephant extends southward down the Malay Peninsula to Singapore and is sandwiched between the Indian Ocean and the Gulf of Thailand. The "head" is bordered by Burma and Laos to the north, Cambodia and Laos to the east, Burma to the west, and the Gulf of Thailand to the south.

Thailand is mountainous in its northernmost and southernmost regions, with the center of the country forming a delta that drains into the Gulf of Thailand. Thailand has over 1,600 miles of coastline and is rich with internal waterways, ponds, lakes, and rice paddies.

Weather

Thailand has a monsoon climate. The peninsula has two seasons: wet from November through July, and dry from August through October. The mainland experiences three seasons: wet from May through November, dry and cool from November through February, and dry and hot from March through April. Yet, these definitions are deceiving. From a Western perspective, Thailand is hot and humid all year round; it just varies in degrees. The only real escape from the heat is heading to the mountains.

Agriculture

Thailand's fertile delta region, in combination with its hot and humid climate, makes for very good growing conditions, especially for rice. Archeologists believe that what is now central Thailand was the site of the first true agriculture on the planet and that rice has been cultivated there since between 4000 and 3500 B.C. Agricultural products account for

66 percent of Thailand's exports, and Thailand produces 36 percent of the world's rice. Other important products include coconut, tapioca, rubber, sugar, pineapple, jute, soybeans, and palm oil. Sixty-five percent of the Thai labor force is involved in agriculture.

Food Culture

Harmony is the name of the game when it comes to Thai cooking. The balance of sweet, salty, sour, bitter, and hot flavors is essential, not only within most dishes, but also within the context of the overall Thai meal. The key flavoring agents found in a Thai kitchen include coconut, lime, chili, garlic, ginger, cilantro, and dried fish (to make fish sauce). These ingredients are as basic as salt and pepper are to a Western kitchen. All of these foodstuffs are indigenous to the Asian continent with one notable exception: chilies, which the Portuguese introduced to Asia in the sixteenth century after "discovering" them in the New World. This is perhaps one of the most profound influences on Thai cuisine, as modern Thai cooking is almost impossible to imagine without the heat of chilies. However, the Portuguese are not the only people to have significantly influenced Thai cuisine as we know it today. The Chinese introduced the concept of stir-frying, the Indians brought curry, and the Indonesians introduced numerous spices.

Thai cuisine reflects the country's ample waterborne resources. Both saltwater and freshwater fish are eaten in abundance. Fish sauce is as common as ketchup and is used as a condiment, a salt substitute, and a general flavoring agent. Shrimp paste is used as we use anchovy paste, and dried fish are eaten as snacks.

The cuisine also reflects Thailand's tropical climate with an almost endless supply of exotic fruits that are eaten in salads, savory dishes, desserts, and by themselves. But by far the most important foodstuff in Thailand is rice. It is farmed everywhere and comes in endless varieties suitable for every growing condition from mountaintops to floodplains. It is Thailand's number one export.

Rice is so important in Thai culture that the word for rice is the same as the word for food. It is eaten with every meal and made into endless forms, from gruel to beverages to puffed cakes and desserts. Rice is believed to have a soul, called Mae Posop, or "The Rice Mother." She is born from rice, becomes pregnant when the rice flowers, and gives birth to rice. Rice farmers pay homage to Mae Posop, offering her food and shelter throughout the year.

Rice is a type of grass, the grain of which can only be extracted by milling or pounding. Thai people take great pride in the quality of their rice, and the whiter and more perfumed the better. For this reason, Jasmine rice is the long-grained variety preferred above all others.

Meat, although readily consumed, is not the centerpiece of a Thai meal, but instead is looked upon as a special treat. Theravada Buddhism, which forbids the killing of animals but not the eating of meat, is practiced by 95 percent of the population of Thailand. To make meat more palatable to the Buddhist psyche, meat is almost always shredded or cut into very small pieces. Rarely will you find a steak or chop served.

Dinner in Thailand is not served in courses, but rather soups, starters, rice, noodles, side dishes, and main courses are all served together to allow the cook to enjoy his or her guests. Only dessert is served separately. Condiments such as dried chilies, chili paste, chopped peanuts, fish sauce, and soy sauce are usual additions to the Thai table, just as salt and pepper are in the West. Fresh fruits are the typical end to a Thai meal. Desserts as we know them are usually served only at the end of a fancy banquet.

Heavy in fish, vegetables, fruits, and rice, and low in meats and dairy, Thai cuisine is just what the doctor ordered. These foods are rich in carotinoids, flavonoids, and antioxidative vitamins, all known to reduce cancer. In fact, the Thai have the lowest incidence of digestive tract cancer of all people.

Some Cooking Basics

The following are some guidelines, which should make your cooking experience more satisfying no matter what your level of expertise. They are not all Thai-food specific, but are all important for the recipes in this book.

- Read the recipe in its entirety before you begin—twice is even better.
- Make sure you have all of the ingredients, pans, and utensils, have enough time, and understand the methodology.
- Always use seasonal ingredients—out of season produce is often tasteless and has an off texture. Inferior ingredients lead to inferior dishes. If the ingredients you are looking for are substandard, either choose a substitute ingredient or a substitute recipe.
- Be prepared. Have your ingredients prepped before you begin cooking—veggies diced, sliced, etc., dry and wet ingredients properly measured, etc.
- Use homemade stocks, curries, and sauces when at all possible: They will give you the greatest depth of flavor. But if time is of the essence, by all means use some prepared products that are on the market. Some of them are quite good.
- When measuring dry ingredients, level them off with the straight edge of a knife.
- Use standard measuring spoons, cups, etc.
- Wash all vegetables and fruits thoroughly and pat or spin dry.
- Take meat out of the refrigerator about fifteen minutes before you are going to cook it, allowing it to come to room temperature. It will cook faster and more evenly.
- Use freshly ground pepper, if you can. Pepper begins to lose its flavor and pungency as soon as it is ground.

Basic Cooking Methods

The following are some of the more common cooking methods used, not only in Thai cooking, but throughout the world. A brief understanding of these methods will help you with all of your cooking.

Stir-Frying and Sautéing

Stir-frying and sautéing are very similar cooking processes that involve cooking in an open pan over high temperatures and with a minimal amount of cooking oil. Sautéing is usually done in either a slope-sided gourmet pan (or skillet) or a straight-sided sauté pan. Stir-frying is usually done in a wok.

The best meats for either method are boneless chicken; tender cuts of beef, pork, or lamb; fillets of fish; and shellfish. For stir-fries, the meat should be cut into thin, bite-sized pieces to allow for quick and even cooking. Thicker pieces can be browned in a sauté pan and then finished cooking in the oven at a low heat. Vegetables should also be thinly sliced or cut into bite-sized pieces.

Cooking fats should be relatively free of flavor and have a high smoking point. The best are canola oil and peanut oil. (If you insist on using some butter for flavor, use equal parts of oil and butter.) The oil must be hot, but not smoking before you begin to cook. To check, you can sprinkle a drop or two of water into the pan: It should spatter. Please be careful! The spatters can burn! Shaking the pan for sautéing or quickly tossing the ingredients in stir-frying prevents the food from sticking as it sears.

Grilling and Broiling

Grilling and broiling are methods by which food is cooked by exposing it to direct (usually intense) heat over hot coals or some other heat source. This method is typically fast; the direct heat chars the surface of the food, giving it great flavor. The fuel used in a grill can also impart a nuance of flavor. Adding aromatic wood chips such as mesquite or applewood or certain herbs such as lemongrass or fennel will provide additional flavor tones. (This is not an option when using a broiler.)

The grill itself may be traditional, using some type of charcoal, gas, or in some instances electric. The best grills will allow for somewhat controllable heat. To prepare your grill for cooking, heat it until very hot, and then use a long-handled brush to scrape away any residue. Just before placing food on the grill, rub a wad of paper towels dipped in oil onto the grate. This will significantly reduce sticking.

Almost all food can be grilled: tender cuts of meat, poultry, game birds, seafood, fish, or vegetables. The food will grill more evenly if it is allowed to come to room temperature just before cooking. Seasoning, especially with salt, should be done just prior to cooking, as salt tends to draw out moisture, rendering your final product less juicy. In addition, foods that are naturally low in fat should be brushed with oil or butter or basted with a sauce to keep them from drying out. Marinades are a great way to add additional flavor to grilled foods.

To test when your grilled meat is done, it is best to use an instant-read thermometer. Alternatively, you can insert the point of a knife to visually see if your food is done. Always remember that your food continues to cook even after you remove it from the grill. In addition, meats will reabsorb some of their juices after they are done cooking. Make sure to allow your meats to rest for five to ten minutes before serving.

Cooking in Water

Simmering and poaching are both techniques that involve cooking food in liquid. With both techniques, the cooking liquid is first brought to a boil and then the heat is reduced in order to obtain less active bubbling. Poaching should have slightly less bubbling action than simmering, but it's a tough call when something is simmering versus poaching. Some recipes call for a covered cooking vessel, others for an open one. As something simmers or poaches, it is important to skim the surface every once in a while to remove the residue that accumulates. Fish, rice, and poultry are all good candidates for poaching and simmering.

Only a few foods are actually boiled—noodles and potatoes being the most obvious. Boiling water is also used to blanch or parboil fruits and vegetables before they are exposed to another cooking method or if you want to keep them tender-crisp. Blanching involves placing the ingredients in boiling water briefly and then plunging them into cold water to help retain color and flavor or to help remove their skins. Ingredients that are parboiled actually stay in the boiling water a bit longer, in order to slightly soften them.

Another cooking process that involves water is steaming. With this method, the ingredients are not in the water, but rather above it on a rack. The pot is always covered. Steaming is a very gentle cooking method and it is usually the most nutritious. Steamed ingredients don't lose much of their nutrients, texture, or individual flavor. Vegetables and sticky rice are perfect candidates for steaming.

Roasting

Roasting is another core cooking method used around the world. It is a very simple method performed in an oven, usually with high heat. (You can also use indirect heat from a grill and obtain similar results.) Essentially anything can be roasted: meats, fishes, vegetables, or fruits.

Roasting meat involves seasoning it in some fashion, sometimes searing it before you place it in the oven and sometimes basting it while it cooks—depending on the recipe—and always letting it rest. Resting allows the meat to reabsorb some of its juices, making your roast more juicy and easier to carve. To rest your roast, you simply remove it from the oven, cover it with foil, and let it sit.

A very handy gadget to have when roasting is an ovenproof meat thermometer. This will let you know when your roast is done to your liking, without cutting into it. For an accurate reading, you must insert the tip of the thermometer into the deepest part of the meat without touching bone, fat, or the bottom of the pan. Roasting charts usually come with the thermometers.

What You'll Need

Knife Types and Their Uses

PARING KNIFE—a short-bladed knife (usually 2 to 4 inches) used to trim fruits and vegetables

CHEF'S KNIFE—a medium-bladed knife used for chopping, slicing, and mincing

SLICING KNIFE—a long-bladed knife, either smooth-edged or serrated used for slicing meats or breads

Other useful knives include: boning, utility, cleaver, and fillet.

Specialty Utensils

Thai cooking really doesn't require a kitchen-full of fancy gadgets: Most often you will use standard mixing bowls and measuring cups, pots and pans, wooden and slotted spoons, and knives. But there are a few items that will make your Thai cooking easier and more enjoyable. So if you are in the mood to splurge, here's the wish list:

WOK—a high-sided, sloping, small-bottomed pan—the quintessential Asian utensil

RICE COOKER—an electric gizmo that takes the guessing out of rice

FOOD PROCESSOR—the workhorse of the kitchen when it comes to mixing, chopping, puréeing, and shredding

BLENDER—great for making sauces and purées

CHINOIS—a sieve perfect for straining stocks, sauces, and purées

HAND BLENDER—great for making sauces and purées right in the pot

COLANDER—perfect for straining noodles

MORTAR and PESTLE—a stone bowl and club used to crush spices and herbs

MANDOLINE—an extremely sharp utensil used for precise paper-thin cutting

Using a Blender with Hot Ingredients
Hot (as in temperature, not spiciness) ingredients in a blender can expand causing its lid to blow off. Instead of the lid, use a kitchen towel as a cover.

Basic Food Substitutions

There are three very common ingredients in Thai cooking that can be rather difficult to find in the United States. Luckily they have very inexpensive and common substitutions. In this book I have always used brown sugar in place of palm sugar, ginger in place of galangal, and vegetable oil in place of peanut oil. Substitutions for some common Thai ingredients are found in the following chart.

THAI INGREDIENT	SUBSTITUTION
Fish sauce	Soy sauce
Cilantro	Parsley
Kaffir lime leaves	Lime peel
Lemongrass	Lemon peel
Rice vinegar	Dry sherry or white vinegar
Long beans	Green beans
Thai eggplant	Green peas
Shallots	Small onions
Homemade curry paste	Store-bought curry paste

CHAPTER 1

Thai Curry Pastes, Marinades, and Other Concoctions

Green Curry Paste—1	2
Green Curry Paste—2	3
Red Curry Paste—1	4
Red Curry Paste—2	5
Southern (or Massaman) Curry Paste	6
Northern (or Jungle) Curry Paste	7
Chili Tamarind Paste	8
Yellow Bean Sauce	9
Minty Tamarind Paste	9
Black Bean Paste	10
Thai Marinade—1	11
Thai Marinade—2	11
Thai Marinade—3	12
Asian Marinade—1	12
Asian Marinade—2	13
Tamarind Marinade	13
Coconut Marinade	14
Malaysian Marinade	14
Thai Vinegar Marinade	15
Lemongrass Marinade	16
Shredded Fresh Coconut	17
Lemon Chili Vinegar	17
Chili Vinegar	18
Tamarind Concentrate	18
Thai Grilling Rub	19

Green Curry Paste—1

10 green serrano chilies
3 shallots, coarsely chopped
5 cloves garlic
1 (1½-inch) piece gingerroot, peeled and chopped
1 stalk lemongrass, tough outer leaves removed, inner tender portion chopped
2 teaspoons grated lime zest
½ teaspoon shrimp paste

2 teaspoons ground coriander
2 teaspoons ground nutmeg
1 teaspoon ground cumin
1 teaspoon black pepper
½ teaspoon ground cloves
1 teaspoon salt
½ cup chopped cilantro
¼ cup vegetable oil

Place the first 6 ingredients in a food processor and process until well mixed. Add the remaining ingredients, except the vegetable oil, and process until smooth. Slowly add the oil until a thick paste is formed. May be refrigerated up to 4 weeks.

Curry Paste

Curry pastes are the foundation of most Thai preparations and are essentially concentrated flavoring agents meant to add complexity and depth. They are usually relatively moist concoctions of chili peppers, lime, and various herbs. Typically, curry pastes are mixed with either broth or coconut milk to create a sauce or cooking liquid.

Thai curries are famous throughout the world. But the Western term curry powder isn't indicative of a spice at all. Instead, it's a varying mixture of ingredients such as cumin, turmeric, garlic, paprika, ginger, clove, coriander, etc. If you find a store-bought variety that you like, stick with it. Each brand can taste completely different.

Green Curry Paste—2

3 tablespoons coriander seeds,
    toasted
2 teaspoons cumin seeds,
    toasted
2–4 green jalapeño chilies,
    seeded and chopped
2 green bell peppers, seeded
    and chopped
1 medium onion, chopped
3 cloves garlic, chopped
1 teaspoon shrimp paste

4 tablespoons chopped cilantro
2 teaspoons chopped
    lemongrass
1 (1-inch) piece ginger,
    peeled and chopped
4 tablespoons Tamarind
    Concentrate (see recipe
    on page 18)
3 teaspoons water
2 tablespoons vegetable oil
1 teaspoon salt

> **Yields approx. 1 cup**
>
> Green pastes tend to be a bit more pungent than their red cousins simply because chilies sweeten somewhat as they ripen and become red.

1. Place all the ingredients in a food processor and blend until smooth. Transfer to a small saucepan and bring to a simmer over medium-low heat. Reduce heat to low and cook, stirring frequently, for 5 minutes.
2. Stir in 1 cup of water and bring the mixture to a boil. Reduce heat, cover, and simmer for 30 minutes.

🌶 Storing Pastes

Making homemade curry pastes can be a bit time-consuming. Luckily, they store very well. They can be refrigerated in an airtight container for a month or frozen for up to a year. To freeze, place the paste in an ice cube tray. After they are frozen, remove the cubes from the tray and store them in freezer bags.

Red Curry Paste—1

3 tablespoons coriander seeds, toasted

2 teaspoons cumin seeds, toasted

6–8 red serrano chilies, seeded and chopped

1 medium onion, chopped

2 garlic cloves, chopped

1 stalk lemongrass, outer leaves removed and discarded, inner core finely chopped

1 (½-inch) piece ginger, finely chopped

3 kaffir lime leaves or the peel of 1 lime, chopped

2 teaspoons paprika

4 tablespoons water

2 tablespoons Tamarind Concentrate (see recipe on page 18)

3 tablespoons vegetable oil

1 teaspoon salt

1. Place all the ingredients in a food processor and blend until very smooth.
2. Transfer to a small saucepan and bring to a simmer over medium-low heat. Reduce heat to low and cook, stirring frequently, for 5 minutes.
3. Stir in 1 cup of water and bring the mixture to a boil. Reduce heat, cover, and simmer 30 minutes.

Red Curry Paste—2

3 large dried red California chilies, seeded and chopped

5 dried Thai bird or similar chilies, seeded and chopped

2 stalks lemongrass, tough outer leaves removed and discarded, inner core finely minced

1 (2-inch) piece ginger, peeled and finely minced

2 cloves garlic, minced

1 small onion, chopped

2 tablespoons ground turmeric

> **Yields approx. 1 cup**
>
> Curry pastes that feature dried chilies tend to have a smoky, complex nuance, whereas those made mostly from fresh chilies have a cleaner, crisper taste.

1. Place the chilies in a bowl and cover them with hot water. Let stand for at least 30 minutes. Drain the chilies, reserving 1 cup of the soaking liquid.
2. Place all the ingredients and 2–3 tablespoons of the soaking liquid in a food processor. Process to form a thick, smooth paste. Add additional liquid if necessary.

Red Curry Paste Applications

While green curry paste is usually used for specific purposes, red curry paste is often treated as a "general purpose" paste that can be added to almost any Thai recipe. Whenever you see a recipe call for "common" or "plain" curry paste, it is almost always referring to the red. And if not, you'll be safe using it!

Southern (or Massaman) Curry Paste

6–8 large dried red chilies (often called California chilies), soaked in hot water for 5 minutes and drained

2 tablespoons coriander seeds, toasted

2 teaspoons cumin seeds, toasted

½ teaspoon cardamom seeds, toasted

2 whole cloves

¼ teaspoon whole black peppercorns

¼ teaspoon ground cinnamon

1 teaspoon shrimp paste (optional)

1 stalk lemongrass, tough outer leaves removed and discarded, inner core finely chopped

1 (1-inch) piece ginger, peeled and minced

1 teaspoon salt

1 teaspoon lime peel

2 teaspoons brown sugar

2 tablespoons vegetable oil

3 tablespoons Tamarind Concentrate (see recipe on page 18)

3 tablespoons water

1. Place all ingredients in a food processor and blend until smooth.
2. Transfer to a small saucepan and bring to a simmer over medium-low heat. Reduce heat to low and cook, stirring frequently, for 5 minutes.
3. Stir in 1 cup of water and bring the mixture to a boil. Reduce heat, cover, and simmer 30 minutes.

The Chili Infusion

Chilies are not indigenous to Asia. They arrived in Thailand from South America with the Portuguese traders and missionaries. Today, the Thai people eat more chilies on the average per person than any other country in the world.

Northern (or Jungle) Curry Paste

2 tablespoons vegetable oil
12 serrano chilies, seeded
   and chopped
6–8 Thai bird chilies, seeded
   and chopped
1 tablespoon shrimp paste
1 stalk lemongrass, tough outer
   leaves removed and discarded, inner core minced

1 (3-inch) piece ginger,
   peeled and chopped
4 shallots, chopped
1 cup chopped basil
½ cup chopped mint
¼ cup chopped chives
¼ cup chopped arugula

Yields approx. 2 cups

This curry has the look of a pesto. In fact, you can use it in a similar manner, tossing a tablespoon or so to taste with hot pasta.

1. In a medium-sized sauté pan, heat the oil on medium. Add the chilies, shrimp paste, lemongrass, ginger, and shallots, and sauté until the shallots begin to turn translucent and the mixture is very fragrant.
2. Transfer the mixture to a food processor and process until smooth, adding 1 or 2 tablespoons of water to help with the grinding.
3. Add the remaining ingredients and more water if necessary and continue to process until coarsely blended.

Arugula

Arugula is a specialty green with a peppery, somewhat bitter taste. Although we Westerners associate it with Italian cuisine, it was originally cultivated in Western Asia. If you can't find it (check in the herb section), you can substitute spinach in this recipe, although with a slightly less flavorful result.

Chili Tamarind Paste

Yields approx. 3 cups

This paste is a study of contrasts. The searingly hot Thai chilies are balanced by the sweetness of the tamarind and brown sugar and the saltiness of the dried shrimp and fish sauce.

½ cup dried shrimp
1¾ cups vegetable oil, divided
⅓ cup garlic
1 cup sliced shallots
12 small Thai chilies or
* 6 serrano chilies*

3 tablespoons Tamarind
* Concentrate (see recipe*
* on page 18)*
3 tablespoons brown sugar
1 tablespoon fish sauce

1. Place the dried shrimp in a small bowl. Cover the shrimp with water, stir briefly, and drain; set aside.
2. Pour 1½ cups of the vegetable oil in a medium-sized saucepan. Bring the oil to approximately 360 degrees over medium-high heat.
3. Add the garlic and fry until golden brown. Using a slotted spoon, transfer the garlic to a bowl lined with paper towels.
4. Add the shallots to the saucepan and fry for 2 to 3 minutes; transfer the shallots to the bowl with the garlic.
5. Fry the reserved shrimp in the saucepan for 2 minutes; transfer to the bowl.
6. Fry the chilies until they become brittle, about 30 seconds; transfer them to the bowl. (Allow oil to cool to room temperature before discarding.)
7. Combine the fried ingredients, the remaining oil, and the tamarind in a food processor; process to form a smooth paste.
8. Place the paste in a small saucepan over medium heat. Add the sugar and fish sauce, and cook, stirring occasionally, for about 5 minutes.
9. Allow the paste to return to room temperature before placing in an airtight container.

Yellow Bean Sauce

2 tablespoons vegetable oil
1 medium to large onion,
    minced
2 serrano chilies, seeded and
    chopped
1 (½-inch) piece ginger, peeled
    and chopped

1 teaspoon ground coriander
4 tablespoons fermented yellow
    beans (fermented soy beans)
2 tablespoons lime juice
2 tablespoons water

> **Yields approx. 1 cup**
>
> This bean sauce is often used in Thai recipes to add depth, not only of flavor but also of texture.

1. In a medium-sized sauté pan, heat the oil over medium heat. Add the onion and chilies, and sauté until the onion becomes translucent. Stir in the ginger and coriander, and continue to cook for 30 seconds.
2. Add the beans, lime juice, and water, and simmer over low heat for 10 minutes.
3. Transfer the mixture to a blender and process until smooth.

Minty Tamarind Paste

1 bunch mint leaves
1 bunch cilantro leaves
¼ cup peanuts
½ cup Tamarind Concentrate
    (see recipe on page 18)

4–5 Thai bird peppers or
    2 serrano chilies, seeded
    and chopped

> **Yields approx. 2 cups**
>
> This is a perfect way to use a lot of those extra herbs growing in your garden—to make a curry paste bursting with the tastes of summer.

Place all the ingredients in a food processor and blend to form a paste.

Black Bean Paste

Yields approx. ½ cup

Fermented soybeans remind me of garbanzo beans. When they are cooked and ground they have a somewhat mealy texture and the fermentation process yields a slightly sharp, vinegary taste.

2 tablespoons vegetable oil
1 medium to large onion, minced
2 jalapeños, seeded and chopped
2 cloves garlic, chopped
3 green onions, trimmed and sliced

4 tablespoons canned black beans or black soy beans
1 teaspoon brown sugar
1 tablespoon fish sauce
2 teaspoons lime juice

1. In a medium-sized sauté pan, heat the oil over medium-high heat. Add the onions, jalapeños, garlic, and green onions, and sauté until the onion becomes translucent.
2. Using a slotted spoon, transfer the sautéed vegetables to a food processor or blender (set aside the oil in the sauté pan). Add the remaining ingredients and process briefly to create a not-too-smooth paste.
3. Reheat the reserved oil in the sauté pan. Transfer the paste to the pan and heat for 5 minutes, stirring constantly. If the paste seems too thick, add a bit of water.

 Marinating Safely
When you marinate foods, you should always do it in the refrigerator to reduce the possibility of bacteria growth unless otherwise directed in a recipe.

Thai Marinade—1

2 tablespoons fish sauce
¼ cup fresh lime juice
½ cup sesame oil
1 large stalk lemongrass,
    crushed

¼ teaspoon hot pepper flakes
2 tablespoons chopped peanuts
3 cloves garlic, minced
¼ cup chopped cilantro
1 tablespoon brown sugar

Combine the fish sauce and lime juice in a small bowl. Slowly whisk in the sesame oil, then stir in remaining ingredients.

Yields approx. 1 cup

This marinade contains the classic ingredients of Thai cuisine: fish sauce, lime juice, peanuts, chili peppers, and lemongrass. It works well with chicken, pork, or beef.

Thai Marinade—2

3 tablespoons fish sauce
1 tablespoon sweet soy sauce
½ cup rice wine
¼ cup peanut oil
¼ cup chopped basil leaves
¼ cup chopped mint leaves

3 cloves garlic, minced
1 tablespoon chopped
    gingerroot
1 small onion, chopped
2 tablespoons chopped
    lemongrass

Combine the fish sauce, sweet soy sauce, and the rice wine in a small bowl. Slowly whisk in the peanut oil, then stir in remaining ingredients.

Yields approx. 1½ cups

The basil and mint in this recipe are more traditional, but you can substitute almost any slightly spicy herb.
Try parsley or arugula, or, for a milder version, baby spinach works well, too.

Thai Marinade—3

Yields approx. 2 cups

This marinade is infused with the flavors of India. In addition to the lemongrass, lime juice, and fish sauce, curry paste and coconut milk add to the complexity of the flavors.

1 (12-ounce) can coconut milk
½ cup Red Curry Paste (see recipes on pages 4 and 5)
1 stalk lemongrass, roughly chopped
6 kaffir lime leaves, finely sliced
1 teaspoon fresh gingerroot, chopped
¼ cup chopped cilantro leaves
¼ cup lime juice
2 tablespoons fish sauce
1 tablespoon sweet soy sauce

1. Combine the coconut milk, curry paste, lemongrass, and kaffir leaves in a small saucepan; bring to a simmer over medium heat.
2. Reduce heat and continue to simmer for 15 minutes.
3. Remove from heat and allow to cool to room temperature.
4. Stir in all the remaining ingredients.

Asian Marinade—1

Yields approx. 1¼ cups

This recipe uses ingredients more common to other Asian countries, yet still has Thai overtones. Soy sauce, which is more characteristic of China and Japan, smooths out the bite of the fish sauce.

¼ cup fish sauce
¼ cup soy sauce (preferably low-sodium)
½ cup freshly squeezed lime juice
2 tablespoons crunchy peanut butter
1 tablespoon light brown sugar
1 tablespoon curry powder
1 teaspoon minced garlic
Crushed dried red pepper

Combine all the ingredients in a blender or food processor and blend until smooth.

Asian Marinade—2

½ cup lime juice
¼ cup soy sauce
2 tablespoons hoisin sauce
1 tablespoon honey
⅓ cup vegetable oil
2 tablespoons sesame oil
¼ teaspoon ground anise

1 teaspoon Chinese 5-spice
  powder
1 tablespoon freshly grated
  gingerroot
3 cloves garlic, minced
3 tablespoons chopped cilantro
¼ cup chopped green onion

> **Yields approx. 1¼ cups**
>
> This recipe has a definite Chinese influence, featuring soy sauce, hoisin sauce, 5-spice powder, and sesame oil.

Combine the lime juice, soy sauce, hoisin sauce, and honey, and blend well. Slowly whisk in the vegetable and sesame oils. Add the remaining ingredients and mix thoroughly.

Tamarind Marinade

1½ cups Tamarind Concentrate
  (see recipe on page 18)
4 pieces lime peel (approximately ½-inch by 2-inches)
¼ cup fresh lime juice
1 tablespoon soy sauce
¼ cup vegetable oil
1 shallot, chopped

2 garlic cloves, minced
1 tablespoon diced fresh
  gingerroot
1 tablespoon brown sugar
¼ cup toasted, unsweetened
  coconut
½ cup chopped cilantro leaves

> **Yields approx. 2 cups**
>
> This slightly sweet marinade works well with chicken or shellfish. Let some of the coconut and cilantro stick to your food while cooking.

1. Combine the tamarind and lime peel in a small saucepan and bring to a simmer; cook for 5 minutes.
2. Remove from heat and cool to room temperature. Stir in the remaining ingredients.

Coconut Marinade

Yields approx. ½ cup

This wonderful marinade is ideal for shellfish such as scallops and prawns. The acidity of the lime is perfectly balanced with the sweetness of the coconut, sugar, and curry.

3 tablespoons rice wine
    vinegar
2 tablespoons shredded,
    unsweetened coconut
1 tablespoon minced fresh
    ginger
3 tablespoons lime juice

1 tablespoon grated lime zest
¼–½ teaspoon red chili pepper
    flakes
2 teaspoons sugar
⅛ teaspoon curry powder

1. Warm the vinegar over low heat. Add the coconut and ginger to soften.
2. Remove from heat and stir in the remaining ingredients.

Malaysian Marinade

Yields approx. 1 cup

Muslim traders brought with them the sweet spices of the West as they ventured into what is now Singapore and Indonesia. Try this fragrant marinade with any poultry.

2 tablespoons honey
3 tablespoons lime juice
1 teaspoon grated lime zest
¼ cup soy sauce
¼ cup vegetable oil
2 tablespoons grated gingerroot

1 green onion, trimmed and
    thinly sliced
½ teaspoon ground cumin
½ teaspoon coriander
¼ cup chopped cilantro

1. Combine the honey, lime juice, lime zest, and soy sauce in a small bowl.
2. Slowly whisk in the oil.
3. Stir in the remaining ingredients.

Thai Vinegar Marinade

4 cloves garlic, minced
6 dried red chilies, seeded and
    crumbled
3 tablespoons chopped green
    onion
1 tablespoon fresh grated
    gingerroot
2–3 tablespoons vegetable oil

3½ cups rice wine vinegar
1 tablespoon sugar
¼ cup chopped lemongrass

Yields approx. 3 cups

The rice wine in this marinade packs a terrific flavor surprise. Try it with beef or pork.

1. Place the garlic, chilies, green onions, and ginger in a food processor or blender and process to form a paste.
2. Heat the oil in a wok or frying pan, add the paste, and stir-fry for 4 to 5 minutes. Remove from heat and allow the mixture to cool to room temperature.
3. In a small saucepan, bring the vinegar to a boil. Add the sugar and the lemongrass; reduce heat and simmer for 20 minutes.
4. Stir in the reserved paste.

The Elements of a Marinade

Most marinades will include three specific elements: an acid, such as a citrus juice or vinegar, acts as a softening agent; an oil, which adds flavor and moisture; and the spices, which impart aroma and flavor to your dish.

Lemongrass Marinade

Yields approx. 1⅓ cups

What is more Thai than lemongrass? If you are a lemongrass fan, this marinade is for you. I think it works well with poultry, beef, and pork, especially if you plan to grill.

1 cup extra-virgin olive oil
2 stalks lemongrass, trimmed
*   and smashed*
2 cloves garlic, minced
¼ tablespoon soy sauce
1 tablespoon fish sauce
2 tablespoons lime juice

1 jalapeño chili pepper, seeded
*   and chopped*
2 tablespoons chopped cilantro

1. Pour the olive oil into a pan and heat until warm. Add the lemongrass and garlic, and cook for 1 minute. Remove from heat and let cool to room temperature.
2. Stir in the remaining ingredients.

Toasted Coconut
Toasted coconut is a nice item to have on hand—and not only as an ingredient for Thai recipes. Try sprinkling some over the top of a frosted cake or over a fruit salad, or stir some into your favorite tuna salad. Place 1 cup of dried, unsweetened coconut flakes in a heavy skillet over low heat, stirring frequently for 8 to 10 minutes, until golden brown.

Shredded Fresh Coconut

1 heavy coconut, with liquid

1. Preheat the oven to 400 degrees.
2. Pierce the eye of the coconut with a metal skewer or screwdriver and drain the coconut water (reserve it for later use if you like).
3. Bake the coconut for 15 minutes, then remove and let cool.
4. When the coconut is cool enough to handle, use a hammer to break the shell. Using the tip of a knife, carefully pull the flesh from the shell. Remove any remaining brown membrane with a vegetable peeler.
5. Shred the coconut using a 4-sided grater. Fresh coconut will keep in the refrigerator for up to 1 week.

Yields approx. 1 cup

This is a good activity for anger management. Take out your aggressions on a coconut—it's amazing how satisfying it can be!

Lemon Chili Vinegar

1 quart white wine vinegar   *8–10 serrano chilies*
Peel of 4 limes

1. Combine all the ingredients in a medium-sized saucepan and bring to a simmer over medium heat.
2. Reduce heat and simmer for 10 minutes.
3. Cool to room temperature, then strain.

Yields approx. 1 quart

Try using this tasty vinegar as a substitute for white vinegar—use it to make salad dressing, in mayonnaise, or to liven up soup.

Chili Vinegar

½ cup white vinegar
2 teaspoons fish sauce

3 serrano chilies, seeded
  and finely sliced

Place all of the ingredients in a bowl. Let sit at least 20 minutes to allow the flavors to develop.

Tamarind Concentrate

2 ounces seedless tamarind
  pulp (sold in Asian markets)

1 cup warm water

1. Place the tamarind pulp and water in a small bowl for 20 minutes or until the pulp is soft.
2. Break the pulp apart with the back of a spoon and stir to combine.
3. Pour the mixture through a fine-mesh sieve, pushing the soft pulp through the strainer. Discard any fibrous pulp remaining in the strainer.

Thai Grilling Rub

4 teaspoons salt
1 teaspoon ground ginger
1 teaspoon dried lime peel

1 teaspoon freshly ground
  black pepper

> **Yields approx.
> 7 teaspoons**
>
> I love spice rubs. They may be the easiest way to add flavor quickly to anything you put on the grill (or under the broiler). This rub is ideal for pork or chicken.

1. Combine all the ingredients and mix thoroughly. Store in an airtight container.
2. To use, rinse the meat of your choice under cool water and pat dry; sprinkle the meat with the spice mixture (to taste) and rub it in along with some olive oil, then grill or broil to your liking.

Spice Rubs

There is a virtually infinite number of spice rub combos and variations. One helpful hint for creating your own spice rub: Check out some of the seasonings used in your favorite sauces, then mix together roughly equal parts of these ingredients to use as a rub for the meat, poultry, fish, or vegetable that was also involved in that recipe. You should also feel free to experiment!

CHAPTER 2

Dipping Sauces, Salsas, and Vinaigrettes

Peanut Dipping Sauce—1	22
Peanut Dipping Sauce—2	23
Peanut Dipping Sauce—3	23
Minty Dipping Sauce	24
Quick Hot Dipping Sauce	24
Sweet-and-Sour Dipping Sauce	25
Thai-Style Plum Dipping Sauce	25
5-Minute Dipping Sauce	26
Mango-Pineapple Salsa	26
Mango-Cucumber Salsa	27
Banana, Tamarind, and Mint Salsa	27
Spicy Thai Dressing	28
Peanut Pesto	28
Jalapeño-Lime Vinaigrette	29
Ginger-Lemongrass Vinaigrette	29
Mint-Cilantro "Chutney"	30

Peanut Dipping Sauce—1

⅔ cup crunchy peanut butter
1½ cups coconut milk
¼ cup lemon juice
2 tablespoons soy sauce
2 tablespoons brown sugar
1 teaspoon grated gingerroot
4 cloves garlic, pressed
3–4 dashes (or to taste)
  Tabasco

¼ cup chicken or vegetable
  stock
¼ cup heavy cream

1. Combine the peanut butter, coconut milk, lemon juice, soy sauce, brown sugar, ginger, garlic, and Tabasco in a small saucepan over medium heat. Cook, stirring constantly, until the sauce has the consistency of heavy cream, about 15 minutes.
2. Transfer the mixture to a blender and purée briefly.
3. Add the stock and cream, and blend until smooth.

 Allergy Alert
There are a fair number of people who are allergic to peanuts. Before inviting guests over for a Thai dinner, you should ask—just in case.

Peanut Dipping Sauce—2

$2/3$ cup crunchy peanut butter
$1\frac{1}{2}$ cups unsweetened canned
   coconut milk
$\frac{1}{4}$ cup fresh lime juice
2 tablespoons soy sauce
2 tablespoons brown sugar
1 teaspoon grated gingerroot

2 teaspoons minced garlic
Ground cayenne or crushed
   red pepper flakes to taste
$\frac{1}{4}$ cup low-sodium beef broth
$\frac{1}{4}$ cup half-and-half or heavy
   cream

> **Yields approx. 2 cups**
>
> This peanut sauce can be used as a dip for any type of meat, but, because it is made with beef broth, it goes best with beef, lamb, or chicken.

1. In a medium-sized saucepan, combine the peanut butter, coconut milk, lime juice, soy sauce, brown sugar, ginger, garlic, and cayenne.
2. Stirring constantly, cook over medium heat until the sauce thickens, about 15 minutes.
3. Remove the sauce from the heat and add the beef broth and cream. Using a hand mixer, blend until smooth. Heat briefly just prior to serving.

Peanut Dipping Sauce—3

3 shallots
1 cup canned coconut milk
$\frac{1}{2}$ cup smooth peanut butter
2 teaspoons light brown sugar
1 teaspoon Tabasco

1 tablespoon fish sauce
2 teaspoons soy sauce
1 teaspoon fresh lemon juice
2 tablespoons fresh lime juice

> **Yields approx. 2 cups**
>
> This quick peanut sauce is a delicious dip for fish, shrimp, or chicken satays. It can also be used as a base for a variety of Thai dishes—or simply toss it with rice noodles for a quick snack.

1. Roast the shallots in an oven preheated to 325 degrees for about 5 minutes or until soft. Let them cool to roughly room temperature.
2. Place all ingredients in a blender or food processor and blend until smooth.

Minty Dipping Sauce

Yields approx. ⅓ cup

Don't be afraid to substitute items in this recipe. For example, you can use basil instead of the mint, jalapeño instead of the serrano, lemon instead of lime, and soy instead of fish sauce.

¼ cup chopped mint leaves
1 serrano chili, seeded and
*   diced*
2 cloves garlic, minced

1 tablespoon grated lime zest
¼ cup lime juice
2 tablespoons fish sauce

Place all the ingredients in a blender and process until smooth. Serve with a variety of grilled, skewered meats and raw or blanched vegetables.

Quick Hot Dipping Sauce

Yields approx. ½ cup

This sauce is an ideal dip for any type of meat. I always have a jar of chili-garlic sauce in the pantry. You can find it in almost any grocery store these days, either in the Asian department or in specialty foods.

1 heaping tablespoon prepared
*   chili-garlic sauce*

½ cup white vinegar

Combine the 2 ingredients and serve.

Sweet-and-Sour Dipping Sauce

½ cup white vinegar
1 cup sugar
½ teaspoon salt

1 heaping tablespoon prepared
    chili-garlic sauce

1. Combine the vinegar, sugar, and salt in a small saucepan over medium-high heat; bring to a boil, reduce to a simmer, and cook for 8 to 10 minutes, stirring occasionally.
2. Stir in the chili sauce and remove from heat. Let cool to room temperature before serving.

Yields approx. 1½ cups

You can vary the sweet and sour of this recipe by playing with the amount of sugar and/or chili sauce. Or you can substitute different brands or types of chili sauce—even Cajun or Jamaican!

Thai-Style Plum Dipping Sauce

⅔ cup plum preserves
⅔ cup white vinegar
⅔ cup water

2 tablespoons honey
Tabasco to taste

1. Place all the ingredients except the Tabasco in a food processor or blender, and process until smooth.
2. Transfer the mixture to a small saucepan and bring to a boil over medium heat; reduce heat and simmer until thick, about 12 to 15 minutes.
3. Allow to cool to room temperature, then stir in the Tabasco.

Yields approx. 2 cups

Traditionally used in Chinese cooking—think Moo Shu—plum sauce has a sweet-and-sour taste that is a perfect complement to poultry.

5-Minute Dipping Sauce

**Yields approx.
4 tablespoons**

This simple sauce is delicious as a dip for rice balls. I particularly like the pungency of the fresh ginger.

1 teaspoon sugar
1 tablespoon lime juice
1 tablespoon fish sauce

1 teaspoon minced fresh ginger
½ teaspoon dried red pepper
   flakes

In a small bowl, dissolve the sugar in 1 tablespoon of water. Stir in the remaining ingredients; adjust seasonings if necessary. Serve at room temperature.

Mango-Pineapple Salsa

Yields approx. 4 cups

A salsa is a condiment usually composed of roughly chopped fresh ingredients that are meant to enliven whatever they are served with. This salsa is perfect served with grilled shrimp, chicken, or fish.

1 cup mango pieces
1 cup diced pineapple
1 cup seeded and chopped
   tomato
½ cup diced red onion
¼ cup snipped chives

3 tablespoons chopped cilantro
1 serrano chili, seeded and
   chopped
2 tablespoons lime juice
2 tablespoons vegetable oil
Salt and pepper to taste

Combine all the ingredients in a small bowl. Cover and refrigerate for at least 2 hours before serving.

Mango-Cucumber Salsa

1 firm, ripe mango, peeled,
    seeded, and cut into
    ¼-inch dice
1 medium cucumber, seeded
    and cut into ¼-inch dice

¼ cup sliced green onion
¼ cup orange juice
2 teaspoons lime juice
1 teaspoon vegetable oil
Salt and pepper to taste

Combine all the ingredients in a small bowl.

Yields approx. 2 cups

This salsa can be served alongside grilled fish or used as a small salad.

Banana, Tamarind, and Mint Salsa

4 ripe bananas, peeled and
    finely diced
¼ cup Tamarind Concentrate
    (see recipe on page 18)
1 roasted red jalapeño, seeded
    and chopped

1 tablespoon chopped
    fresh mint
1 teaspoon brown sugar
1 tablespoon lime juice

Gently fold all the ingredients together.

Yields approx. 2 cups

This unique salsa goes perfectly with roasted or grilled poultry or game.

Spicy Thai Dressing

2 tablespoons soy sauce
1 tablespoon plus 1 teaspoon
   rice wine vinegar
1 tablespoon sesame oil
3 tablespoons water
1 teaspoon sugar
2 cloves garlic

1 teaspoon grated gingerroot
1 fresh red cayenne pepper or
   2 Thai peppers, stemmed,
   seeded, and cut into pieces

Place all the ingredients in a blender and process until smooth.

Peanut Pesto

1 cup unsalted roasted peanuts
½ cup soy sauce
¼ cup honey
⅓ cup water
2–3 cloves garlic, minced

½ cup sesame oil
¼ teaspoon (or to taste)
   red pepper flakes

Place the peanuts in a food processor fitted with a metal blade; process until fine. While continuing to blend, add the remaining ingredients one at a time through the feed tube until well blended.

Jalapeño-Lime Vinaigrette

1 jalapeño, seeded and
    chopped
⅓ cup lime juice
1 tablespoon sugar

Salt and pepper to taste
1 cup vegetable or canola oil

Place the jalapeño, lime juice, sugar, and salt and pepper in a food processor; blend for 1 minute. While continuing to blend, slowly add the oil; blend for 30 seconds or until well emulsified.

**Yields approx.
1⅓ cups**

Serve over grilled fish or vegetables or a fresh salad.

Ginger-Lemongrass Vinaigrette

1 quart rice wine vinegar
2 stalks lemongrass,
    outer leaves removed
    and discarded, inner core
    slightly mashed

¼ cup grated fresh gingerroot

Combine all the ingredients in a nonreactive pot and simmer over low heat for 30 minutes. Remove from heat and let stand overnight. Strain before serving.

Yields approx. 1 quart

This vinaigrette is fantastic as a dressing for salad or as a marinade for crudités.

Mint-Cilantro "Chutney"

Yields approx. 2 cups

I like to spoon some of this chutney on a plate and top it with roasted cauliflower. The cauliflower acts as a sponge, soaking up every last drop.

$\frac{1}{3}$ cup unsalted peanuts, toasted
$\frac{3}{4}$ cup packed mint leaves
$\frac{3}{4}$ cup packed cilantro
3 tablespoons sour cream
2 teaspoons honey

$\frac{1}{2}$ teaspoon minced honey
Salt and pepper to taste

Place the peanuts in a food processor and finely grind. Add the remaining ingredients to the processor and blend until well combined.

What's a Chutney?

A chutney is a traditional accompaniment to Indian foods. It is a coarse relish or condiment usually made from tropical fruits, ginger, and herbs. Chutneys usually have notes of spicy, sweet, and sour, and can be used as a dipping sauce, a bread spread, or as a glaze.

CHAPTER 3

Appetizers

Rice Paper Rolls	32
Crab Spring Rolls	33
Pork, Carrot, and Celery Spring Rolls	34
Omelet "Egg Rolls"	35
Basil and Shrimp Wedges	36
Crispy Mussel Pancakes	37
Chicken, Shrimp, and Beef Satay	38
Shrimp Toast	40
Pork Toast Triangles	41
Mee Krob	42
Son-in-Law Eggs	43
Salt-Cured Eggs	44
3-Flavor Rice Sticks	44
Thai Fries	45
Spicy Coconut Bundles	46
Curried Fish Cakes	47
Spicy Scallops	48
Spicy Ground Pork in Basil Leaves	49
Skewered Thai Pork	50
Fried Won Tons	51
Fried Tofu with Dipping Sauces	52
Cold Sesame Noodles	52
Chinese-Style Dumplings	53

Rice Paper Rolls

Serves 2–4

This healthy appetizer is the perfect finger food and is a great introduction to Thai cuisine: There are no scary ingredients, it isn't tongue-numbingly hot, and yet it is definitely not Western in style or flavor.

1 cup thin rice noodles
8–10 medium to large cooked shrimp, cut in half
4 (8" × 10") sheets of rice paper
1 cup grated carrot

2 scallions, thinly sliced
1 small cucumber, shredded
20 mint leaves
1 small bunch cilantro

1. Soak the rice noodles in very hot water until they are soft, usually 10 to 20 minutes; drain. You can leave the noodles whole, or cut them into 2-inch pieces if you prefer.
2. Place a clean kitchen towel on a work surface with a bowl of hot water nearby. Put a sheet of the rice paper in the hot water for approximately 20 seconds, just until soft; lay it out flat on the towel.
3. In the middle of the rice paper, place 2 to 3 pieces of shrimp and ¼ of the noodles, carrots, scallions, and cucumbers. Top with mint and cilantro.
4. Quickly roll up the rice paper, keeping it fairly tight; then roll up the whole thing in plastic wrap, making sure to keep it tight. Refrigerate until ready to serve.
5. To serve, trim the ends off the rolls. Cut the remaining roll into pieces and remove the plastic wrap. Serve with your favorite dipping sauce.

Crab Spring Rolls

*1 pound crabmeat, picked
over to remove any shells,
and shredded
1 tablespoon mayonnaise
¼–½ teaspoon grated lime peel
15 spring roll or egg roll
wrappers*

*2 egg yolks, lightly beaten
Canola oil for deep frying
15 small, tender Boston
lettuce leaves
Mint leaves
Parsley leaves*

Yields 15 rolls

Don't let the deep-frying steer you away from these light, crunchy rolls. The key to keeping the fat to a minimum is using clean, hot cooking oil and immediately transferring the rolls to papers towels.

1. In a small bowl, mix the crabmeat with the mayonnaise and lime peel.
2. Place 1 tablespoon of the crabmeat mixture in the center of 1 spring roll wrapper. Fold a pointed end of the wrapper over the crabmeat, then fold the opposite point over the top of the folded point. Brush a bit of the egg yolk over the top of the exposed wrapper, then fold the bottom point over the crabmeat and roll to form a tight packet; set aside. Repeat with the remaining crabmeat and wrappers.
3. Heat the oil to 365 degrees in a skillet or deep fryer. Deep-fry the rolls 3 to 4 at a time for 2 minutes or so, until they are a golden brown; drain on paper towels.
4. To serve, wrap each spring roll in a wrapper with a single piece of lettuce, and a sprinkling of mint and parsley. Serve with your favorite dipping sauce.

Pork, Carrot, and Celery Spring Rolls

2 tablespoons vegetable oil
1 teaspoon minced garlic
1 cup minced or ground pork
2 cups grated carrots
2 cups chopped celery
¼ cup fish sauce
2 tablespoons sugar
¼ teaspoon white pepper
1 cup bean sprouts
20 spring roll wrappers
2 egg yolks, beaten
Vegetable oil for deep frying

1. In a large skillet, heat the 2 tablespoons of vegetable oil over medium-high heat. Add the garlic and pork, and sauté until the pork is cooked through.
2. Add the carrots, celery, fish sauce, sugar, and white pepper. Increase heat to high and cook for 1 minute.
3. Drain any liquid from the pan and allow the mixture to cool to room temperature, then stir in the bean sprouts.
4. On a clean, dry work surface, place the egg roll wrapper with an end pointing toward you, forming a diamond. Place approximately 2 tablespoons of the filling on the lower portion of the wrapper. Fold up the corner nearest you and roll once, then fold in the sides. Brush the remaining point with the egg yolk and finish rolling to seal. Repeat with the remaining wrappers and filling.
5. Heat 2 to 3 inches of oil to 350 degrees. Deep-fry the spring rolls until golden brown; remove immediately to drain on paper towels.
6. Serve with sweet-and-sour sauce.

Omelet "Egg Rolls"

For the filling:

1 teaspoon vegetable oil
½ pound ground pork or
    chicken
2 green onions, trimmed and
    thinly sliced
1 cup shredded Chinese
    cabbage
½ teaspoon sugar
1 tablespoon fish sauce
1 tablespoon minced cilantro

For the omelets:

8 eggs
6 tablespoons water
1 tablespoon soy or fish sauce
1 teaspoon vegetable oil
Bibb lettuce
Soy sauce, fish sauce, and/or
    hot sauce
Garnish of your choice

Yields 16–20 pieces

Using omelets in place of the usual egg roll wrapper is a fun twist on a classic favorite. These rolls use traditional filling ingredients and dipping sauces.

1. To make the filling: In a medium-sized skillet, warm the vegetable oil over medium heat. Add the ground meat and sauté until it is no longer pink. Add the green onions and cabbage and cook until soft. Add the sugar, fish sauce, and cilantro; cook for 1 more minute. Set the filling aside, keeping it warm.
2. To make the omelets: Combine the eggs, water, and soy sauce in a medium-sized bowl. Place an omelet pan over medium heat for 1 minute. Add approximately ¼ teaspoon of vegetable oil, swirling it to coat the pan evenly. Pour approximately ¼ of the egg mixture into the pan, then let it rest for approximately 30 seconds. When the bottom is firm, flip the omelet and cook until done. Remove to a plate and cover with foil to keep warm. Repeat to make 3 more omelets.
3. To fill the "egg rolls," place 1 omelet in the center of a plate. Place ¼ of the filling slightly off-center and then roll up. Trim the ends and cut the rolls into bite-sized pieces.
4. To serve, use Bibb lettuce leaves to pick up the rolls. Dip in additional soy sauce, fish sauce, hot sauce, or other favorite dipping sauce, and add the garnish of your choice.

Basil and Shrimp Wedges

Serves 4–6
as an appetizer or
2 as a brunch item

When is basil not just plain old basil? When it's Horapa, Ga-prow, or Manglug. Don't be afraid to experiment with different basils. They all taste great!

1½ teaspoons vegetable oil, divided
½ pound cooked salad shrimp
1 green onion, trimmed and thinly sliced
½ cup julienned basil
1 teaspoon fish sauce
4 eggs
2 tablespoons water
Salt and pepper to taste

1. Place 1 teaspoon of the vegetable oil in a sauté pan over medium heat. Add the shrimp and green onion, and sauté until the shrimp are warmed through, approximately 2 minutes. Add the basil and fish sauce and cook for 1 more minute. Set aside.
2. In a large bowl, whisk together the eggs, water, and salt and pepper, then stir in the shrimp mixture.
3. Place the remaining ½ teaspoon of vegetable oil in an omelet pan over medium heat. Add the egg mixture and cook until the omelet begins to brown. Flip over the omelet and continue to cook until set.
4. To serve, slide the omelet onto a serving plate and cut it into wedges. Serve it with your favorite Thai dipping sauce.

Crispy Mussel Pancakes

1 cup shelled mussels (about
   1 pound before shelling)
½ cup tapioca flour
¼ cup all-purpose flour
¼ teaspoon salt
1 teaspoon baking powder

¾ cup water
2 cups bean sprouts
2 tablespoons chopped cilantro,
   plus extra for garnish
Salt and ground pepper
   to taste

Serves 2–4

I know these sound weird, but you have to trust me on this. They're great! The slightly herbed pancakes make a perfect foil for the subtle taste of the mussels.

1. To prepare the mussels, rinse them quickly under cold running water. Debeard the mussels by pulling out the brown membrane that is sometimes still attached. Discard any mussels that are already open. Fill a large skillet with ½ to 1 inch of water. Bring the water to a boil, then add the mussels, cover, and let steam about 4 minutes or until the mussels have opened, shaking the pan every so often. Drain the mussels through a colander. Let cool to room temperature and then use a small fork to pull the meat from the shell; set aside on paper towels.
2. In a medium-sized mixing bowl, stir together the flours, the salt, and the baking powder. Whisk in the water to form a thin batter.
3. Preheat the oven to 200 degrees. In a large, heavy-bottomed skillet, heat the vegetable oil over medium-high heat. Pour half of the batter into the skillet and top with half of the mussels. Cook until the batter has set and turned golden, about 2 minutes. Carefully flip the pancake over and continue cooking until golden. Remove the pancake to a baking sheet lined with some foil and place it in the oven to keep warm. Repeat to make a second pancake with the remaining batter and mussels.
4. Add 1 teaspoon of vegetable oil to the skillet if it is dry, and increase the heat to high. Add the bean sprouts, sprinkle with salt and ground pepper to taste, and stir-fry quickly just to heat through, about 30 seconds.
5. To serve, place each pancake in the center of a plate. Top with the bean sprouts, some cilantro, and a grind of fresh pepper. Serve with a sweet-and-sour sauce of your choice.

Chicken, Shrimp, and Beef Satay

Makes 4–6 chicken skewers or 6–8 shrimp or beef skewers

Satays are served hot but are almost as delicious at room temperature, and they go great with a cold beer. Don't forget to have a lot of peanut sauce!

Chicken

1 recipe Thai Marinade (see recipes in Chapter 1)
3 whole boneless, skinless chicken breasts, cut into long
   strips about ½-inch wide
1 recipe Peanut Dipping Sauce
   (see recipes in Chapter 2)

1. Thread the chicken strips onto presoaked bamboo skewers or onto metal skewers. Place the skewers in a flat pan and cover with marinade. Marinate the chicken in the refrigerator overnight.
2. Cook the skewers on the grill or under the broiler, basting and turning them until they are cooked through, about 6 to 8 minutes.
3. Serve with the peanut sauce for dipping.

Shrimp

1 recipe Thai Marinade
24 large shrimp, shelled and deveined
1 recipe Peanut Dipping Sauce

1. Thread the shrimp onto presoaked bamboo skewers or onto metal skewers (about 3 shrimp per skewer). Place the skewers in a flat pan and cover with marinade. Marinate the shrimp for at least 15 minutes, but no longer than 1 hour.
2. Cook the skewers on the grill or under the broiler, basting and turning them often until just opaque, about 3 to 4 minutes.
3. Serve with the peanut sauce for dipping.

(recipe continues on the next page)

Chicken, Shrimp, and Beef Satay

(continued)

Beef

1 recipe Thai Marinade
1–1½ pounds sirloin steak, fat and sinew removed,
   cut into ½-inch-wide strips
1 recipe Peanut Dipping Sauce

1. Thread the beef strips onto presoaked bamboo skewers or onto metal skewers. Place the skewers in a flat pan and cover with marinade. Marinate the beef in the refrigerator overnight.
2. Cook the skewers on the grill or under the broiler, basting and turning them often until done to your liking, about 6 to 8 minutes for medium.
3. Serve with the peanut sauce for dipping.

 The Origin of Satay

Satay was first introduced to Thailand by Arab traders from the Middle East.

Shrimp Toast

Yields 32 pieces

The pork in this recipe not only adds a bit of extra flavor, but also helps to bind the ingredients together. You could also use ground chicken or turkey if you don't want the pork.

8 slices of white bread, left to sit out overnight, crusts removed
½ pound shrimp, cleaned, deveined, and coarsely chopped
¼ pound ground pork
1 tablespoon chopped cilantro
2 cloves garlic, minced
⅛ teaspoon cayenne
¼ teaspoon salt
1 egg, beaten
2 teaspoons soy sauce
2 tablespoons sesame seeds
2 teaspoons vegetable oil, divided
32 slices cucumber

1. In a small bowl, combine the shrimp and pork; set aside.
2. In another small bowl, combine the cilantro, garlic, cayenne, and salt. Pour the spice mixture over the shrimp and pork, and combine.
3. Stir in the beaten egg and soy sauce; mix well. Divide the mixture into 8 parts.
4. Smoothly spread a thin layer of the mixture on each slice of bread and sprinkle with sesame seeds.
5. Heat ¼ teaspoon vegetable oil in nonstick skillet. When it is very hot, place 1 piece of bread, meat side down, in the oil. Cook until golden in color, then remove to a paper towel, blotting any excess oil. Repeat for all of the bread sides.
6. Cut each slice of bread into quarters and top each quarter with a cucumber slice.

Pork Toast Triangles

*¼ pound of large shrimp,
   peeled and deveined*
1 tablespoon dried shrimp
1 tablespoon chopped cilantro
2 cloves garlic, peeled
*1 pound ground pork
   (the leaner the better)*

1 egg
1 tablespoon fish sauce
*6 slices day-old bread, crusts
   trimmed off*
Vegetable oil for frying

Yields 24 pieces

Similar in concept to the Shrimp Toast, this recipe features pork and uses the shrimp as the primary accent flavor, resulting in a milder overall taste.

1. Fill a medium-sized saucepan with water and bring it to a boil. Reduce the heat, add the shrimp, and simmer until the shrimp are opaque. Drain the shrimp and let cool to room temperature. Coarsely chop and set aside.
2. Place the dried shrimp, cilantro, and the garlic in a food processor and blend until a smooth paste is formed. Add the reserved shrimp and ground pork; process again. Add the egg and fish sauce and process once more.
3. Spread the mixture evenly over each slice of bread. Cut the bread into 4 equal slices, either from corner to corner forming triangles or from top to bottom forming squares.
4. Add approximately ½ inch of vegetable oil to a large skillet. Bring the oil to approximately 375 degrees over medium-high heat. Place 4 to 5 toasts in the oil, filling side down. Make sure that the toasts are not crowded in the oil or they will not brown evenly. After the filling side is nicely browned, use a slotted spoon or metal strainer to flip the toasts. Watch the toasts carefully, as the bottoms will brown quickly. Remove the toasts to a stack of paper towels to drain. Carefully pat the tops of the toasts with paper towels to remove any oil.
5. Serve the toasts with sweet-and-sour or plum sauce.

Mee Krob

⅓ cup honey
⅓ cup rice or white vinegar
5 tablespoons sugar
2–3 drops red food coloring
1 tablespoon Tamarind Concentrate (see recipe on page 18)

Vegetable oil for deep-frying
2 eggs, beaten
½ pound thin rice stick noodles, broken into handfuls
½ cup dried shrimp
1 cup bean sprouts
10 small lime wedges

1. Combine the honey, vinegar, sugar, food coloring, and tamarind in a medium-sized saucepan. Bring the mixture to a boil over medium heat, stirring occasionally. Reduce heat and simmer for 2 to 3 minutes or until the mixture begins to thicken; remove from heat and set aside.
2. Bring about 3 inches of vegetable oil to 360 degrees in a deep fryer or skillet. Drop a single layer of the rice stick noodles into the hot oil, making sure to leave enough room for them to cook evenly. Turn the noodles with a slotted spoon as soon as they begin to puff up. As soon as the noodles are golden, remove them to paper towels to drain. Repeat until all of the noodles are cooked.
3. Add the dried shrimp to the oil and cook for 45 seconds or so. Remove to paper towels.
4. Pour out all but a thin coat of the oil from the skillet. Add the beaten eggs and stir-fry them quickly, shirring them into long strips. As soon as they are cooked, remove them to paper towels.
5. Bring the sauce back to a boil. Stir in the shrimp and continue to boil for 2 minutes.
6. Place about ⅓ of the noodles on a serving platter and spoon about ⅓ of the sauce over the top; gently toss to coat the noodles evenly being careful not to crush the noodles. Repeat until all of the noodles are coated in sauce.
7. To serve, mound the noodles, place the egg strips over them, and top with the bean sprouts. Pass the lime wedges.

Son-in-Law Eggs

¼ cup vegetable oil
10 hard-boiled eggs, cooled
   and peeled
2 shallots, thinly sliced
⅓ cup light brown sugar
3 tablespoons fish sauce

⅓ cup Tamarind Concentrate
   (see recipe on page 18)
¼ cup chopped cilantro
Dried hot chili flakes to taste

> **Yields 20**
>
> A version of deviled eggs with all of the characteristic Thai flavors—sweet, sour, salty, and spicy— these eggs make a delightful addition to a picnic basket, a summer barbecue, or as a quick snack.

1. Heat the vegetable oil in a skillet over medium heat. Place the whole eggs in the skillet and fry until golden brown. Remove the eggs to paper towels and set aside. (If your skillet can't hold all of the eggs comfortably, do this in batches.)
2. Add the shallots to the skillet and sauté until just beginning to brown. Remove the shallots from the oil with a slotted spoon and set aside.
3. Put the brown sugar, fish sauce, and tamarind in the skillet. Stir to combine and bring to a simmer. Cook the mixture, stirring constantly, until the sauce thickens, about 5 minutes; remove from heat.
4. Cut the eggs in half vertically and place them face-up on a rimmed serving dish. Spread the shallots over the eggs and then drizzle the eggs with the sauce. Garnish with cilantro and chili pepper flakes.

The Secret to Making Perfect Hard-Boiled Eggs

The perfect hard-boiled egg has a delicate white and a fully cooked yolk, without even a hint of the unattractive gray shadow that affects an improperly cooked egg. The perfect hard-boiled egg is also easy to peel. To achieve this, put the eggs in enough cold water to cover them by 1 inch and boil for 1 minute only. Then remove from heat, cover, and let them sit for 15 minutes. Then, transfer the eggs to a bath of ice water for 15 to 20 minutes. They should then peel easily.

Salt-Cured Eggs

Yields 1 dozen eggs

6 cups water
1½ cups salt

1 dozen eggs

Salt-cured eggs are delicious as is—just peel and eat. I used them for Easter eggs this year, much to the delight of my husband, who is a real hard-boiled egg fan. They were beautiful and tasted great.

1. Combine the water and the salt in a large saucepan and bring to a boil over high heat. Remove from heat and let cool to room temperature.
2. Carefully place the eggs in a container. Pour the salt water over the eggs and seal the container tightly. Place the container in the refrigerator and let the eggs cure for at least 1 month.
3. To serve, hard-boil the eggs, let cool to room temperature, then peel, slice, and enjoy.

3-Flavor Rice Sticks

Serves 4–6

1 pound rice sticks, broken into 3-inch segments
Vegetable oil for frying
Salt to taste

Curry powder to taste
Cayenne pepper to taste

These crunchy sticks are irresistible: I challenge you to eat just a handful! Don't be shy about experimenting with other spice blends or flavoring agents.

1. Pour 2 to 3 inches of vegetable oil into a large skillet and heat to 350 degrees. Fry the rice sticks in batches (making sure not to overcrowd the pan), turning them quickly as they puff up. After they stop crackling in the oil, transfer the puffed sticks to paper towels to drain.
2. While the rice sticks are still hot, sprinkle salt on 1 batch; sprinkle a second batch with curry powder; and a third batch with cayenne pepper to taste.

Thai Fries

2 medium-sized sweet potatoes
4 green plantains
1 pound taro root
1 cup rice flour
1 cup sticky rice flour
Water
1 teaspoon black pepper
1 teaspoon salt

2 tablespoons sugar
3 tablespoons black sesame
  seeds
1 14-ounce bag shredded
  sweetened coconut

1. Peel the root vegetables and cut them into flat ⅓-inch-thick strips about 3 inches long and 1 inch wide.
2. Combine the flours in a large mixing bowl and stir in ½ cup of water. Continue adding water ¼ cup at a time until a mixture resembling pancake batter is formed. Stir in remaining ingredients.
3. Fill a medium-sized saucepan a third to a half full with vegetable oil. Heat the oil over high heat until very hot, but not smoking.
4. Add some of the vegetables to the batter, coating them well. Using a slotted spoon or Asian strainer, place the vegetables in the hot oil. (Be careful here: The oil may spatter.) Fry the vegetables, turning them occasionally, until golden brown. Transfer the fried vegetables to a stack of paper towels to drain, then serve immediately.

Spicy Coconut Bundles

1 cup shredded fresh coconut
$2/3$ cup brown sugar
$1/3$ cup shrimp paste
$1/2$ cup diced red onion
$1/2$ cup chopped lime segments
$1/2$ cup chopped peanuts
$1/2$ cup dried shrimp

1–2 jalapeños, seeded and sliced
20–25 medium-sized spinach leaves, washed and patted dry

1. Place the coconut in a medium-sized sauté pan and cook over medium heat until browned, about 20 minutes; set aside to cool.
2. In a small saucepan, melt the brown sugar over medium heat, stirring constantly. Mix in the shrimp paste until well combined. Set the sauce aside.
3. Place the coconut, onion, lime pieces, peanuts, dried shrimp, and jalapeños in a medium-sized serving bowl; gently toss to combine.
4. To serve, place 4 to 5 spinach leaves (depending on the size of the leaves) on each serving plate. Top each leaf with approximately 1 tablespoon of the coconut mixture and drizzle a bit of sauce over the coconut.
5. To eat, roll up the spinach leaf around the coconut mixture and pop the whole bundle in your mouth. Pass additional sauce separately.

Curried Fish Cakes

¼ cup chopped shallots
¼ cup chopped garlic
¼ cup chopped lemongrass,
   inner portion only
1 tablespoon chopped ginger
½ teaspoon peppercorns
1 teaspoon grated lime peel
1 tablespoon shrimp paste
5–10 dried chilies, seeded,
   soaked, and shredded

½ tablespoon salt
1 pound boneless whitefish
   steak, minced
1 egg, beaten
½ pound French beans,
   trimmed and finely chopped
Vegetable oil for frying

**Yields 15–20
small cakes**

One of my favorite dishes growing up was my mother's salmon cakes. Here is a Thai version. Whitefish is used so that the lemongrass and ginger aren't overpowered by the fish.

1. Place the shallots, garlic, lemongrass, ginger, peppercorns, lime peel, shrimp paste, chilies, and salt in a food processor or blender and process to form a smooth paste.
2. Add the fish to the food processor and pulse until well combined with the spice paste. Add the beaten egg and combine once more. Transfer the fish mixture to a large mixing bowl and stir in the green beans.
3. Using approximately 1 tablespoon of fish mixture, form a flat, round cake; repeat until all of the mixture is used.
4. Heat approximately ⅛ to ¼ inch of vegetable oil to 350 degrees over medium-high heat in a skillet or deep fryer; fry the fish cakes until golden.
5. Serve with your favorite dipping sauce.

Spicy Scallops

1 teaspoon vegetable oil
1 clove garlic, minced
1 jalapeño, seeded and minced
1 (½-inch) piece of ginger, peeled and minced
⅛ teaspoon ground coriander

2 tablespoons soy sauce
2 tablespoons water
8 large scallops, cleaned

1. In a pan large enough to hold all of the scallops, heat the oil over medium heat. Add the garlic, jalapeño, and ginger, and stir-fry for about 1 minute.
2. Add the coriander, soy sauce, and water, stirring to combine; simmer for 2 to 3 minutes. Strain the liquid through a fine-mesh sieve. Allow the pan to cool slightly.
3. Add the scallops to the pan and spoon the reserved liquid over the top of them. Return the pan to the stove, increasing the heat to medium-high. Cover the pan and let the scallops steam for about 2 to 3 minutes, or until done to your liking. Serve immediately.

Cleaning Out Whole Scallops
If you buy scallops whole, there is an easy way to clean out the meat! Simply put the scallops on ice for about 10 minutes, which will cause them to open up. Then, using a sturdy tablespoon, slide the spoon in-between the open shell and twist open. Then use the spoon to scoop out the meat—that's it!

Spicy Ground Pork in Basil Leaves

Juice of 1–2 limes
½ pound ground pork
3 tablespoons fish sauce
1 shallot, thinly sliced
¼ tablespoon (or to taste)
    ground dried chili pepper
5 sprigs cilantro, chopped

1 tablespoon toasted rice
    powder (available in Asian
    specialty stores)
Lettuce and/or large basil
    leaves

Serves 4

I remember the first time I went to an Ethiopian restaurant and was encouraged to eat using flatbread instead of utensils. This Thai dish is eaten using basil and lettuce leaves as utensils.

1. Squeeze the juice of half of a lime over the ground pork and let marinate for a few minutes.
2. Heat a large skillet on high. Add a couple of tablespoons of water and then immediately add the pork; stir-fry until the pork is cooked through. (Don't worry if the pork sticks at first—it will eventually loosen.)
3. Pour off any fat that has accumulated in the pan and then put the pork in a large mixing bowl. Add the remaining lime juice (to taste), fish sauce, shallot, ground chili pepper, cilantro, and toasted rice; stir to combine thoroughly.
4. To serve, place the mixture in a serving bowl and let guests use the lettuce and basil leaves to scoop out the mixture.

Skewered Thai Pork

Serves 2–3

This recipe is similar to satay, but the coconut milk in this dish infuses it with a certain tropical nuance, and it is rarely served with peanut sauce. Although, if peanut sauce is your thing, don't let me stop you.

2 tablespoons sugar
1 teaspoon salt
3 cloves garlic, minced
1 tablespoon fish sauce
1 tablespoon coconut milk

1 pound pork, thinly sliced into
   long strips
20–30 bamboo skewers,
   soaked in water for 1 hour

1. In a medium-sized bowl, combine the sugar, salt, garlic, fish sauce, and coconut milk.
2. Toss the pork strips in the mixture to coat thoroughly. Cover the bowl and marinate for at least 30 minutes, but preferably overnight in the refrigerator.
3. Thread the pork strips onto the bamboo skewers.
4. Grill the skewers for about 3 to 5 minutes per side.
5. Serve with your favorite sauce or as is.

Using Bamboo Skewers

When using bamboo skewers for grilling, always be sure to soak them in water for at least an hour (to prevent them from catching on fire or charring badly). Another way to reduce charring of the skewers is to make sure as much of the skewer is covered by food as possible—leave only ¼–½ inch of space at the end.

Fried Won Tons

1 clove garlic, minced
2 tablespoons minced cilantro
1 tablespoon soy sauce
½ cup chopped white
   mushrooms
Pinch white pepper

½ pound ground pork
25 won ton skins
Vegetable oil for frying

Yields approx. 25 won tons

Although won tons and spring rolls often have similar fillings, their wrappers set them apart. Spring rolls use rice flour wrappers; won ton wrappers are made with wheat flour.

1. In a medium-sized mixing bowl, thoroughly combine the garlic, cilantro, soy sauce, mushrooms, white pepper, and ground pork.
2. To make the won tons, place approximately ½ teaspoon of the filling in the middle of a won ton skin. Fold the won ton from corner to corner, forming a triangle. Press the edges together to seal closed. Repeat with the remaining skins and filling.
3. Add about 2 to 3 inches of vegetable oil to a deep fryer or wok. Heat the oil on medium until it reaches about 350 degrees. Carefully add the won tons, 2 or 3 at a time. Fry until they are golden brown, turning them constantly. Transfer the cooked won tons to drain on paper towels as they are done.
4. Serve the won tons with either sweet-and-sour sauce or the sauce of your choice.

Fried Tofu with Dipping Sauces

Serves 2–4

Although this recipe calls for frying, it is one of the healthiest dishes you can eat. Tofu, which is made from soybeans, is one of the best foods on the planet—low fat, high protein, no dairy, and no sodium.

1 package of tofu, cut into
   bite-sized cubes
Vegetable oil for frying

Dipping sauces of your choice

1. Add about 2 to 3 inches of vegetable oil to a deep fryer or wok. Heat the oil on medium until it reaches about 350 degrees. Carefully add some of the tofu pieces, making sure not to overcrowd them; fry until golden brown, turning constantly. Transfer the fried tofu to paper towels to drain as each batch is cooked.
2. Serve the tofu with a choice of dipping sauces, such as Sweet-and-Sour, Peanut, and Minty Dipping Sauce (see recipes in Chapter 2).

Cold Sesame Noodles

Serves 2–4

I first made this tasty, inexpensive dish back when I was in college, My roommates and I would make huge bowlfulls of sesame noodles and chase it down with a cold beer.

1 pound angel hair pasta
2 tablespoons sesame oil
¼ cup creamy peanut butter
   or tahini
2 tablespoons rice vinegar

1 tablespoon grated ginger
¼–½ teaspoon dried red
   pepper flakes
1–2 green onions, trimmed and
   thinly sliced (optional)

1. Cook the pasta according to package directions. Rinse under cold water, then set aside.
2. Vigorously whisk together the remaining ingredients; pour over pasta, tossing to coat.
3. Garnish with green onion if desired.

Chinese-Style Dumplings

¼ cup sticky rice flour
1 cup rice flour
½ cup water
¼ cup tapioca flour
1 teaspoon vegetable oil

2 cups chives, cut into ½-inch
  lengths
1 tablespoon soy sauce

> **Yields 15–20 dumplings**
>
> If you prefer your dumplings pan-fried, follow steps 1 through 6, then fry them in a sauté pan with a bit of vegetable oil over medium-high heat until browned to your liking.

1. In a medium-sized saucepan, stir together the sticky rice flour, the rice flour, and the water. Turn the heat to medium and cook, stirring constantly until the mixture has the consistency of glue. (If the mixture becomes too sticky, reduce the heat to low.) Remove the batter from the heat and quickly stir in the tapioca flour. Set aside to cool to room temperature.

2. Meanwhile, add the vegetable oil to a skillet large enough to easily hold the chives, and heat on high. Add the chives and the soy sauce. Stir-fry the chives just until they wilt. Be careful not to let the chives cook too much. Remove from heat and set aside.

3. Once the dough has reached room temperature, check its consistency. If it is too sticky to work with, add a bit more tapioca flour.

4. To make the dumplings, roll the batter into balls 1 inch in diameter. Using your fingers, flatten each ball into a disk about 4 inches across. Spoon about 1 tablespoon of the chives into the middle of each disk. Fold the disk in half and pinch the edges together to form a half-moon-shaped packet.

5. Place the dumplings in a prepared steamer for 5 to 8 minutes or until the dough is cooked. Serve with a spicy dipping sauce of your choice.

Chapter 4
Soups

Tom Yum	56
Tom Ka Kai	57
Chicken Soup with Lemongrass	58
Asian Chicken Noodle Soup	59
Lemony Chicken Soup	60
Spicy Seafood Soup	61
Pumpkin Soup	62
Thai-Spiced Beef Soup with Rice Noodles	64
Vegetarian Lemongrass Soup	65
Chilled Mango Soup	66

Tom Yum

Serves 4–6

You can substitute chicken for the shrimp in this dish. Cut up 1 boneless, skinless chicken breast into bite-sized pieces, add the pieces during step 2, and poach for about 8 minutes before proceeding.

4–5 cups water
3 shallots, finely chopped
2 stalks lemongrass, bruised and cut into 1-inch-long segments
2 tablespoons fish sauce
2 tablespoons minced fresh ginger
20 medium-sized shrimp, shelled but with tails left on
1 can straw mushrooms, drained
2–3 teaspoons sliced kaffir lime leaves or lime zest
3 tablespoons lime juice
2–3 Thai chili peppers, seeded and minced

1. Pour the water into a medium-sized soup pot. Add the shallots, lemongrass, fish sauce, and ginger. Bring to a boil, reduce heat, and simmer for 3 minutes.
2. Add the shrimp and mushrooms, and cook until the shrimp turn pink. Stir in the lime zest, lime juice, and chili peppers.
3. Cover and remove from the heat. Let the soup steep for 5 to 10 minutes before serving.

Tom Yum Soup for Life
A joint study by Thailand's Kasetsart University and Japan's Kyoto and Kinki Universities has found that the ingredients in Tom Yum soup are 100 times more effective in inhibiting cancerous tumor growth than other foods. No wonder it's Thailand's bestselling soup!

Tom Ka Kai

2 cups chicken broth

1 teaspoon sliced kaffir lime
   leaves

1 (2-inch) piece of lemongrass,
   bruised

1 (1-inch) piece ginger, sliced
   thinly

4 tablespoons fish sauce

2 tablespoons lime juice

1 boneless, skinless chicken
   breast, cut into bite-sized
   pieces

5 ounces coconut milk

2–4 Thai chilies (to taste),
   slightly crushed

Serves 4–6

This soup can be
served as is or ladled
over mounds of rice in
individual serving
bowls. I love it with
some cooked noodles
thrown in.

1. In a medium-sized soup pot, heat the broth on medium. Add the lime
   leaves, lemongrass, ginger, fish sauce, and lime juice.
2. Bring the mixture to a boil, add the chicken and coconut milk, and
   bring to a boil again.
3. Reduce the heat, add the chilies, and cover; let simmer until the
   chicken is cooked through, about 3 to 5 minutes.
4. Remove the chilies and the lemongrass stalk with a slotted spoon
   before serving.

Handling Lemongrass

*Lemongrass is a very popular ingredient in Thai and other
Asian recipes. It can usually be found fresh in most well-stocked
supermarkets and can be stored in the fridge for about 3 weeks or
frozen for up to 6 months. Many recipes call for lemongrass to be
"bruised." This helps add more flavor to your recipe. If you like the
strong flavor, feel free to bruise lemongrass even when not called
for in a recipe.*

Chicken Soup with Lemongrass

Serves 4–6

This soup is an explosion of flavors—spicy from the curry paste and ginger, sweet from the coconut milk, and sour from the lime leaves. The mushrooms and the chicken let these vibrant flavors shine.

1 tablespoon vegetable oil
1 medium onion, minced
1 clove garlic, minced
1 stalk lemongrass, trimmed, bruised, and cut into 2 to 3 pieces
2 teaspoons prepared Red Curry Paste (see recipes in Chapter 1) or curry powder
1 (1-inch) piece ginger, cut into 6 pieces
3 lime leaves (fresh or dried)
4 cups chicken broth

1 (14-ounce) can unsweetened coconut milk
3/4 pound boneless, skinless chicken breast, trimmed and cut into bite-sized pieces
2 cups wild or domestic mushrooms, cut into bite-sized pieces (if necessary)
Juice of 2 limes
2 tablespoons fish sauce
Salt and pepper to taste

1. In a medium-sized saucepan, combine the oil, onion, and garlic. Cook over medium heat for 1 minute. Add the lemongrass, curry paste, ginger, and lime leaves.
2. Cook, stirring, for 3 minutes, then add the broth. Bring to a boil, reduce heat to medium, and continue to cook for 10 more minutes.
3. Add the coconut milk, the chicken pieces, and the mushrooms. Continue to cook for 5 minutes or until the chicken is done.
4. Stir in the lime juice and fish sauce. Season to taste with salt and pepper.
5. Remove the lemongrass, lime leaves, and ginger pieces before serving.

Asian Chicken Noodle Soup

2 tablespoons vegetable oil
½ cup chopped onion
2 tablespoons chopped ginger
3 cloves garlic, minced
1 cup chopped cilantro
2 cups chicken broth
5 cups water, divided
2 star anise
1 carrot, peeled and julienned
3 ounces snow peas, trimmed
1 medium-sized sweet red
    pepper, seeded and julienned

2 whole boneless, skinless
    chicken breasts, cut into
    long strips
4 ounces, cellophane noodles,
    soaked in boiling water for
    5 minutes and drained
2 tablespoons fish sauce
Peanuts, coarsely chopped
Lemon or lime wedges

Serves 4 to 6

No matter where you are, there's something comforting about chicken noodle soup. This soup is definitely Thai—together, the ginger, anise, and fish sauce create a delightful broth.

1. In a large saucepan, heat the oil on high. Add the onion and sauté until translucent. Add the ginger, garlic, and cilantro, and sauté for 1 more minute. Stir in the broth and 2 cups of the water. Add the star anise. Bring to a boil, reduce heat, and cover; simmer for 20 to 30 minutes.

2. In another saucepan, bring the remaining water to a boil. Add the vegetables and blanch for 1 minute or until tender-crisp. Drain and run very cold water over the vegetables to stop the cooking process; set aside.

3. Strain the broth into a clean soup pot and bring to a boil. Add the chicken strips and reduce heat. Poach the chicken over low heat until opaque, approximately 10 minutes. Add the cellophane noodles and reserved vegetables, and continue to simmer for 2 more minutes. Season to taste with fish sauce.

4. To serve, ladle the soup into warm bowls. Sprinkle with peanuts and garnish with lime wedge.

Lemony Chicken Soup

Serves 4–6

This soup is sure to make you pucker! The lemon and the chilies brighten the broth of this easy-to-make and oh-so-flavorful soup. If you like lemon, this soup is for you.

½ cup lemon slices, including peel
3 tablespoons fish sauce
1½ teaspoons fresh hot chili pepper, seeded and chopped
2 green onions, thinly sliced
1½ teaspoons sugar
1½ cups coconut milk
2 cups chicken broth

3 teaspoons lemongrass, peeled and chopped
1 cup straw mushrooms
1 tablespoon minced fresh ginger
1 whole boneless, skinless chicken breast, poached and shredded

1. Combine the lemon slices, fish sauce, chili pepper, green onion, and sugar in a small glass bowl; set aside.
2. Combine the coconut milk, chicken broth, lemongrass, mushrooms, and ginger in a saucepan. Bring to a boil, reduce heat, and simmer for 20 to 25 minutes. Add the chicken and lemon mixture; heat through.
3. To serve, ladle into warmed bowls.

Spicy Seafood Soup

1 tablespoon vegetable oil

1 pound medium-sized raw shrimp, peeled and deveined, shells reserved

2 quarts fish or chicken stock

1 quart water

3 stalks lemongrass, peeled and chopped

Zest of 1 lime, grated

6–8 kaffir lime leaves

10 (⅛-inch-thick) slices fresh ginger

2 fresh serrano chilies, seeded and chopped

24 fresh mussels, cleaned

2 tablespoons lime juice

2 tablespoons fish sauce

3 tablespoons chopped fresh cilantro

Red pepper flakes to taste

¼ cup sliced green onions

Salt

Serves 4–6

This soup is a Thai version of the French classic bouillabaisse—although frankly I would bet that the Thai version has been around longer than the French one. Either way, it's a great way to serve seafood.

1. Heat the vegetable oil in a large saucepan. Add the shrimp shells and sauté until they turn bright pink. Add the stock, water, lemongrass, lime zest, lime leaves, ginger, and serrano chilies. Bring to a boil, reduce heat, and simmer for 30 minutes. Strain the broth into a clean soup pot.

2. Bring the broth to a boil. Add the mussels, cover, and cook until the shells open, about 2 minutes. Use a slotted spoon to remove the mussels, discarding any that have not opened. Remove the top shell of each mussel and discard. Set aside the mussels on the half shell.

3. Add the shrimp to the boiling broth and cook until they are opaque, about 2 minutes. Reduce heat to low.

4. Add the mussels to the pot. Stir in the lime juice, fish sauce, cilantro, red pepper flakes, and green onions. Simmer for 1 to 2 minutes. Season to taste with salt.

5. Serve immediately.

Pumpkin Soup

For the broth:

2 tablespoons butter
1 small pumpkin, peeled, seeded, and cut into small chunks
1 medium-sized leek, sliced
1½ stalks celery, sliced
1 small banana, sliced
1 red chili pepper, cut in half and seeded
3 stalks lemongrass, peeled and thinly sliced

1 clove of garlic, halved
1 tablespoon finely chopped ginger
3¼ cups vegetable broth
⅓ cup half-and-half
⅓ cup coconut milk
1 tablespoon Green Curry Paste (see recipes in Chapter 1)
Salt and pepper to taste

For the chicken and vegetables:

2 tablespoons butter
1 whole boneless, skinless chicken breast, trimmed and cut into strips
2 teaspoons finely chopped ginger
2 kaffir lime leaves, cut into strips
2 teaspoons prepared Green Curry Paste (see recipes in Chapter 1)
1 tablespoon vegetable oil

1 small Japanese eggplant, cut into 4 pieces
2 red chili peppers, cut in half and seeded (optional)
¾ cup cooked rice
Thai basil

(recipe continues on the next page)

Pumpkin Soup
(continued)

To prepare the broth:

1. In a large pot, melt the butter over medium heat. Add the pumpkin, leeks, celery, bananas, chili pepper, lemongrass, garlic, and ginger; sweat for 5 minutes.
2. Add the vegetable broth and heat until warm.
3. Add the half-and-half, coconut milk, and curry paste; simmer for 15 to 20 minutes.
4. Remove the chili pepper halves. Transfer the broth mixture to a blender or food processor and purée until smooth. Strain if desired, and season to taste with salt and pepper. Pour the mixture into a clean pot and keep warm.

To prepare the chicken and vegetables:

5. Melt the butter in a heavy-bottomed sauté pan over medium heat. Add the chicken strips, ginger, lime leaves, and curry paste. Sauté until the chicken is cooked, but not browned. Add the chicken mixture to the broth.
6. In another sauté pan, heat the vegetable oil. Add the eggplant and sauté until just warmed through.
7. To serve, divide the rice among 4 soup bowls. Spoon the broth over the rice. Top with a piece of eggplant, a chili pepper half (if desired), and some basil.

Thai-Spiced Beef Soup with Rice Noodles

Serves 4–6

I like using leftover pot roast for the beef because I prefer the more tender texture, but any cooked beef will do. And frankly, you could leave out the meat entirely and still have a really great dish.

8 cups beef broth
1 whole star anise, crushed
1 (2-inch) cinnamon stick
2 (¼-inch) pieces peeled gingerroot
8 ounces rice noodles, soaked in hot water for 10 minutes, strained and rinsed in cold water
1 stalk lemongrass, tough outer leaves removed, inner core crushed and minced

¾ cup leftover beef roast, chopped or shredded
¼ cup fish sauce
1 tablespoon prepared chili-garlic sauce
2½ tablespoons lime juice
3–4 teaspoons (or to taste) salt
Freshly ground black pepper to taste

1. In a medium-sized saucepan, simmer the beef broth, star anise, cinnamon stick, and ginger over low heat for 30 to 40 minutes.
2. Strain the stock and return to the saucepan.
3. Add the noodles, lemongrass, shredded beef, fish sauce, chili sauce, and garlic. Bring the soup to a boil over medium heat. Reduce heat and simmer for 5 minutes. Stir in the lime juice, salt, and pepper.

Vegetarian Lemongrass Soup

8 cups low-sodium vegetable
  broth
1 teaspoon (or to taste)
  crushed red peppers
4–6 stalks lemongrass, bruised
4 tablespoons soy sauce
Juice of ½ lime or to taste
1 can straw mushrooms,
  drained

1 cup snow peas, trimmed
½ cup coarsely shredded
  carrots
½ cup sliced celery
1 red serrano chili, seeded
  and thinly sliced

> **Serves 4–6**
>
> The original recipe for this Lemongrass Soup calls for chicken broth and fish sauce, but I regularly use vegetable broth and soy sauce instead, and still enjoy this soup very much.

1. Bring the broth to a simmer in a large saucepan. Add the crushed red peppers, lemongrass, soy sauce, and lime juice. Simmer for 10 minutes.
2. Add the remaining ingredients. Continue to simmer until the vegetables are just done, about 2 to 3 minutes. Remove the lemongrass stalks before serving.

Vegetarian Thai Food

If you're a vegetarian, or just trying to cut back on your meat consumption, then Thai food is for you! Most Thai dishes start with rice or noodles with vegetables—meat and sauce are placed on top. Meat is rarely the main focus of the meal, and the flavors of the dish mostly come from the spices and vegetables. Generally, you can substitute tofu in any recipe that includes meat.

Chilled Mango Soup

2 large mangoes, peeled, pitted, and chopped
1½ cups chilled chicken or vegetable broth
1 cup plain yogurt
1 teaspoon sugar (optional)
1 tablespoon dry sherry
Salt and white pepper to taste

Place all of the ingredients in a blender or food processor and process until smooth. Adjust seasonings. This soup may be served immediately or refrigerated until needed. If you do refrigerate the soup, let it sit at room temperature for 10 minutes or so before serving to take some of the chill off.

CHAPTER 5
Salads

Fiery Beef Salad	68
Spicy Rice Salad	69
Spicy Shrimp Salad	70
Shrimp and Noodle Salad	71
Thailand Seafood Salad	72
Asian Noodle and Vegetable Salad	73
Grilled Calamari Salad	74
Thai Dinner Salad	75
Sweet-and-Sour Cucumber Salad	76
Cucumber Salad with Lemongrass	77
Papaya Salad	78
Zesty Melon Salad	79
Crunchy Coconut-Flavored Salad	79
Thailand Bamboo Shoots	80

Fiery Beef Salad

Serves 2–4

This entrée salad is one of my favorites—somehow hearty and light at the same time. If the weather doesn't permit grilling, the steak can be broiled instead—and it will still be good.

For the dressing:

¼ cup basil leaves
2 tablespoons chopped serrano chilies
2 cloves garlic
2 tablespoons brown sugar
2 tablespoons fish sauce
¼ teaspoon black pepper
¼ cup lemon juice

For the salad:

1 pound beef steak
Salt and pepper to taste
1 stalk lemongrass, outer leaves removed and discarded, inner stalk finely sliced
1 small red onion, finely sliced
1 small cucumber, finely sliced
1 tomato, finely sliced
½ cup mint leaves
Bibb or romaine lettuce leaves

1. Combine all of the dressing ingredients in a blender and process until well incorporated; set aside.
2. Season the steak with salt and pepper. Over a hot fire, grill to medium-rare (or to your liking). Transfer the steak to a platter, cover with foil, and let rest for 5 to 10 minutes before carving.
3. Slice the beef across the grain into thin slices.
4. Place the beef slices, any juices from the platter, and the remaining salad ingredients, except the lettuce, in a large mixing bowl. Add the dressing and toss to coat.
5. To serve, place lettuce leaves on individual plates and mound the beef mixture on top of the lettuce.

Spicy Rice Salad

For the dressing:

½ cup rice vinegar
½ cup fish sauce
¼ cup sesame oil
¼ cup hot chili oil
¼ cup lime juice

For the salad:

2 cups long-grained rice
    (preferably Jasmine)
4–6 green onions, trimmed and
    thinly sliced
2 carrots, peeled and diced
1 sweet red pepper, seeded
    and diced
1 serrano chili pepper, seeded
    and minced
¼–½ cup chopped mint
¼–½ cup chopped cilantro
1 pound cooked shrimp
⅓ cup chopped unsalted
    peanuts
Lime wedges

> **Yields approx. 8 cups**
>
> This salad is equally delicious with shredded chicken or turkey instead of the shrimp. Or if you would prefer a vegetarian salad, simply omit the shrimp! I like to have this confetti-like salad for a light lunch.

1. Whisk together all of the dressing ingredients; set aside.
2. Cook the rice according to the package directions. Fluff the rice, then transfer it to a large mixing bowl. Allow the rice to cool slightly.
3. Pour approximately ⅓ of the dressing over the rice and fluff to coat. Continue to fluff the rice every so often until it is completely cooled.
4. Add the green onions, carrots, red pepper, serrano chili pepper, mint, cilantro, and shrimp to the rice. Toss with the remaining dressing to taste.
5. To serve, place on individual plates and garnish with peanuts and lime wedges.

Vinegar Distinctions
Rice wine vinegar has a less sharp flavor than distilled white vinegar and matches particularly well with sesame oil.

Spicy Shrimp Salad

Serves 2–4

The cooked shrimp add great color and texture to this salad, but it's equally tasty if you substitute cooked mussels or scallops. Why not try combining all of them?

For the dressing:

3 tablespoons sugar
4 tablespoons fish sauce
⅓ cup lime juice
2 tablespoons prepared
    chili sauce

For the salad:

¾ pound cooked shrimp
¼ cup chopped mint
1 small red onion, thinly sliced
2 green onions, trimmed and
    thinly sliced
2 cucumbers, peeled and thinly
    sliced
Bibb lettuce leaves

1. In a small bowl, combine all the dressing ingredients. Stir until the sugar dissolves completely.
2. In a large bowl, combine all of the salad ingredients except the lettuce. Pour the dressing over and toss to coat.
3. To serve, place the lettuce leaves on individual plates. Mound a portion of the shrimp salad on top of the leaves. Serve immediately.

 Peeling Tomatoes
The trick to peeling tomatoes is to quickly blanch them in boiling water before removing the skin. Bring a pan of water to boil, then throw in the tomato for 15 to 30 seconds. Using a slotted spoon, remove the tomato from the water and run it under cold water until it is cool enough to handle. Using the tip of a knife, pull up a small piece of skin, then simply pull the skin off the flesh.

Shrimp and Noodle Salad

8 ounces rice noodles

1 stalk lemongrass, finely minced (inner core only)

1 cup citrus fruit (oranges, grape-fruit, tangerines, etc.) peeled, sectioned, and chopped

1/3 cup chopped peanuts, plus extra for garnish

1 medium tomato, peeled, seeded, and chopped

3 green onions, sliced

1/3 cup chopped mint leaves

1/3 cup chopped cilantro, plus extra for garnish

1/2–1 teaspoon dried red pepper flakes

1 clove garlic, minced

1 tablespoon brown sugar

3/4 cup lime juice (approximately 4–5 limes)

2 tablespoons fish sauce

24 medium shrimp, peeled and deveined

1 tablespoon vegetable oil

Salt and ground pepper to taste

Serves 6

I like the noodle and fruit mixture in this recipe so much, I even eat it without the shrimp. Or, you can top the noodles with anything you like— grilled scallops, grilled chicken, or grilled pork tenderloin.

1. Soak the rice noodles in hot water for 10 to 20 minutes or until soft. While the noodles are soaking, bring a large pot of water to boil.
2. Meanwhile, in a large bowl, mix together the lemongrass, citrus, peanuts, tomato, scallions, mint, and cilantro.
3. In a small bowl, combine the red pepper flakes, garlic, sugar, lime juice, and fish sauce. (Adjust seasoning to your taste.)
4. Drain the noodles from their soaking liquid and add them to the boiling water. When the water returns to a boil, drain them again and rinse thoroughly with cold water. Allow the noodles to drain thoroughly.
5. Add the noodles and the dressing to the citrus mixture and toss to combine. Set aside.
6. Brush the shrimp with the vegetable oil and season with salt and pepper. Grill or sauté for approximately 2 minutes per side or until done to your liking.
7. To serve, mound the noodles in the center of a serving platter. Place the grilled shrimp on top and garnish with peanuts and cilantro.

Thailand Seafood Salad

½ pound squid rings, poached in salted water for 30 seconds
½ pound salad shrimp
1 (6-ounce) can chopped clams, drained
2 medium cucumbers, peeled, halved, seeded, and very thinly sliced
1 stalk celery, cleaned and thinly sliced
1 small onion, finely chopped
1 stalk lemongrass, outer leaves removed, inner core minced
1 small serrano chili, seeded and finely chopped
2 tablespoons chopped mint
1 clove garlic, minced
1 green onion, trimmed and thinly sliced
¼ cup fish sauce
Sugar to taste
Bibb lettuce leaves

1. In a large mixing bowl, gently combine the squid, shrimp, clams, cucumber, and celery; set aside.
2. In a small mixing bowl, stir together the onion, lemongrass, serrano chili, mint, garlic, green onion, and fish sauce. Add sugar to taste.
3. Pour the dressing over the seafood mixture, tossing to coat. Cover and let sit for at least 30 minutes before serving.
4. To serve, place lettuce leaves in the center of 4 to 6 plates. Mound the seafood salad on top of the lettuce leaves.

Asian Noodle and Vegetable Salad

8 ounces dried rice noodles,
   cooked al dente and rinsed
   under cold water
2 teaspoons vegetable oil
1 teaspoon sesame oil
1 teaspoon soy sauce
¼ pound snow peas, trimmed
   and cut on the diagonal
1 small red bell pepper, cored,
   seeded, and cut into thin
   strips

1 medium carrot, peeled and
   thinly sliced on the diagonal
1 recipe Spicy Thai Dressing
   (see recipe on page 28)
10 basil leaves, shredded
   (preferably Thai or lemon)
4 green onions, thinly sliced
1 cup bean sprouts
1 lime, cut into 6–8 wedges
½ cup toasted peanuts,
   chopped

Serves 4–6

The riot of colors and the intense flavors of the lime, peanuts, and dressing in this salad will have you so impressed, you'll forget you were ever an omnivore.

1. In a large bowl, toss the noodles with the oils and the soy sauce.
2. Blanch the snow peas in boiling water for 30 seconds and then rinse them under cold water.
3. Add the snow peas, bell pepper, and the carrot to the noodles and toss.
4. Drizzle the Spicy Thai Dressing over the noodle mixture to taste, add the basil, half of the green onions, and half of the bean sprouts, and toss well.
5. To serve, place the noodle salad on a chilled serving platter. Scatter the remaining green onions, remaining bean sprouts, and the peanuts over the top. Squeeze the juice of 2 lime wedges over the whole dish, and use the remaining wedges as garnish. Serve immediately.

Grilled Calamari Salad

Serves 2–4

When I was a kid I thought that calamari was disgusting, but now I'm a huge fan. This recipe features calamari grilled with a light vinaigrette that I'm sure will please even the most conservative eaters.

For the dressing:

1 tablespoon fish sauce
⅓ cup water
1 stalk lemongrass, inner core finely chopped
3 kaffir lime leaves, chopped or 1 tablespoon lime zest
1 small onion, thinly sliced
5 teaspoons lime juice
1–5 red chili peppers, seeded and chopped (the more you use, the spicier it'll be!)

For the salad:

1 pound calamari, cleaned
15–20 mint leaves, chopped
6–8 sprigs cilantro, chopped
1 green onion, thinly sliced
Baby greens (optional)

1. Combine all the dressing ingredients in a small bowl; set aside.
2. Prepare a grill or broiler. Place the calamari on a broiler pan or in a grill basket and cook over high heat until tender, about 3 minutes per side. Let cool to room temperature.
3. Place the grilled calamari in a mixing bowl. Stir the dressing and pour it over the calamari.
4. If serving immediately, add the mint, cilantro, and green onions. Alternatively, allow the calamari to marinate for up to 1 hour before serving, and then add the additional ingredients.
5. To serve: Use individual cups or bowls to help capture some of the wonderful dressing. Alternatively, mound the calamari mixture over a bed of baby greens and spoon additional dressing over the top.

What Is Calamari?

Calamari is squid! Sometimes you will see the smallest ones sold whole. Otherwise it comes in pearly white pieces that you slice into bite-sized morsels. Calamari has a sweet, mild flavor and only becomes chewy when overcooked.

Thai Dinner Salad

For the dressing:

2 tablespoons fish sauce
1 tablespoon lemon juice
1 clove garlic, minced
2 teaspoons sugar
1 tablespoon water
¾ teaspoon rice wine vinegar
Pinch of red pepper flakes

For the salad:

1 small head of romaine or
  Bibb lettuce, torn into bite-
  sized pieces
2 small carrots, grated
1 cucumber, peeled, seeded,
  and diced
¼ cup chopped cilantro
¼ cup chopped mint leaves
Chopped unsalted peanuts
  (optional)

Serves 2–4

This salad gets its Thai character from the mint and cilantro in the salad and the fish sauce, rice wine vinegar, and red pepper flakes in the dressing. It's not fancy, but it's a great start to any meal.

1. In a small bowl, stir together all of the salad dressing ingredients; set aside.
2. In a large bowl, toss together all of the salad ingredients. Add dressing to taste and toss until well coated. Sprinkle chopped peanuts over the top of each salad, if desired.

Thai Salads

Thai salads are often light, flavorful, and work fantastically to get you ready for the main meal. Many of the all-vegetable salads are too light to be a meal of their own, but by simply adding some sautéed chicken, shrimp, or tofu to any salad, you've got yourself a nice lunch!

Sweet-and-Sour Cucumber Salad

5 tablespoons sugar
1 teaspoon salt
1 cup boiling water
½ cup rice or white vinegar
2 medium cucumbers, seeded and sliced

1 small red onion, sliced
2 Thai chilies, seeded and minced

1. In a small bowl, combine the sugar, salt, and boiling water. Stir to thoroughly dissolve sugar and salt. Add the vinegar and allow the vinaigrette to cool to room temperature.
2. Place the cucumbers, onion slices, and the chili peppers in a medium-sized bowl. Pour the dressing over the vegetables. Cover and let marinate in the refrigerator at least until cold, preferably overnight.

 Seeding Cucumbers
Seeding a cucumber is simple! Cut the cucumber in half lengthwise. Using a small spoon, scoop out the soft inner flesh and seeds in one quick swoop. That's it!

Cucumber Salad with Lemongrass

½ cup white vinegar

1 Thai chili, very finely minced

1 garlic clove, very finely
   minced

2 stalks lemongrass

3 cups thinly sliced cucumber

1 cup bean sprouts

1 cup cubed tart apple (such
   as Granny Smith)

½ cup shredded carrot

¼ cup minced mint

¼ cup minced parsley

1 tablespoon fish sauce

1 tablespoon vegetable oil

> **Serves 6–8**
>
> I think the Thai have figured out more ways to use cucumber than anyone else on the planet, and each one seems better than the last. The cucumber and apple in this salad yield a great contrast of flavors.

1. In a small saucepan, combine the vinegar, chili, and garlic. Bring the mixture to a boil. Cover the pan, remove it from the heat, and let cool.
2. Trim and finely chop 1 lemongrass stalk. Place it in a small saucepan with ½ cup of water, cover, and bring to a boil. Turn off heat and let cool.
3. Trim the remaining lemongrass stalk, peel off the tough outer layers, and finely mince the white portion of the tender stalk within. Reserve approximately 1 tablespoon.
4. Combine the cucumber, bean sprouts, apple, carrot, mint, and parsley in a large mixing bowl. In a small bowl combine the fish sauce, oil, minced lemongrass, the vinegar mixture, and the lemongrass water.
5. Toss the vegetables with the lemongrass vinaigrette to taste.

Preserving Fresh-Cut Apples

To keep the apple pieces from turning brown before you use them, put them in a small container of cool water to which you have added a couple of drops of lemon or lime juice. The citric acid prevents the apple from discoloring.

Papaya Salad

Serves 4–6

This recipe calls for salting the papaya in order to extract some of its liquid. This is the same method used to prepare eggplant slices for the grill or for use in an Eggplant Parmesan.

1 medium papaya, peeled and julienned, or cut into small pieces
½–1 teaspoon salt
3 jalapeño peppers, seeded and thinly sliced
4–6 cloves of garlic, chopped coarsely
½ cup long beans (green beans), cut into 1-inch pieces
2 teaspoons fish sauce
4 tablespoons Tamarind Concentrate (see recipe on page 18)
2 tomatoes, thinly sliced
Sticky rice, cooked according to package directions

1. Place the papaya on a sheet pan and sprinkle it with salt. Let the papaya stand for 30 minutes. Pour off any juice and then squeeze the fruit with your hands to extract as much fluid as possible. Place the pulp of the papaya in a large food processor.
2. Add the chilies and pulse briefly to combine. Add the remaining ingredients except the tomato and pulse again until mixed.
3. Transfer the papaya mixture to a serving bowl and garnish with tomato slices. Serve with sticky rice.

Zesty Melon Salad

6 cups assorted melon cubes
2 cucumbers, peeled, halved,
   seeded, and sliced
6–8 tablespoons lime juice
Zest of 1 lime

¼ cup honey
1 serrano chili, seeded and
   minced (for a hotter salad,
   leave the seeds in)
¼ teaspoon salt

1. In a large mixing bowl, combine the melon and the cucumber.
2. Mix the remaining ingredients together in a small bowl. Pour over the fruit and toss well to coat.
3. Serve immediately, or if you like a zestier flavor, let the salad sit for up to 2 hours to allow the chili flavor to develop.

> **Serves 4–6**
>
> A lively looking and tasting salad, it's a sure winner at a picnic. Using a hollowed out watermelon as a serving dish makes an impressive, yet easy and inexpensive, serving dish.

Crunchy Coconut-Flavored Salad

1 cup julienned jicama
1 medium cucumber, peeled,
   seeded, and julienned
2–3 tablespoons chopped fresh
   basil

1 recipe Coconut Marinade
   (see recipe on page 14)

Place the jicama, cucumber, and basil in a large bowl. Pour the marinade over the vegetables and let rest in the refrigerator for at least 2 hours before serving.

> **Serves 2–3**
>
> The cucumber and the jicama offer very different crunches—one rather juicy and one rather snappy—in this appealing salad. The basil adds just enough bite to balance the sweetness of the coconut marinade.

 Jicama

Jicama is indigenous to the Americas and looks like a big brown, rather unappetizing, root. But beneath the ugly skin is a light, crunchy vegetable with a slightly sweet taste reminiscent of apple.

Thailand Bamboo Shoots

Serves 4

Bamboo is a great plant. Humans throughout the world have used it as a food, a building material, and in hats, just to name a few uses. Here we use it as a simple salad ingredient.

1 20-ounce can of bamboo shoots, shredded, liquid reserved
Juice of ½ lime
1 teaspoon ground dried chili pepper
2 green onions, sliced
1 teaspoon fish sauce

2 tablespoons finely crushed peanuts, divided
Sticky rice, cooked according to package directions

1. Place the shredded bamboo shoots and approximately ¼ cup (half) of the reserved bamboo liquid in a medium-sized saucepan. Bring the contents of the pan to a boil, reduce heat, and let simmer until tender, about 5 minutes. Remove from heat.
2. Stir in the lime juice, chili pepper, green onions, fish sauce, and 1 tablespoon of the peanuts.
3. Serve with sticky rice, sprinkled with the remaining peanuts.

CHAPTER 6

Meat Dishes

Green Curry Beef	82
Curried Beef and Potato Stew	83
Red Beef Curry	84
Hot and Sour Beef	85
Grilled Ginger Beef	86
Thai Beef with Rice Noodles	87
Minty Stir-Fried Beef	88
Chilied Beef	89
Pork and Eggplant Stir-Fry	90
Pork with Garlic and Crushed Black Pepper	91
Bangkok-Style Roasted Pork Tenderloin	92
Chiang Mai Beef	93
Barbecued Pork on Rice	94
Lemongrass Pork	95
Pork and Spinach Curry	96
Thai-Style Beef with Broccoli	97
Pork with Tomatoes and Sticky Rice	98
Cinnamon Stewed Beef	99

Green Curry Beef

Serves 4–6

This quick and easy curry is a great introduction to Thai cuisine. It contains most of the key Thai ingredients—coconut milk, fish sauce, chilies, and basil. Serve with lots of steamed Jasmine rice.

2 cans coconut milk, thick cream separated from the milk

¼ cup (or to taste) Green Curry Paste (see recipes in Chapter 1)

1½ pounds sirloin, cut into thin strips

¼ cup brown sugar

¼ cup fish sauce

1 pound eggplant (Japanese, Thai, or a combination), cut into ¼-inch slices

6 serrano chilies, stemmed, seeded, and cut in half lengthwise

1 cup basil

1. Place the thick cream from the coconut milk and the curry paste in a large soup pot and stir to combine. Place over medium-high heat and bring to a boil. Reduce heat and simmer for 2 to 3 minutes.
2. Add the beef and the coconut milk, stirring to combine. Return the mixture to a simmer.
3. Add the sugar and the fish sauce, stirring until the sugar dissolves, about 2 minutes.
4. Add the eggplant and simmer for 1 to 2 minutes.
5. Add the serrano chilies and cook 1 minute more.
6. Remove from heat and stir in the basil.

Hot Stuff

Let your guests know that the chilies are hot and are not to be eaten by the faint of heart. They add plenty of heat and flavor just being on the plate!

Curried Beef and Potato Stew

2–3 tablespoons vegetable oil
1½ pounds beef stew meat,
    cut into bite-sized cubes
1 large onion, chopped
1 large russet potato, peeled
    and cut into bite-sized cubes
2 (14-ounce) cans coconut milk
½–¾ cup prepared Massaman
    Curry Paste (see recipe on
    page 6)

½ cup brown sugar
7 tablespoons fish sauce
¼ cup Tamarind Concentrate
    (see recipe on page 18)
1 cup chopped fresh pineapple
Jasmine rice, cooked according
    to package directions
½ cup unsalted roasted
    peanuts, chopped

> **Serves 4**
>
> Who doesn't like beef stew on a cold winter evening? This one isn't quite like Mom used to make (unless your mother is Thai), but it's still satisfying and comforting with tender chunks of beef and silky potatoes.

1. Heat the oil in a large soup pot over medium-high heat. When the oil is hot, brown the meat on all sides. Add the onion and cook until translucent, about 2 to 3 minutes.
2. Add enough water to just cover the meat and onions. Bring to a boil, reduce heat, cover, and simmer for 30 to 60 minutes.
3. Add the potatoes and continue to simmer for 15 more minutes. (The potatoes will not be quite cooked through at this point.)
4. Strain the solids from the broth, reserving both.
5. In another soup pot, combine the coconut milk with the curry paste until well blended. Bring the contents to a simmer over medium-high heat and cook for 2 to 3 minutes.
6. Add the reserved meat and potato mixture, the sugar, fish sauce, and tamarind, stirring until the sugar dissolves. Add some of the reserved broth to thin the sauce to desired consistency.
7. Stir in the pineapple and continue to simmer until the potatoes are cooked through.
8. To serve, place some Jasmine rice in the middle of individual serving plates and spoon the stew over the top. Garnish with the chopped peanuts.

Red Beef Curry

1 tablespoon vegetable oil
2 tablespoons Red Curry Paste (see recipes in Chapter 1)
½ cup plus 2 tablespoons coconut milk
1 pound lean beef, cut into thin strips
2 tablespoons (roughly) ground peanuts
1–3 tablespoons (to taste) fish sauce

Sugar to taste
1 green or red sweet pepper, seeded and cubed
¼ cup chopped basil
Rice, cooked according to package directions

1. Heat the oil in a large sauté pan over low heat. Add the curry paste and cook, stirring constantly, until fragrant, about 1 minute.
2. Stir in the ½ cup of coconut milk and bring the mixture to a simmer. Add the beef strips and poach for 5 minutes.
3. Add the peanuts and continue to poach for an additional 5 minutes.
4. Add the fish sauce and sugar to taste; continue to cook until the mixture is almost dry, then add the sweet pepper and basil and cook for 5 more minutes.
5. Serve with rice.

 Chili Varieties

The most typical fresh chilies used in Thai cuisine include jalapeños, serranos, Thai bird, and Scotch bonnet. The jalapeño is the mildest of the bunch, adding more flavor than actual heat. Serranos are a bit more searing.

Hot and Sour Beef

1 tablespoon lime juice
1 tablespoon fish sauce
1 tablespoon dark, sweet soy
   sauce
3 tablespoons chopped onion
1 teaspoon honey
1 teaspoon dried chili powder
1 green onion, trimmed and
   thinly sliced

1 teaspoon chopped cilantro
1½ pound sirloin steak
Salt and pepper to taste

> **Serves 1–2**
>
> This flavorful dish couldn't be any easier. It's great to serve when you are introducing your guests to Thai flavors, because they can add as little or as much of the sauce as they prefer.

1. Make the sauce by thoroughly combining the first 8 ingredients; set aside.
2. Season the steak with salt and pepper, then grill or broil it to your preferred doneness. Remove the steak from the grill, cover with foil, and let rest for 5 to 10 minutes.
3. Thinly slice the steak, cutting across the grain.
4. Arrange the pieces on a serving platter or on 1 or 2 dinner plates. Spoon the sauce over the top. Serve with rice and a side vegetable.

Adjusting Flavors

Don't be afraid to adjust the amount of curry paste you put in a recipe. If you want the end product to be a bit more flavorful, add a bit more; if you are looking for a more delicate taste, reduce the amount a bit

Grilled Ginger Beef

Serves 6

This may be my favorite recipe in this book. Its complex, aromatic overtones will make your taste buds beg for more. It's well worth the effort.

8 cups low-salt beef broth
2 stalks lemongrass
5 cloves garlic
1 (3-inch) piece ginger, cut in half
1 onion, cut in half
1 cinnamon stick
2 dried red chili peppers
1 (2-inch) piece of ginger, minced

1 small package of rice noodles
1 pound green vegetables
2 tablespoons (or to taste) soy sauce
6 (6-ounce) strip steaks
Salt and pepper to taste
6 scallions, minced

1. Place the beef broth, lemongrass, and garlic in a large pot; bring to a boil.
2. In the meantime, place the ginger and onion halves, cut-side down, in a dry skillet over high heat and cook until black. Add the onion and ginger to the broth mixture.
3. Place the cinnamon and dried chili peppers in the dry skillet and toast over medium heat for 1 minute; add to the broth mixture.
4. Reduce the heat and simmer the broth for 1 to 2 hours. Cool, strain, and refrigerate overnight.
5. Before you are ready to eat, remove the broth from the refrigerator and skim off any fat that may have accumulated. Bring the broth to a simmer and add the minced ginger.
6. Soak the rice noodles in hot water for 10 to 20 minutes or until soft; drain.
7. Blanch the vegetables for about a minute. Using a slotted spoon, remove them from the boiling water and shock them in cold water.
8. Season the broth to taste with the soy sauce. Season the steaks with salt and pepper and grill or broil to your liking.
9. To serve, slice the steaks into thin strips (cutting across the grain) and place them in 6 large bowls. Add a portion of noodles and vegetables to the bowls and ladle the broth over the top.

Thai Beef with Rice Noodles

¾ pound sirloin, trimmed of all
   fat, rinsed and patted dry
½ pound dried rice noodles
¼ cup soy sauce
2 tablespoons fish sauce
2 tablespoons dark brown sugar
Freshly ground black pepper
5 tablespoons vegetable oil,
   divided
2 tablespoons minced garlic

1 pound greens (such as
   spinach or bok choy), cleaned
   and cut into ½-inch strips
2 eggs, beaten
Crushed dried red pepper flakes
   to taste
Rice vinegar to taste

> **Serves 2–4**
>
> I like to use a bag of organic baby spinach leaves for the greens in this recipe because they are prewashed and small enough that you can skip the process of cutting them into strips.

1. Slice the meat into 2-inch-long, ½-inch-wide strips.
2. Cover the noodles with warm water for 5 minutes, then drain.
3. In a small bowl, combine the soy sauce, fish sauce, brown sugar, and black pepper; set aside.
4. Heat a wok or heavy skillet over high heat. Add approximately 2 tablespoons of the vegetable oil. When the oil is hot, but not smoking, add the garlic. After stirring for 5 seconds, add the greens and stir-fry for approximately 2 minutes; set aside.
5. Add 2 more tablespoons of oil to the wok. Add the beef and stir-fry until browned on all sides, about 2 minutes; set aside.
6. Heat 1 tablespoon of oil in the wok and add the noodles. Toss until warmed through, approximately 2 minutes; set aside.
7. Heat the oil remaining in the wok. Add the eggs and cook, without stirring until they are set, about 30 seconds. Break up the eggs slightly and stir in the reserved noodles, beef, and greens, and the red pepper flakes. Stir the reserved soy mixture, then add it to the wok. Toss to coat and heat through. Serve immediately with rice vinegar to sprinkle over the top.

Minty Stir-Fried Beef

7–14 (to taste) serrano chilies, seeded and coarsely chopped
¼ cup chopped garlic
¼ cup chopped yellow or white onion
¼ cup vegetable oil

1 pound flank steak, sliced across the grain into thin strips
3 tablespoons fish sauce
1 tablespoon sugar
½–¾ cup water
½ cup chopped mint leaves

1. Using a mortar and pestle or a food processor, grind together the chilies, garlic, and onion.
2. Heat the oil over medium-high heat in a wok or large skillet. Add the ground chili mixture to the oil and stir-fry for 1 to 2 minutes.
3. Add the beef and stir-fry until it just begins to brown.
4. Add the remaining ingredients, adjusting the amount of water depending on how thick you want the sauce.
5. Serve with plenty of Jasmine rice.

 Peeling Garlic
To peel garlic, place the clove on a cutting board and smash it with the back or side of a knife, which will split the skin.

Chilied Beef

3 serrano chilies, stems
  removed and sliced
¼ cup white vinegar
1 pound flank steak
1 large red onion, sliced
4 scallions, trimmed and thinly
  sliced

Juice of 1 large lime
2 tablespoons fish sauce
1 teaspoon dried red pepper
  flakes
Bibb or romaine lettuce leaves

> **Serves 4–6**
>
> This one is a zinger!
> Between the serranos
> and the dried pepper
> flakes, it really packs a
> punch. Luckily the lime
> juice helps to quench
> the fire, as does a
> cold beer or even a
> margarita!

1. Place the sliced chilies in a small bowl with the vinegar; let stand for at least 15 minutes.
2. Grill or broil the flank steak to your desired doneness. Remove from the grill, cover with foil, and let stand 10 minutes. Thinly slice the streak across the grain.
3. Place the beef slices in a large bowl. Add the red onion, scallions, lime juice, and red pepper flakes; toss all of the ingredients together. Cover the dish, place in the refrigerator, and let marinate for at least 1 hour.
4. Before serving, let the beef return to room temperature. Mound the beef on top of lettuce leaves and serve with white rice. Pass the serrano/vinegar sauce separately.

Grill Safety

Be careful around a grill. Do not add lighter fluid to a fire or hot coals. Keep your grill clean of excess grease to guard against fires. Don't forget to turn off the gas after you are finished cooking. Don't throw water on a fire to douse a flame. Instead, move the food away from the fire and let the fire burn itself out.

Pork and Eggplant Stir-Fry

3 tablespoons vegetable oil
5–10 cloves garlic, mashed
½ pound ground pork
½ teaspoon freshly ground pepper
1 tablespoon fish sauce
1 tablespoon Yellow Bean Sauce (see recipe on page 9)

1 pound Japanese eggplant, cut into ¼-inch slices
¼ cup chicken stock
2 tablespoons (or to taste) sugar

1. Heat the oil in a wok or large skillet over medium-high heat. When the oil is hot, add the garlic and stir-fry until fragrant, about 30 seconds.
2. Add the pork and continue to stir-fry until the pork loses its color, about 1 minute.
3. Add the pepper, fish sauce, bean sauce, and eggplant; cook for 1 minute.
4. Add the chicken stock. Continue to stir-fry for 2 minutes.
5. Stir in the sugar to taste and cook until the eggplant is cooked through, about 2 more minutes.

Meat Grades

Meats are graded prime, choice, and select. For dishes that cook quickly, like stir-fries, choose prime or choice. For slow-cooked dishes, like a braise, select meat will be just fine.

Pork with Garlic and Crushed Black Pepper

10–20 garlic cloves, mashed
2–2½ teaspoons black pepper-
    corns, coarsely ground
4 tablespoons vegetable oil
1 pork tenderloin, trimmed of
    all fat and cut into medal-
    lions about ¼-inch thick

¼ cup sweet black soy sauce
2 tablespoons brown sugar
2 tablespoons fish sauce

Serves 2

Be sure to use the freshest, highest quality pepper you can find. I like the rich Tellicherry pepper-corns from India. Also, make sure it is freshly ground in order to achieve its maximum flavor potential.

1. Place the garlic and the black pepper in a small food processor and process briefly to form a coarse paste; set aside.
2. Heat the oil in a wok or large skillet over medium-high heat. When the oil is hot, add the garlic-pepper paste and stir-fry until the garlic turns gold.
3. Raise the heat to high and add the pork medallions; stir-fry for 30 seconds.
4. Add the soy sauce and brown sugar, stirring until the sugar is dissolved.
5. Add the fish sauce and continue to cook until the pork is cooked through, about another 1 to 2 minutes.

Slicing Meat Paper Thin
To make thinly slicing meat easier, wrap the meat in plastic wrap and place it in the freezer until it's very cold, but not frozen. Always use the sharpest knife possible.

Bangkok-Style Roasted Pork Tenderloin

1 teaspoon salt
¼ teaspoon ground ginger
¼ teaspoon ground cardamom
¼–½ teaspoon freshly ground
    black pepper

2 (1-pound) pork tenderloins,
   trimmed
Olive oil
½ cup chicken, pork, or
   vegetable stock, or water

1. Place rack on bottom third of the oven, then preheat the oven to 500 degrees.
2. Combine the spices in a small bowl.
3. Rub each of the tenderloins with half of the spice mixture and a bit of olive oil. Place the tenderloins in a roasting pan and cook for 10 minutes.
4. Turn the tenderloins over and roast for 10 more minutes or until done to your liking.
5. Transfer the pork to a serving platter, cover with foil, and let rest.
6. Pour off any fat that has accumulated in the roasting pan. Place the pan on the stovetop over high heat and add the stock (or water). Bring to a boil, scraping the bottom of the pan to loosen any cooked-on bits. Season with salt and pepper to taste.
7. To serve, slice the tenderloins into thin slices. Pour a bit of the sauce on top, passing more separately at the table.

Chiang Mai Beef

3¼ cups water
2 cups uncooked long-grained
   rice
1 pound lean ground beef
3–4 tablespoons soy sauce
1 tablespoon vegetable oil
1 tablespoon chopped garlic

1 tablespoon small dried chilies
2 green onions, trimmed and
   sliced
Fish sauce

Serves 4–6

Chiang Mai is the principal city in Northern Thailand, known for its mountain scenery, fertile valleys, and handicrafts. This is one of the main starting points for tourists interested in jungle treks and elephant rides.

1. In a large saucepan, bring the water to a boil, then stir in the rice. Cover, reduce heat to low, and cook until the water is absorbed, about 20 minutes.
2. Put the cooked rice in a large mixing bowl and let cool to room temperature.
3. Add the ground beef and soy sauce to the rice, mixing thoroughly. (I find using my hands works best.)
4. Divide the rice-beef mixture into 8 to 12 equal portions, depending on the size you prefer, and form them into loose balls. Wrap each ball in foil, making sure to seal them well.
5. Steam the rice balls for 25 to 30 minutes or until cooked through.
6. While the rice is steaming, heat the vegetable oil in a small skillet. Add the garlic and the dried chilies and sauté until the garlic is golden. Transfer the garlic and the chilies to a paper towel to drain.
7. To serve, remove the rice packets from the foil, slightly smash them, and put on serving plates. Pass the garlic-chili mixture, the green onions, and the fish sauce separately to be used as condiments at the table.

Barbecued Pork on Rice

1 pork tenderloin, trimmed of excess fat
2 tablespoons sugar
2 tablespoons soy sauce
1 teaspoon Chinese 5-spice powder
1 hard-boiled egg, peeled
2 tablespoons flour
1½ cups water

2 tablespoons rice vinegar
1 tablespoon sesame seeds, toasted
Jasmine rice, cooked according to package directions
1 cucumber, thinly sliced
1 green onion, trimmed and thinly sliced

1. Slice the tenderloin into medallions approximately ¼-inch thick. Place the medallions in a mixing bowl.
2. Combine the sugar, soy sauce, and 5-spice powder in a small bowl.
3. Pour the soy mixture over pork strips and toss the strips until thoroughly coated. Let marinate at least 30 minutes, but preferably overnight.
4. Preheat the oven to 350 degrees. Place the pork pieces in a single layer on a baking sheet lined with foil. Reserve any leftover marinade.
5. Bake the pork for approximately 1 hour. The pork with be firm and rather dry, but not burned. It will also have a reddish color.
6. Place the reserved marinade in a small saucepan and heat to boiling. Turn off the heat and add the peeled egg, rolling it in the sauce to color it. Remove the egg and set it aside. When cool enough to handle, slice it into thin pieces.
7. Combine the flour and water, and add it to the marinade. Bring to a boil to thicken, then remove from heat.
8. Add the vinegar and the sesame seeds. Adjust seasoning by adding additional sugar and/or soy sauce.
9. To serve, place some Jasmine rice in the center of each plate. Fan a few pieces of the pork around 1 side of the rice. Fan some cucumber slices and sliced hard-boiled egg around the other side. Spoon some of the sauce over the pork and sprinkle with the green onion slices.

Lemongrass Pork

½ cup brown sugar
½ cup fish sauce
½ cup dark soy sauce
½ cup chopped lemongrass stalks
    (inner white portion only)
¼ cup whiskey
¼ cup chopped shallots
¼ cup minced garlic

¼ cup coconut milk
3 tablespoons sesame oil
1 teaspoon cayenne pepper
1 pound lean pork, cut into
    bite-sized pieces

Serves 2

You don't run across many Asian recipes that call for liquor. The whiskey complements the lemongrass in this dish incredibly well, while adding a complexity that only a fermented beverage can.

1. In a medium-sized saucepan, combine the brown sugar, fish sauce, soy sauce, lemongrass, whiskey, shallots, and garlic. Over medium heat, bring to a boil and cook until the mixture is reduced by half. Remove the marinade from the heat and allow it to cool to room temperature. Stir in the coconut milk, sesame oil, and cayenne pepper.
2. Place the pork and the marinade in a large Ziplock bag. Marinate the pork in the refrigerator for at least 3 hours, or overnight.
3. Drain the meat, reserving the marinade. Thread the meat onto metal skewers (or soaked bamboo skewers), and grill or broil to your liking.
4. Place the reserved marinade in a small saucepan and bring it to a boil over medium-high heat. Reduce the heat and simmer the marinade for 2 to 3 minutes. Use the marinade as a dipping sauce for the pork.

Pork and Spinach Curry

Serves 1–2

Some meat departments actually offer meats precut into strips, which dramatically reduces prep time. If pork strips are not available, try this recipe with beef, chicken, or turkey.

1 cup coconut milk, divided
1 tablespoon Red Curry Paste
   (see recipes in Chapter 1)
½ cup lean pork strips
2 cups water
½ lime
3–4 kaffir lime leaves, crumbled
4 tablespoons fish sauce
2 tablespoons sugar
½ pound baby spinach
Rice, cooked according to
   package directions

1. In a medium-sized saucepan, heat ½ cup of the coconut milk and the curry paste over medium-low heat, stirring to combine thoroughly. Cook for 5 minutes, stirring constantly, so that the sauce does not burn.
2. Add the pork cubes, the remaining coconut milk, and the water. Return the mixture to a simmer and let cook for 5 minutes. Squeeze the juice of the lime half into the curry. Add the lime half.
3. Stir in the kaffir lime leaves, fish sauce, and sugar. Continue simmering for 5 to 10 more minutes or until the pork is cooked through. Remove the lime half.
4. Add the baby spinach and cook for 1 minute.
5. Serve over rice.

Spinach
Spinach is an amazingly healthy leaf vegetable. Spinach is low in calories, and is a good source of vitamin C, vitamin A, and minerals, especially iron.

Thai-Style Beef with Broccoli

3 tablespoons vegetable oil
1 medium shallot, chopped
1 teaspoon chili powder
2 tablespoons brown sugar
2 tablespoons fish sauce
2 tablespoons sweet soy sauce
1 tablespoon preserved soy
   beans (optional)
1 pound lean beef, cut into
   bite-sized pieces

2 cups water
½ of a 7–8-ounce package
   of rice sticks
1 cup broccoli pieces
Lime wedges (optional)
Hot sauce (optional)

Serves 2–4

I enjoy traditional Chinese-style beef with broccoli, but I like the spiciness of this Thai version better. To make this a vegetarian dish, I omit the beef and use 3 cups of broccoli instead of only 1.

1. Heat the vegetable oil in a wok over medium-high heat. Add the shallot and stir-fry until it begins to soften. Add the chili powder and continue to stir-fry until well combined.
2. Add the brown sugar, fish sauce, soy sauce, and soy beans; stir-fry for 30 seconds.
3. Add the beef and continue to stir-fry until the beef is almost done, approximately 2 minutes.
4. Stir in the water and bring it to a boil. Add the rice sticks, stirring until they start to cook. Reduce the heat to medium, cover, and let cook for 30 seconds. Stir and reduce the heat to medium-low, cover, and let cook for 3 minutes.
5. Add the broccoli pieces, cover, and cook for 1 minute. Remove the wok from the heat and adjust seasoning to taste.
6. Serve with wedges of lime and hot sauce passed separately at the table.

Pork with Tomatoes and Sticky Rice

7 small dried chilies
½ teaspoon salt
½ teaspoon shrimp paste
2 tablespoons chopped shallot
1 tablespoon chopped garlic
1 tablespoon vegetable oil
*½ pound coarsely chopped
   lean pork*

20 cherry tomatoes, quartered
1 tablespoon fish sauce
1 teaspoon brown sugar
*Sticky rice, cooked according
   to package directions*

1. Trim the chilies of their stems and shake out the seeds. Cut them into small pieces, cover them with warm water, and let them soak for 20 minutes to soften; drain.
2. Using a food processor or mortar and pestle, grind (or process) the chilies and salt together until a thick paste is formed. Add the shrimp paste, shallot, and garlic. Process until well combined; set aside.
3. Heat a wok or heavy-bottomed skillet over low heat. Add the vegetable oil and heat for 1 minute. Add the chili purée and cook for approximately 3 minutes or until the color of the paste deepens.
4. Increase the heat to medium and add the pork; stir-fry for 1 minute. Add the tomatoes and continue to cook for 3 to 4 minutes, stirring frequently.
5. Stir in the fish sauce and brown sugar; simmer for 2 minutes. Adjust seasoning to taste.
6. Serve this beef dish with sticky rice either warm or at room temperature.

Cinnamon Stewed Beef

1½ quarts water
2 tablespoons sugar
2 whole star anise
5 tablespoons soy sauce
1 clove garlic, smashed
2 tablespoons sweet soy sauce
1 (2-inch) piece of cinnamon
   stick

5 sprigs cilantro
1 celery stalk, sliced
1 pound beef sirloin, trimmed of
   all fat and cut into 1-inch
   cubes
1 bay leaf

> **Serves 4**
>
> Cinnamon is not a spice we Westerners typically use in savory dishes, but it is great at balancing spice or salt.

1. Place the water in a large soup pot and bring to a boil. Reduce heat to low and add the remaining ingredients.
2. Simmer, adding more water if necessary, for at least 2 hours or until the beef is completely tender. If possible, let the stewed beef sit in the refrigerator overnight.
3. To serve, place noodles or rice in the bottom of 4 soup bowls. Add pieces of beef and then ladle broth over. Sprinkle with chopped cilantro or sliced green onions if you like. Pass a vinegar-chili sauce of your choice as a dip for the beef.

CHAPTER 7

Chicken Dishes

Siamese Roast Chicken	102
Tamarind Stir-Fried Chicken with Mushrooms	103
Chili-Fried Chicken	104
Thai-Style Green Curry Chicken	105
Ginger Chicken	106
Red Chili Chicken	107
Basil Chicken	108
Fragrant Roast Chicken	109
Sweet-and-Sour Chicken	110
Thai Cashew Chicken	111
Lemongrass Chicken Skewers	112
Brandied Chicken	113
Thai Glazed Chicken	114
Chicken with Black Pepper and Garlic	115
Jungle Chicken	116

Siamese Roast Chicken

Serves 2–4

The longer you let the bird take on the flavor nuances of the spice rub, the more aromatic your roast chicken will be. So if you can plan ahead, do so. It will be well worth the wait.

2 stalks lemongrass, thinly sliced (tender inner core only)
1 medium onion, chopped
1 clove garlic, minced
1 teaspoon (or to taste) dried red pepper flakes
1 tablespoon fish sauce
1 whole roasting chicken
Salt and pepper to taste
Vegetable oil

1. To prepare the marinade, place the lemongrass, onion, garlic, red pepper, and fish sauce in a food processor. Process until a thick paste is formed. Refrigerate for at least 30 minutes, overnight if possible.
2. Spread the marinade throughout the chicken cavity and then sprinkle the cavity with salt and pepper. Rub the outside of the bird with a bit of vegetable oil (or butter if you prefer) and season with salt and pepper. Place the bird in a roasting pan, and cover it with plastic wrap. Refrigerate for a few hours to marinate, if possible. Remove the chicken from the refrigerator approximately 30 minutes before roasting.
3. Preheat the oven to 500 degrees. Remove the plastic wrap and place the bird in the oven, legs first, and roast for 50 to 60 minutes or until the juices run clear.

Using Pan Drippings

Pan drippings from any roasted poultry or meat make a great "sauce" for pouring over potatoes or noodles. After you have removed the roast from the pan, pour off any fat. Place the roasting pan on a burner over medium-high heat. Add approximately ½ cup of liquid—water, stock, wine—and bring to a boil. Scrape up the browned bits off the bottom of the roaster. Cook until the liquid is reduced by about half. Remove from heat and check seasonings; adjust if necessary.

Tamarind Stir-Fried Chicken with Mushrooms

2 tablespoons vegetable oil
1–2 whole boneless, skinless
  chicken breasts, cut into
  bite-sized cubes
Salt and freshly ground black
  pepper
1 teaspoon sugar
4 ounces domestic mushrooms,
  sliced
½ cup sliced onions
1 clove garlic, minced

2 tablespoons Tamarind
  Concentrate (see recipe
  on page 18)
2 tablespoons water
1 cup bean sprouts
1 small jalapeño, seeded and
  minced
¼ cup chopped basil

Serves 1–2

This recipe calls for domestic mushrooms and it's great as is. But don't hesitate to experiment—try portobellos, creminis, shitakes, or morels. Just cut them into bite-sized pieces and go for it!

1. Heat the vegetable oil in a large sauté pan or wok over high heat. Season the chicken with the salt, pepper, and sugar.
2. Add the chicken to the pan and stir-fry for 2 minutes. Add the mushrooms, onions, and garlic; continue to cook for an additional 2 to 3 minutes. Add the tamarind and water; stir.
3. Add the remaining ingredients. Adjust seasonings to taste and serve.

Chili-Fried Chicken

3 tablespoons Tamarind
   Concentrate (see recipe on
   page 18)
Pinch of turmeric
½ teaspoon ground coriander
1½ teaspoons salt, divided
½ teaspoon white pepper
3 pounds chicken pieces,
   rinsed and patted dry

2 tablespoons vegetable oil
8 large red chilies, seeded and
   chopped
2 small onions, thinly sliced
Vegetable oil for deep-frying

1. In a small bowl combine the tamarind, turmeric, coriander, 1 teaspoon of the salt, and the pepper.
2. Place the chicken pieces in a large Ziplock bag. Pour the tamarind mixture over the chicken, seal the bag, and marinate at least 2 hours or overnight in the refrigerator.
3. In a small sauté pan, heat 2 tablespoons of vegetable oil over medium heat. Add the red chilies, onions, and the remaining salt; sauté for 5 minutes. Set aside to cool slightly.
4. Transfer the chili mixture to a food processor and pulse briefly to form a coarse sauce.
5. Drain the chicken and discard the marinade. Deep-fry the chicken pieces in hot oil until the skin is golden and the bones are crispy. Remove the cooked chicken to paper towels to drain.
6. Place the cooked chicken in a large mixing bowl. Pour the chili sauce over the chicken and toss until each piece is evenly coated.

Thai-Style Green Curry Chicken

¼ cup vegetable oil
3 whole boneless, skinless
    chicken breasts, cut into
    bite-sized pieces
¼ cup Green Curry Paste
    (see recipes in Chapter 1)
2 cups coconut milk

3 tablespoons fish sauce
¼ cup (or to taste) chopped
    cilantro leaves
Steamed white rice

Serves 4–6

Vegetables can easily be added to this dish if you like: Stir in snow peas 5 minutes before the curry is done cooking and a handful of baby spinach leaves just at the last moment.

1. Heat 2 tablespoons of vegetable oil in a large sauté pan or wok over medium heat. Add the chicken and sauté until lightly browned on all sizes. Remove the chicken and set aside.
2. Add the remaining vegetable oil to the sauté pan. Stir in the curry paste and cook for 2 to 3 minutes. Add the coconut milk and continue to cook for 5 minutes. Add the reserved chicken and fish sauce. Reduce heat and simmer until chicken is tender, 15 to 20 minutes. Stir in the cilantro.
3. Serve with steamed white rice.

Reducing Chili Fire
Roasting chilies is another way to tone down their heat, as is soaking them in ice water for an hour.

Ginger Chicken

Serves 2

Ginger is one of the most well-known of all of the Asian flavoring agents. Its bright, clean, slightly sweet, slightly hot flavor is found in everything from savory stir-fries like this one to desserts to beverages.

2 tablespoons fish sauce
2 tablespoons dark soy sauce
2 tablespoons oyster sauce
3 tablespoons vegetable oil
1 tablespoon chopped garlic
1 whole boneless, skinless chicken breast, cut into bite-sized pieces
1 cup sliced domestic mushrooms
3 tablespoons grated ginger

Pinch of sugar
3 tablespoons chopped onion
2–3 habanero or bird's eye chilis
Jasmine rice, cooked according to package directions
3 green onions, trimmed and cut into 1-inch pieces
Cilantro

1. In a small bowl combine the fish, soy, and oyster sauces; set aside.
2. Heat the oil in a large wok until very hot. Add the garlic and chicken, and stir-fry just until the chicken begins to change color.
3. Add the reserved sauce and cook until it begins to simmer, stirring constantly.
4. Add the mushrooms, ginger, sugar, onion, and chilies; simmer until the chicken is cooked through, about 8 minutes.
5. To serve, ladle the chicken over Jasmine rice and top with green onion and cilantro.

Poultry Protection

Be careful with raw poultry. It often contains bacteria that can cause food-borne illness. Keep it refrigerated at all times, even when thawing it, in a leak-proof container. Thoroughly clean all utensils and cutting boards. Sanitize them in a dishwasher or with a bleach solution. Thoroughly wash your hands with hot water and soap after handling raw poultry.

Red Chili Chicken

1 tablespoon vegetable oil
1–3 tablespoons Red Curry Paste
    (see recipes in Chapter 1)
½ cup coconut milk
1 whole boneless, skinless
    chicken breast, cut into
    bite-sized pieces
2 kaffir lime leaves or 2
    (2-inch-long, ½-inch wide)
    pieces of lime zest

1 tablespoon basil leaves
2 tablespoons fish sauce
1 tablespoon brown sugar
4 ounces Thai eggplant (green
    peas can be substituted)

Serves 2

This relatively mild curry is a perfect example of basic Thai cooking—simple ingredients and simple cooking methods leading to a flavor-packed result. No wonder Thai cooking is becoming so popular!

1. In a large skillet or wok, heat the oil over medium-high heat. Stir in the curry paste and cook until fragrant, about 1 minute.
2. Reduce the heat to medium-low and add the coconut milk. Stirring constantly, cook until a thin film of oil develops on the surface.
3. Add all of the remaining ingredients except the eggplant. Bring to a boil, reduce heat, and simmer until the chicken begins to turn opaque, about 5 minutes.
4. Add the eggplant and continue to cook until the chicken is done to your liking, about 3 minutes more.

Is a Thai Eggplant the Same as a Japanese Eggplant?

No. A Japanese eggplant is long and narrow, almost the shape and size of a large banana, but with a deep purple color. They have a mild flavor and a smooth texture. Thai eggplants, on the other hand, are green and shaped like small cherries. They have a firmer bite than the Japanese variety and can be very difficult to find. Green peas make a fine substitute.

Basil Chicken

2 tablespoons fish sauce
1½ tablespoons soy sauce
1 tablespoon water
1½ teaspoons sugar
2 whole boneless, skinless
  chicken breasts, cut into
  1-inch cubes
2 tablespoons vegetable oil
1 large onion, cut into thin
  slices

3 Thai chilies, seeded and
  thinly sliced
3 cloves garlic, minced
1½ cups chopped basil leaves,
  divided

1. In a medium-sized bowl, combine the fish sauce, the soy sauce, water, and sugar. Add the chicken cubes and stir to coat. Let marinate for 10 minutes.
2. In a large skillet or wok, heat oil over medium-high heat. Add the onion and stir-fry for 2 to 3 minutes. Add the chilies and garlic and continue to cook for an additional 30 seconds.
3. Using a slotted spoon, remove the chicken from the marinade and add it to the skillet (reserve the marinade.) Stir-fry until almost cooked through, about 3 minutes.
4. Add the reserved marinade and cook for an additional 30 seconds. Remove the skillet from the heat and stir in 1 cup of the basil.
5. Garnish with the remaining basil, and serve with rice.

Fragrant Roast Chicken

For the marinade:

½ cup fish sauce
½ cup sweet dark soy sauce
2 tablespoons crushed garlic
2 tablespoons freshly grated
   gingerroot
1 tablespoon freshly ground
   black pepper

For the stuffing:

½ cup freshly grated ginger
½ cup fresh grated galangal
½ cup sliced bruised lemongrass stalks
½ cup chopped cilantro
½ cup chopped mushrooms
1 roasting chicken, cleaned and
   patted dry

> **Serves 2–4**
>
> The stuffing in this recipe is certainly edible, but is really used for the flavor it will give to the chicken.

1. Combine all of the marinade ingredients in a plastic bag large enough to hold the whole chicken. Add the chicken, making sure to coat the whole bird with the marinade. Place the chicken in the refrigerator and leave overnight.
2. Remove the chicken from the plastic bag, reserving the marinade.
3. Place all of the stuffing ingredients in a large mixing bowl. Stir in the reserved marinade.
4. Stuff the bird's cavity and place it breast side up in a roasting pan. Place the roasting pan in a preheated 400 degree oven and roast for 50 to 60 minutes, or until the juices run clear.

Picking Lemongrass

To choose fresh lemongrass, look for stalks that are firm, full, and pale green. The color indicates freshness. Bend the stalk slightly and smell it. It should be very fragrant.

Sweet-and-Sour Chicken

Serves 4

A classic Asian dish that we have all tried at one time or another. The green and red peppers complement the sweetness of the pineapple. The chili sauce offsets the plum sauce.

2 tablespoons soy sauce
2 cloves garlic, minced
1 (1-inch) piece of ginger, peeled and minced
1–2 tablespoons prepared chili sauce
1 pound boneless, skinless chicken breasts, cut into 1-inch cubes
1 tablespoon vegetable oil
1 small onion, thinly sliced

1 green and 1 red bell pepper, seeded and cut into 1-inch pieces
8 ounces canned pineapple pieces, drained
4–6 tablespoons prepared Plum Sauce (see recipe on page 25)
Jasmine rice, cooked according to package directions

1. In a small bowl, combine the soy sauce, garlic, ginger, and chili sauce. Add the chicken pieces, stirring to coat. Set aside to marinate for at least 20 minutes.
2. Heat the oil in a wok or large skillet over medium heat. Add the onion and sauté until translucent, about 3 minutes.
3. Add the chicken mixture and continue to cook for another 3 to 5 minutes.
4. Add the bell peppers, the pineapple, and plum sauce. Cook for an additional 5 minutes or until the chicken is cooked through.
5. Serve over lots of fluffy Jasmine rice.

Thai Cashew Chicken

3 tablespoons vegetable oil

5–10 dried Thai chilies

5–10 cloves garlic, mashed

1 large whole boneless, skinless chicken breast, cut into
thin strips

4 green onions, trimmed and
cut into 1-inch lengths

1 small onion, thinly sliced

2–3 teaspoons Chili Tamarind
Paste (see recipe on page 8)

¼ cup chicken broth

1 tablespoon oyster sauce

1 tablespoon fish sauce

2 tablespoons sugar

¾ cup whole cashews

> **Serves 2–4**
>
> This is a rather pun-
> gent curry. To tone it
> down, reduce the
> number of chilies and
> garlic, and warn
> guests not to eat the
> dried chilies.

1. In a wok or large skillet, heat the oil over medium-high heat until hot.
2. Add the chilies and stir-fry briefly until they darken in color. Transfer
   the chilies to a paper towel to drain; set aside.
3. Add the garlic to the wok and stir-fry until just beginning to turn
   golden.
4. Raise the heat to high and add the chicken. Cook, stirring constantly,
   for approximately 1 minute.
5. Add the green onions and onion slices and cook for 30 seconds.
6. Add the Chili Tamarind Paste, broth, oyster sauce, fish sauce, and
   sugar. Continue to stir-fry for 30 more seconds.
7. Add the reserved chilies and the cashews; stir-fry for 1 more minute
   or until the chicken is cooked through and the onions are tender.

Chili Nutrition

*Fresh chilies are rich in vitamins A, C, and E. Red chilies
(i.e., ripe) have the most nutritional value. Cooking chilies lessens
their vitamin levels and drying them destroys most of their vitamins.*

Lemongrass Chicken Skewers

Serves 4

These skewers are based on a recipe from award-winning chef Jean-Georges Vongerichten, whose Thai cuisine has won praise worldwide. He has a line of tasty sauces and marinades that is available in stores.

5 stalks lemongrass, trimmed
12 large cubes chicken breast meat, a little over 1 ounce each
Black pepper
2 tablespoons vegetable oil, divided
Pinch of dried red pepper flakes
Juice of 1 lime
2 teaspoons fish sauce
Pinch of sugar
Sea salt to taste

1. Remove 2 inches from the thick end of each stalk of lemongrass; set aside. Bruise 4 of the lemongrass stalks with the back of a knife. Remove the tough outer layer of the fifth stalk, exposing the tender core; mince.
2. Skewer 3 cubes of chicken on each lemongrass stalk. Sprinkle the skewers with the minced lemongrass and black pepper, and drizzle with 1 tablespoon of oil. Cover with plastic wrap and refrigerate for 12 to 24 hours.
3. Chop all of the reserved lemongrass stalk ends. Place in a small saucepan and cover with water. Bring to a boil, cover, and let reduce until approximately 2 tablespoons of liquid is left; strain. Return the liquid to the saucepan and further reduce to 1 tablespoon.
4. Combine the lemongrass liquid with the red pepper flakes, lime juice, fish sauce, sugar, and remaining tablespoon of oil; set aside.
5. Prepare a grill to high heat. Grill the chicken skewers for approximately 2 to 3 minutes per side, or until done to your liking.
6. To serve, spoon a little of the lemongrass sauce over the top of each skewer and sprinkle with sea salt.

Brandied Chicken

1 whole roasting chicken,
rinsed and trimmed of
excess fat
¼ cup vegetable oil
6 tablespoons soy sauce
2 tablespoons black soy sauce
1 teaspoon salt

8 cloves garlic, minced
2 shots brandy
1 (1-inch) piece ginger, sliced

Serves 4–6

Be careful when you are lowering the bird into the scalding water. Instead of using a utensil, I actually grab the legs in my hands and carefully lower the chicken into the water.

1. Fill a pot large enough to hold the whole chicken approximately ⅓ full of water. Bring the water to a boil over high heat. Reduce the heat to medium and carefully add the chicken to the pot. Adjust the heat so that the water is just simmering.
2. Poach the whole chicken for 20 to 30 minutes or until cooked through. Carefully remove the chicken from the pot, making sure to drain the hot water from the cavity of the bird. Set the chicken aside to cool.
3. Remove the skin from the bird and discard. Remove the meat from the chicken and cut it into 1-inch pieces; set aside. (This portion of the recipe can be done 1 or 2 days in advance.)
4. Add the oil to a large skillet or wok and heat on medium. Add the soy sauces, salt, and garlic. Stir-fry until the garlic begins to soften, about 30 seconds to 1 minute.
5. Add the chicken pieces, stirring to coat. Stir in the brandy and the ginger.
6. Cover the skillet or wok, reduce the heat to low, and simmer 5 to 10 more minutes.

Thai Glazed Chicken

Serves 2–4

The marinade for this dish looks rather like watered-down milk, but don't let the blah appearance fool you: It's delicious. Unlike many Thai marinades, this one is not terribly spicy.

1 whole chicken, cut in half (ask your butcher to do this for you)
1 teaspoon salt
4 cloves garlic, chopped
1 teaspoon white pepper
1 tablespoon minced cilantro
2 tablespoons rice wine

2 tablespoons coconut milk
1 tablespoon fish sauce
1 teaspoon chopped ginger
2 tablespoons soy sauce

1. Rinse the chicken under cold water, then pat dry. Trim off any excess fat or skin. Place the chicken halves in large Ziplock bags.
2. Stir the remaining ingredients together in a small bowl until well combined.
3. Pour the marinade into the Ziplock bags, seal closed, and turn until the chicken is evenly coated with the marinade. Let the chicken marinate for 30 minutes to 1 hour in the refrigerator.
4. Preheat the oven to 350 degrees.
5. Remove the chicken from the bags and place them breast side up in a roasting pan large enough to hold them comfortably. (Discard the remaining marinade.)
6. Roast the chicken for 45 minutes.
7. Turn on the broiler and broil for approximately 10 minutes or until done.

Chicken
with Black Pepper and Garlic

*1 tablespoon whole black
   peppercorns*
5 cloves garlic, cut in half
*2 pounds boneless, skinless
   chicken breasts, cut into
   strips*

⅓ cup fish sauce
3 tablespoons vegetable oil
1 teaspoon sugar

> **Serves 4–6**
>
> Serve the chicken with mounds of Jasmine rice. Garnish plates with slices of cucumber and tomato.

1. Using either a mortar and pestle or a food processor, combine the black peppercorns with the garlic.
2. Place the chicken strips in a large mixing bowl. Add the garlic-pepper mixture and the fish sauce, and stir to combine.
3. Cover the bowl, place in the refrigerator, and let marinate for 20 to 30 minutes.
4. Heat the vegetable oil over medium heat in a wok or skillet. When it is hot, add the chicken mixture and stir-fry until cooked through, about 3 to 5 minutes.
5. Stir in the sugar. Add additional sugar or fish sauce to taste.

The Glory of the Mortar (and Pestle)

The grinding action of a mortar and pestle releases the oils and flavor essence of the substances being mashed. Unlike a food processor, a mortar will mash ingredients together completely and fully, creating a much more intense and flavorful combination. However, using a mortar and pestle can sometimes be very tiresome. If you enjoy cooking, using a mortar and pestle will probably be something you'll love—both the process and the results!

Jungle Chicken

Serves 2–3

Like the tiger, this dish can be a bit ferocious and can pack quite a bite! So beware!

2–4 serrano chilies, stems and
   seeds removed
1 stalk lemongrass, inner portion roughly chopped
2 (2-inch-long, ½-inch wide)
   strips of lime peel
2 tablespoons vegetable oil
½ cup coconut milk
1 whole boneless, skinless
   chicken breast, cut into thin
   strips
2–4 tablespoons fish sauce
10–15 basil leaves

1. Place the chilies, lemongrass, and lime peel into a food processor and process until ground.
2. Heat the oil over medium-high heat in a wok or large skillet. Add the chili mixture and sauté for 1 to 2 minutes.
3. Stir in the coconut milk and cook for 2 minutes.
4. Add the chicken and cook until the chicken is cooked through, about 5 minutes.
5. Reduce heat to low and add the fish sauce and basil leaves to taste.
6. Serve with plenty of Jasmine rice.

CHAPTER 8
Fish and Seafood Dishes

Snapper Baked with Fish Sauce and Garlic	118
Lime-Ginger Fillets	119
Baked Redfish with Lime Vinaigrette	120
Broiled Salmon with 5-Spice Lime Butter	121
Roasted Southeast Asian Fish	122
Steamed Red Snapper	123
Marinated Steamed Fish	124
Quick Asian-Grilled Fish	125
Seafood Stir-Fry	126
Curried Mussels	127
Steamed Mussels with Lemongrass	128
Clams with Hot Basil	129
Stir-Fried Shrimp and Green Beans	129
Seared Coconut Scallops	130
Curried Shrimp with Peas	131
Basil Scallops	132

Snapper Baked
with Fish Sauce and Garlic

2 whole small red snappers, cleaned but left whole
¼ cup fish sauce

1 tablespoon sesame oil
2 cloves garlic, minced

1. With a sharp knife, make 3 deep diagonal slits on each side of the fish. Place the fish in an ovenproof baking dish.
2. Combine the fish sauce, sesame oil, and garlic in a small bowl. Spoon the mixture over the fish, making sure it goes into the slits. Let the fish sit at room temperature for 30 minutes.
3. Bake the fish in a 425-degree oven for 30 minutes or until the skin is crisp.

How to Find the Freshest Seafood
The best source for great fish is a great fishmonger, someone who will steer you to the best fish he or she has. If you are on your own, follow your nose. Fresh fish should NOT smell fishy. Instead it should smell clean, and if an ocean fish, like the sea. If there is any fishy smell at all, don't buy it. Other things to look for: Feel the skin; it should be slippery and moist. Press the fish; it should feel firm. Look at the eyes; they should be plump and clear.

Lime-Ginger Fillets

4 tablespoons unsalted butter,
   at room temperature
2 teaspoons lime zest
½ teaspoon ground ginger
½ teaspoon salt

4 fish fillets, such as whitefish,
   perch, or pike
Salt and freshly ground black
   pepper

1. Preheat the broiler.
2. In a small bowl, thoroughly combine the butter, lime zest, ginger, and ½ teaspoon salt.
3. Lightly season the fillets with salt and pepper and place on a baking sheet.
4. Broil for 4 minutes. Brush each fillet with some of the lime-ginger butter and continue to broil for 1 minute or until the fish is done to your liking.

Storing Fish

How to store fresh fish: The best way to store fresh fish is not to store it at all, but rather use it the day you purchase it. If that's not an option, lay the fish on a bed of ice and then cover it. Make sure that the ice has somewhere to drain so that the fish doesn't end up sitting in water, which will cause it to turn mushy.

Baked Redfish
with Lime Vinaigrette

2 (6-ounce) redfish fillets,
  rinsed and patted dry
  (skate, sole, or flounder
  also work well)
1 clove garlic, minced
2 tablespoons lime juice
2 teaspoons soy or fish sauce

½ teaspoon sugar
¼ teaspoon salt
2 tablespoons vegetable oil

1. Place the fillets in a shallow baking dish.
2. In a small bowl, combine the garlic, lime juice, soy sauce, sugar, and salt, then whisk in the oil.
3. Pour the vinaigrette over the fish and bake in a 450-degree oven for 6 to 7 minutes or until done to your liking.

Eco-Friendly Fish Choices
Many types of fish are on their way to extinction due to over-fishing. But here are a few, according to the Audubon Society, that are still plentiful—Alaska salmon, mahi-mahi, striped bass, Pacific halibut, catfish, farmed tilapia, farmed scallops, pole-caught tuna, and rainbow trout.

Broiled Salmon
with 5-Spice Lime Butter

Vegetable oil
2 (6-ounce) salmon fillets,
　　rinsed and patted dry
1 tablespoon unsalted butter

¼–½ teaspoon Chinese 5-spice
　　powder
2 teaspoons lime juice

Serves 2

I'm a salmon fan. I like it poached, grilled, broiled, and smoked—any way really. No matter what variety you buy, they all seem to share that slightly sweet flavor that I haven't found in any other fish.

1. Using paper towels, wipe a thin coat of vegetable oil over a broiler pan.
2. Preheat the broiler on high, with the rack set on the upper third of the oven.
3. Melt the butter over low heat in a small saucepan. Stir in the 5-spice powder and lime juice; keep warm.
4. Place the salmon on the broiler pan, skin side up. Broil for 2 to 4 minutes or until the skin is crispy. Turn the salmon over and broil 2 minutes more or until done to your liking.
5. Transfer the salmon to 2 plates and spoon the butter sauce over the top.

Fatty Fish

Fatty fish are good for you! Fish such as tuna, salmon, and mackerel have high levels of Omega-3, a fatty acid shown to help prevent blood clots. Omega-3 has also been linked to lowering triglycerides and cholesterol.

Roasted Southeast Asian Fish

Serves 4

A great light meal is created when you let the fish in this recipe cool to room temperature and place it on a bed of greens that have been tossed in Thai Vinaigrette (see recipes in Chapter 2).

¼ cup chopped green onion
3 cloves garlic
4 thin slices of gingerroot
4 small fresh red chilies, seeded, 2 left whole and 2 julienned
Zest of 1 lime
1 teaspoon salt

4 (8-ounce) fish fillets (salmon or mackerel are good choices)
4 (12-inch-square) pieces of aluminum foil
12 fresh cilantro sprigs
8 thin lime slices, cut in half

1. In a food processor, combine the green onions, garlic, gingerroot, the 2 seeded whole chilies, the lime zest, and salt.
2. Preheat the oven to 450 degrees.
3. Rinse the fish under cold water and pat dry. Place each fillet in the center of a piece of foil. Rub generously with the green onion paste. Top with the cilantro leaves, lime slices, and julienned chilies. Wrap the fish in the foil.
4. Place the fish on a baking sheet and roast for approximately 10 minutes per inch of thickness.
5. To serve, place unopened packets on each plate. Let guests unwrap.

Roasting Meat

Roasting or grilling meats, poultry, and fish in aluminum foil is a terrific way to seal in juices and flavor. It makes additional fat unnecessary, and—maybe best of all—it makes cleanup a breeze. Give it a try and you may never go back!

Steamed Red Snapper

*1 whole red snapper
(about 2 pounds), cleaned,
but left whole*
Vegetable oil

*1 recipe of sauce, such as
Minty Dipping Sauce (see
page 24), Sweet-and-Sour
Dipping Sauce (see page
25), or Mango-Pineapple
Salsa (see page 26)*

Serves 4

This is a great dinner party dish. Its vibrant color makes a dramatic presentation. Place the whole fish on a serving platter and garnish with lime slices, whole chilies, and coconut wedges. Pass the sauce separately.

1. Quickly rinse the fish under cold water. Pat dry with paper towels. With a sharp knife, deeply score the fish 3 to 4 times on each side.
2. Fill the base of a tiered steamer ⅓ full of water. Bring the water to a boil.
3. In the meantime, lightly coat the steamer rack with vegetable oil. Place the fish on the rack.
4. Place the rack over the boiling water, cover, and let steam for 10 to 12 minutes, until the flesh of the fish is opaque when pierced with a knife.
5. Serve the sauce on the side.

Red Snapper

Red snapper is one of the most cherished of fish. Its moist, white flesh has a delicate, sweet flavor. It can readily be found fresh or frozen, and can be served broiled, baked, steamed, poached, fried, or grilled. If not available, rock cod, white sea bass, and calico bass are popular substitutions.

Marinated Steamed Fish

Serves 4

This fish gets its flavoring from the unique marinade, which is more of a paste than a traditional liquid. The finished fish is packed with flavor, but if you like, a squeeze of lemon or lime juice certainly won't hurt.

1 whole lean flatfish (such as redfish, flounder, or bass), cleaned
1 large mushroom, thinly sliced
2 tablespoons grated ginger
1 tablespoon sliced jalapeño pepper
2 green onions, finely sliced
3 tablespoons fish sauce
1 tablespoon soy sauce
1 tablespoon shrimp paste
1 teaspoon Tabasco
Vegetable oil

1. Quickly rinse the fish under cold water. Pat dry with paper towels. With a sharp knife, deeply score the fish 3 to 4 times on each side.
2. Stir together all of the remaining ingredients except the vegetable oil.
3. Place the fish in a large plastic bag. Pour the marinade over the fish and seal. Let the fish marinate for about 1 hour in the refrigerator.
4. Fill the base of a tiered steamer ⅓ full of water. Bring the water to a boil.
5. In the meantime, lightly coat the rack with vegetable oil. Place the fish on the rack.
6. Place the rack over the boiling water, cover, and let steam for 15 to 20 minutes, until the flesh of the fish is opaque when pierced with a knife.

Don't Over-Marinate
If your fish marinade has an acid in it (such as lemon or lime juice), don't marinate it for more than an hour or the marinade will begin "to cook" your fish. (Unless, of course, you are making cerviche.)

Quick Asian-Grilled Fish

1 whole fish, such as sea
   bass or mackerel, cleaned
4 tablespoons chopped cilantro
3 tablespoons chopped garlic,
   divided
1 teaspoon freshly ground
   black pepper

3 tablespoons lime juice
1 tablespoon sliced jalapeño
   chili peppers
2 teaspoons brown sugar

Serves 4–6
Alternatively, this fish can be cooked on a baking sheet in a 450-degree oven for approximately 10 to 12 minutes. Serve it with a variety of Thai-inspired salads—one featuring rice, one featuring veggies, and one with fruit.

1. Quickly rinse the fish under cold water. Pat dry with paper towels. Set the fish on a large sheet of aluminum foil.
2. Place the cilantro, 2 tablespoons of the garlic, and the black pepper in a food processor and process to form a thick paste.
3. Rub the paste all over the fish, both inside and out. Tightly wrap the fish in the foil.
4. To make the sauce, place the remaining garlic, the lime juice, jalapeños, and brown sugar in a food processor and pulse until combined.
5. Place the fish on a prepared grill and cook for 5 to 6 minutes per side or until the flesh is opaque when pierced with the tip of a knife.
6. Serve the fish with the sauce.

Thai Manners
Cleaning your plate in Thailand makes you a bad dinner guest. It makes your host appear not to be generous.

Seafood Stir-Fry

Serves 2–4

When I'm in the seafood section of the grocery store and everything looks great, I start thinking about this simple stir-fry. I buy a little of every-thing that strikes my fancy, go home, and have a seafood feast.

3 tablespoons vegetable oil
3 teaspoons garlic, chopped
2 shallots, chopped
1 stalk lemongrass, bruised
¼ cup chopped basil
1 can bamboo shoots, rinsed and drained
3 tablespoons fish sauce
Pinch of brown sugar

1 pound fresh shrimp, scal-lops, or other seafood, cleaned
Rice, cooked according to package directions

1. Heat the oil in a skillet or wok over high heat. Add the garlic, shallots, lemongrass, and basil, and sauté for 1 to 2 minutes.
2. Reduce heat, add the remaining ingredients, and stir-fry until the seafood is done to your liking, approximately 5 minutes.
3. Serve over rice.

Bamboo

Bamboo, a favorite of panda bears, is indigenous to Asia. However, bamboo is farmed in California and actually grows wild in some parts of Arizona!

Curried Mussels

2 tablespoons butter
2 shallots, minced
½ cup sweet white wine, such as Riesling
2 pounds mussels, debearded and rinsed well
½ cup sour cream
1 teaspoon (or to taste) curry powder
1 tablespoon lemon juice

Serves 2–4

Make sure to have empty bowls on the table to hold all of the empty shells. Use appetizer forks if you have them. Their smallish size and reduced number of tines make it easier to get at the mussels.

1. In a pan large enough to hold all of the mussels, melt the butter over medium heat. Add the shallots and sauté until softened and translucent.
2. Add the wine and the mussels and increase the heat to high. Cover and cook, shaking the pan occasionally, until the mussels open, approximately 10 minutes.
3. Remove the mussels from the pan, discarding any mussels that haven't opened. Strain the pan liquid through a strainer and return it to the pan. Bring to a boil, then stir in the sour cream and curry powder.
4. Reduce the heat to medium-low and add the lemon juice. Cook for 2 to 3 minutes. Adjust the seasonings of the sauce if necessary with salt and curry powder.
5. Return the mussels to the broth, coating them. Reheat and serve.

Cleaning Mussels

Don't clean the mussels until just before you cook them. Scrape off any barnacles that are on the shells with a knife or scouring pad. Pull off any strands. (This is called debearding.) Throw out any mussels that are open. Place the mussels in a colander and rinse thoroughly under cool water. Use as soon as possible.

Steamed Mussels with Lemongrass

3 cups water
2 stalks lemongrass, outer leaves removed and discarded, inner portion bruised
Peel of 1 lime
5 cloves garlic
3 (½-inch) slices unpeeled ginger
2 pounds mussels, cleaned
1 serrano chili
Tabasco to taste

1. Place the water, lemongrass, lime, garlic, and ginger in a pot large enough to hold all of the mussels. Bring to a boil, reduce heat, and let simmer for 5 minutes.
2. Bring the liquid back to a boil and add the mussels; cover and let steam for 5 minutes, shaking the pan every so often.
3. Transfer the mussels to a serving platter, discarding any mussels that have not opened.
4. Add the chili pepper to the broth and simmer for an additional 2 minutes. Strain the broth, then pour over the mussels.
5. Serve the mussels with Tabasco on the side.

 Closed Mussels
Do not eat any mussels that have not opened during the cooking process. Throw them away!

Clams with Hot Basil

1 tablespoon vegetable oil
2 small dried red chili pep-
    pers, crushed
2 cloves garlic
2 pounds Manila clams, cleaned

4 teaspoons fish sauce
2 teaspoons sugar
1 bunch basil (Thai variety
    preferred), trimmed and
    julienned

1. Heat the oil in a large skillet on high. Add the chili peppers, garlic, and clams. Stir the clams until they open, about 4 to 5 minutes. Discard any clams that remain closed.
2. Add the fish sauce and sugar; stir until well combined.
3. Add the basil and stir until it wilts.
4. Serve immediately either as an appetizer or with rice as a main course.

> **Serves 4–6**
>
> Handle the clams in the same manner you do mussels—rinse them, debeard them, and discard any that are open before you cook them.

Stir-Fried Shrimp and Green Beans

1 tablespoon vegetable oil
1 tablespoon Red Curry Paste
    (see recipes in Chapter 1)
½ cup cleaned shrimp

1½ cups green beans, trimmed
    and cut into 1-inch lengths
2 teaspoons fish sauce
2 teaspoons sugar

1. Heat the vegetable oil over medium heat. Stir in the curry paste and cook for 1 minute to release the fragrance.
2. Add the shrimp and the green beans at the same time, and stir-fry until the shrimp become opaque. (The green beans will still be quite crispy. If you prefer your beans softer, cook an additional minute.)
3. Add the fish sauce and the sugar; stir to combine.
4. Serve immediately with rice.

> **Serves 2–3**
>
> The green beans are the stars of this simple stir-fry, but the shrimp are the highlight. They give the beans a bit more flavor and the dish more color and protein!

Seared Coconut Scallops

Serves 2

These sweet scallops have just a hint of heat and are so good, they may not make it to the dinner table. They may just disappear right off the paper towels!

1½ cups sweetened, flaked coconut
2 cups boiling water
¼ teaspoon cayenne
½ teaspoon salt

10 medium sea scallops, cleaned, rinsed, and patted dry
Salt and pepper
1 large egg, beaten

1. Preheat the oven to 350 degrees.
2. Place the coconut in a small bowl. Pour the boiling water over the coconut, stir, and then drain through a colander. Pat dry.
3. Spread the coconut on a baking sheet and bake for 10 minutes or until golden.
4. Place the toasted coconut in a small bowl and mix in the cayenne and salt.
5. Season the scallops with salt and pepper.
6. Heat a heavy, nonstick pan over high heat until almost smoking.
7. Dip each scallop in the beaten egg, letting most of the egg drip off, then press the scallops into the coconut mixture.
8. Place the scallops in the pan and sear for 1 to 1½ minutes per side until just done.

Choosing Scallops

The best scallops in the world are called "diver scallops" because they are harvested by-you guessed it-scuba divers! This method, although costly, is environmentally superior to the net method for the same reasons the scallops taste better-the entire environment is not disturbed, shells are not cracked, and only the mature scallops are taken.

Curried Shrimp with Peas

1½ teaspoons Red Curry Paste
    (see recipes in Chapter 1)
1 tablespoon vegetable oil
1 (14-ounce) can unsweetened
    coconut milk
4 teaspoons fish sauce
2-3 teaspoons brown sugar
2 pounds large shrimp, peeled
    and deveined

1 cup packed basil leaves,
    chopped
1 cup packed cilantro, chopped
1 (10-ounce) package thawed
    frozen peas
Jasmine rice, cooked according
    to package directions

Serves 4-6
A beautifully colored curry-pink shrimp in a pink sauce peppered with green peas! The shrimp and the peas have a freshness that perfectly complements the silkiness of the Jasmine rice.

1. In a large pot, combine the curry paste, vegetable oil, and ¼ cup of the coconut milk; cook over medium heat for 1 to 2 minutes.
2. Stir in the remaining coconut milk and cook for another 5 minutes.
3. Add the fish sauce and sugar, and cook for 1 minute more.
4. Add the shrimp, basil, and cilantro; reduce heat slightly and cook for 4 to 5 minutes or until the shrimp are almost done.
5. Add the peas and cook 2 minutes more.
6. Serve over Jasmine rice.

Shrimp Sizes
Shrimp are sized according to how many come in a pound. Medium means that there are about 40 shrimp per pound. Large equals 30, extra-large equals 25, jumbo equals 20, and colossal equals about 15. Salad shrimp are too tiny to count, so they are weighed instead.

Basil Scallops

2 tablespoons vegetable oil
3 cloves garlic, chopped
3 kaffir lime leaves, julienned, or the peel of 1 small lime cut into thin strips
½ pound bay scallops, cleaned
1 (14-ounce) can straw mushrooms, drained
¼ cup shredded bamboo shoots
3 tablespoons oyster sauce
15–20 fresh basil leaves

1. In a wok or skillet, heat the oil on high. Add the garlic and lime leaves, and stir-fry until fragrant, about 15 seconds.
2. Add the scallops, mushrooms, bamboo shoots, and oyster sauce; continue to stir-fry for approximately 4 to 5 minutes or until the scallops are done to your liking.
3. Mix in the basil leaves and serve immediately.

CHAPTER 9

Vegetable Dishes

Thai Vegetable Curry	134
Vegetables Poached in Coconut Milk	135
Southeastern Vegetable Stew	136
Vegetarian Stir-Fry	137
Thai Pickled Vegetables	138
Asian Grilled Vegetables	139
Pumpkin with Peppercorns and Garlic	140
Gingered Green Beans	141
Curried Green Beans	141
Green Beans with Macadamia Nut Sauce	142
Roasted Asian Cauliflower	143
Spicy Stir-Fried Corn	143
Grilled Eggplant with an Asian Twist	144
Japanese Eggplant with Tofu	144
Stir-Fried Black Mushrooms and Asparagus	145
Thai-Style Fried Okra	145
Tropical Vegetables	146
Thai-Style Bean Sprouts and Snap Peas	147

Thai Vegetable Curry

Serves 4–6

Don't be afraid to experiment. In this recipe you can add just about any veggies you want. Try substituting sweet potatoes for the boiling potatoes and Brussels sprouts for the broccoli.

2 tablespoons vegetable oil
¼ cup Green Curry Paste
   (see recipes in Chapter 1)
3 cups canned, unsweetened
   coconut milk
3 tablespoons fish sauce
1 pound small boiling potatoes,
   quartered (or halved if large)
1 pound Japanese eggplant,
   cut into 1-inch slices

12 ounces baby carrots
2 cups broccoli florets
3–4 ounces green beans,
   cut into 1-inch lengths
½ cup fresh minced cilantro

1. In a heavy stew pot, heat the oil. Add the curry paste and cook for 2 to 3 minutes.
2. Add the coconut milk and fish sauce; simmer for 5 minutes.
3. Add the potatoes, eggplant, and carrots, and bring to a boil. Reduce heat and simmer for 10 minutes. Add the broccoli and green beans; continue to simmer until the vegetables are cooked through, about 10 minutes.
4. Just before serving stir in the cilantro.

Soy Sauce?
The Thai will know immediately that you are a foreigner if you ask for soy sauce. It's usually available, but it is not a traditional condiment. Fish sauce is the way to go.

Vegetables Poached in Coconut Milk

1 cup coconut milk
1 shallot, finely chopped
1 tablespoon soy sauce
1 tablespoon brown sugar
1 tablespoon Thai chilies,
    seeded and finely sliced
1 tablespoon green pepper-
    corns, tied together in a
    small pouch made from a
    Handi Wipe

½ teaspoon sliced kaffir lime
    leaves
½ cup long beans or green
    beans, broken into 2-inch
    pieces
½ cup sliced mushrooms
1 cup shredded cabbage
½ cup peas
Rice, cooked according to
    package directions

> **Serves 2–4**
>
> Each vegetable in this dish is rather mild in flavor and tends to absorb different amounts of the poaching liquid, giving the diner a slightly different flavor sensation with every bite.

1. In a saucepan bring the coconut milk to a gentle simmer over medium heat. Stir in the shallots, soy sauce, brown sugar, chilies, green peppercorn pouch, and lime leaves. Simmer for 1 to 2 minutes until aromatic.
2. Add the green beans, mushrooms, and cabbage, and return to a simmer. Cook for 5 to 10 minutes or until tender.
3. Add the peas and cook 1 more minute. Remove the pouch of peppercorns before serving over rice.

Kaffir Limes
The kaffir lime tree produces fruit and leaves that make great additions to dishes. It imparts a wonderful tropical fruit flavor to any dish.

Southeastern Vegetable Stew

8 cups vegetable stock
3 tablespoons fish sauce
2 tablespoons dark soy sauce
2 tablespoons brown sugar
4 cups turnip, cut into bite-
sized pieces
1 Chinese cabbage, cut into
bite-sized pieces
1 Western cabbage, quartered,
cored, and cut into bite-
sized pieces
1 cup sliced leeks
2 cups sliced celery

4 cups roughly chopped kale
1 can straw mushrooms,
drained
5 cakes hard tofu, cut into
bite-sized pieces
1 teaspoon vegetable oil
6 tablespoons soybean paste
3 tablespoons chopped garlic
1 tablespoon minced ginger
3 cups bean noodles, soaked,
and cut into short lengths
½ cup chopped cilantro
Freshly ground pepper to taste

1. Bring the stock to a boil and add the fish sauce, soy sauce, and brown sugar.
2. Reduce the heat, add the vegetables and tofu, and simmer until the vegetables are almost tender.
3. In a small sauté pan, heat the oil over medium heat. Add the soybean paste and stir-fry until fragrant. Add the garlic and ginger, and stir-fry until the garlic is golden.
4. Add the soybean paste mixture to the soup. Stir in the noodles and cilantro, and simmer 5 more minutes.
5. Season with the pepper and additional fish sauce to taste.

Vegetarian Stir-Fry

1–2 tablespoons vegetable oil
2 cups bite-sized tofu pieces
2 tablespoons minced garlic
2 tablespoons grated ginger
4 tablespoons seeded and
  sliced Thai chilies
4 tablespoons soy sauce
2 tablespoons dark sweet
  soy sauce
1 small onion, sliced
¼ cup snow peas
¼ cup thinly sliced celery

¼ cup water chestnuts
¼ cup bite-sized pieces
  bell pepper
¼ cup sliced mushrooms
¼ cup cauliflower florets
¼ cup broccoli florets
¼ cup asparagus tips
1 tablespoon cornstarch,
  dissolved in a little water
¼ cup bean sprouts
Rice, cooked according to
  package directions

**Serves 4-6
as a main course**

If your vegetable bin ends up looking like mine, with a bit of this and a bit of that, this is the recipe for you. You can follow the ingredient list precisely, or substitute to your heart's desire.

1. Heat 1 tablespoon of oil in a large skillet or wok over medium-high heat. Add the tofu and sauté until golden brown. Transfer the tofu to paper towels to drain.
2. Add additional oil to the skillet if necessary, and stir-fry the garlic, ginger, and chilies to release their fragrance, about 2 to 3 minutes. Stir in the soy sauces and increase the heat to high.
3. Add the reserved tofu and all the vegetables except the bean sprouts; stir-fry for 1 minute.
4. Add the cornstarch mixture and stir-fry for another minute or until the vegetables are just cooked through and the sauce has thickened slightly.
5. Add the bean sprouts, stirring briefly to warm them.
6. Serve over rice.

Thai Pickled Vegetables

Yields approx. 6 cups

These pickled vegetables are great as a side dish, a snack, or on top of a bed of greens. The longer they sit in the marinade, the spicier and more vinegary they will get.

4 cups water
1 cup baby corn
1 cup broccoli florets
1 cup sliced carrots
½ cup bok choy
1 large cucumber, seeded
   and cut into 3-inch-long,
   ½-inch wide strips

1 recipe Thai Vinegar
   Marinade (see recipe
   on page 15)
½ cup cilantro leaves
2–3 tablespoons toasted
   sesame seeds

1. Bring the water to a boil in a large pan. Add the vegetables and blanch for 2 to 3 minutes. Strain the vegetables and shock with cool water to stop the cooking process.
2. Place the vegetables in a large bowl and pour the Thai Vinegar Marinade over the top. Let cool to room temperature and then refrigerate for at least 4 hours or up to 2 weeks (yes, weeks).
3. Stir in the cilantro and sesame seeds just before serving.

Asian Grilled Vegetables

2 bell peppers (red, yellow, or
green, in any combination),
seeded and cut into 2-inch
squares

1 zucchini, cut into 1-inch slices

1 summer squash, cut into
1-inch slices

12 whole mushrooms, approximately 1-inch in diameter

12 whole pearl onions or
12 (2-inch) pieces of
white onion

1 recipe Asian Marinade
(see recipes in Chapter 1)

Serves 6

If you are planning on serving your vegetables from a bowl, don't bother with the skewers. Simply place the vegetables in a pan, marinate them, and then place them in a grill basket to cook.

1. Alternate the vegetables on 6 skewers (soak the skewers in water until soft if using wooden skewers).
2. Place the skewers in a pan large enough to allow them to lay flat. Pour the marinade over the skewers and let sit for approximately 1 hour.
3. Place the skewers in a lightly oiled grill basket and place on a hot grill. Cook approximately 5 minutes on each side or until vegetables are done to your liking.

Grilling Isn't Just for Meats!

Grilling vegetables may be my favorite way to prepare them. Even when I just baste them in a little olive oil and sprinkle them with salt and pepper, grilling gives them this special taste you just can't get any other way. And if you burn them a little bit—who cares—the charring just adds a little more flavor!

Pumpkin
with Peppercorns and Garlic

Serves 4–6

Pumpkin? Really? Yes, really. The slightly sweet flavor of the pumpkin handles the strong flavors of the peppercorns and the garlic astonishingly well. I like to serve this as an accompaniment to simple grilled meats.

30 peppercorns
2 cloves garlic
1 tablespoon vegetable oil
2 cups fresh pumpkin pieces,
    cut into 1-inch cubes

1 cup water
2 tablespoons fish sauce
1 teaspoon sugar

1. Using a mortar and pestle, crush together the peppercorns and the garlic.
2. Add the vegetable oil to a large sauté pan and heat on high. Add the peppercorn-garlic mixture and stir-fry until the garlic just begins to brown.
3. Add the pumpkin pieces, stirring to coat.
4. Add the water and bring the water to a simmer. After the water has been reduced by half, stir in the fish sauce and sugar.
5. Continue to cook until the pumpkin is tender but not mushy.
6. Serve as a side dish.

 Thai Pumpkins
In Thailand, the differences between pumpkins and squashes are not very well defined—they basically treat them all the same. The Thai version of a pumpkin is Fug Tong, but almost any fleshy hard squash can be substituted (with different, but delicious, results).

Gingered Green Beans

2 tablespoons vegetable oil
1 stalk lemongrass, minced
    (inner tender portion only)
1 tablespoon peeled and
    minced ginger

1–3 (to taste) serrano chilies,
    seeded and minced
½ cup coconut milk
¼ teaspoon salt
½ pound green beans, trimmed

1. In a medium-sized saucepan, heat the oil on medium-high. Stir in the lemongrass, ginger, and chilies; sauté for 1 to 2 minutes.
2. Stir in the coconut milk and the salt until well combined.
3. Add the green beans, raise the heat to high, and cook for 3 minutes or until the beans are done to your liking.

Serves 2–4

This recipe goes well with grilled steak, especially if the beans have been soaked in an Asian marinade. They also complement seared tuna exceedingly well. Or try tossing them into a salad.

Curried Green Beans

2 tablespoons vegetable oil
2 tablespoons Red Curry Paste
    (see recipes in Chapter 1)
6 cups chicken or vegetable
    broth

1 pound green beans, trimmed
Steamed rice

1. In a large saucepan, heat the vegetable oil over medium-high heat.
2. Add the curry paste and stir-fry for 1 minute.
3. Stir in the broth until well combined with the paste. Add the green beans and bring to a low boil. Cook for 15 to 20 minutes to reduce the liquid.
4. Reduce the heat to maintain a hard simmer and continue cooking until the beans are very well done.
5. Serve the beans over steamed rice, ladling the sauce over the top.

Serves 4–6

I usually like my green beans like a really rare steak—just barely heated through. But in this instance, you have to cook the beans almost to a pulp. As the beans break down, they help form the sauce.

Green Beans
with Macadamia Nut Sauce

1 medium onion, chopped
4 whole raw macadamia nuts, chopped
2 cloves garlic, chopped
2 tablespoons vegetable oil
2 tablespoons water
½ teaspoon cayenne pepper
1 teaspoon ground coriander

½ teaspoon ground cumin
1 cup coconut milk
1 bay leaf
½–1 teaspoon salt to taste
1 pound green beans, trimmed

1. Place the onion, macadamia nuts, garlic, vegetable oil, and water in a blender or food processor and process until smooth. Transfer the paste to a small bowl and stir in the cayenne pepper, coriander, and cumin.
2. In a medium-sized saucepan, heat the macadamia nut paste, coconut milk, and bay leaf over medium-high heat. Bring to a simmer, reduce heat, and cook until reduced by half.
3. Stir in the salt. Add the green beans and continue simmering, stirring occasionally, until the beans are done to your liking, about 8 to 10 minutes. Add salt to taste if necessary.

Roasted Asian Cauliflower

1 head cauliflower, broken into
    florets (cut the florets in half
    if large)

1 recipe Asian Marinade
    (see recipes in Chapter 1)

Serves 6–8

Roasting cauliflower?
Yes, another strange
idea, but it's actually
quite good and it
couldn't be much
easier.

1. Place the cauliflower florets in a large Ziplock bag and pour marinade over them; let rest in the refrigerator for 4 to 6 hours.
2. Preheat the oven to 500 degrees.
3. Place the cauliflower florets in a roasting pan. Roast for approximately 15 minutes or until tender, turning after 7 to 8 minutes.

Spicy Stir-Fried Corn

2 tablespoons vegetable oil
1 stalk lemongrass, minced
    (tender inner portion only)
2 teaspoons minced garlic
1 tablespoon butter
1 medium onion, minced

4 cups corn kernels (fresh or
    frozen and thawed are best)
1 cup low-sodium vegetable broth
2 teaspoons lime zest
2 tablespoons fish sauce
Tabasco to taste
2 tablespoons lime juice

Serves 6–8

This corn recipe can
be addicting. So be
warned! Try serving it
with any grilled meat
or fish dish.

1. Place the oil in a large skillet over high heat. Add the lemongrass. As soon as it begins to brown, add the garlic, butter, and onion. Continue to cook on high, letting the ingredients brown somewhat.
2. Add the corn kernels and cook until they brown. Stir in the vegetable stock; stirring constantly, cook the mixture for 2 minutes, scraping the bottom of the pan to loosen any burned-on bits.
3. Stir in the remaining ingredients and cook for 30 more seconds.

Grilled Eggplant with an Asian Twist

Serves 4–6

I like cooking with Japanese eggplant because you don't have to go through the process of salting them in order to extract their extra moisture like you do with our larger, more familiar Western ones.

4–8 Japanese eggplants (about 1½ pounds in all)
Olive oil
Salt and pepper to taste
Juice of 1 lemon or lime
1 tablespoon fish sauce
Basil leaves

1. Prepare a grill or broiler. Allow it to achieve high heat.
2. If the eggplants are relatively large, cut in half vertically. Toss them with a little olive oil just to coat, and season with salt and pepper. Place the eggplant either in a vegetable grilling basket or directly on the grill grate or broiler pan. Cook until tender, about 15 to 20 minutes, turning midway through the cooking process.
3. Remove from the heat. Sprinkle with lemon juice and fish sauce.
4. Garnish with basil leaves. Serve either hot or at room temperature.

Japanese Eggplant with Tofu

Serves: 2–4

Both eggplant and tofu are extremely mild by themselves. The zest from this recipe comes from the garlic, serrano chili, and basil—all of which pack quite a punch.

4–6 tablespoons vegetable oil
2–3 cloves garlic, finely chopped
3 cups sliced Japanese eggplant, about ⅛-inch thick
¼ pound extra-firm tofu, cut into small cubes
1–5 (to taste) serrano chili peppers, seeded and minced
10–15 basil leaves
1–3 tablespoons Yellow Bean Sauce (see recipe on page 9)

1. Heat the oil in a large skillet over medium-high heat. Add the garlic and sauté until it turns golden.
2. Add the eggplant and tofu pieces; sauté, stirring constantly, for 5 to 6 minutes or until the eggplant is done to your liking.
3. Carefully stir in the remaining ingredients.
4. Serve immediately to avoid discoloration of the eggplant and basil.

Stir-Fried Black Mushrooms and Asparagus

*1 ounce dried Chinese black
  mushrooms
1 tablespoon vegetable oil
1–2 cloves garlic, minced*

*3–4 tablespoons oyster sauce
Tabasco (optional)
1 pound asparagus spears,
  trimmed*

Serves 4–6

The unique sauce in this dish is a far cry from the traditional, super-rich hollandaise sauce or butter and nutmeg traditionally served with asparagus in the West.

1. Place the dried mushrooms in a bowl and cover with hot water. Let soak for 15 minutes. Drain, discard the stems, and slice into strips; set aside.
2. Heat the oil on medium-high in a large skillet. Add the garlic and sauté until golden.
3. Stir in the mushrooms and continue cooking, stirring constantly, for 1 minute.
4. Stir in the oyster sauce and a few drops of Tabasco if desired.
5. Add the asparagus spears. Sauté for 2 to 4 minutes or until the asparagus is done to your liking.

Thai-Style Fried Okra

*⅓ cup all-purpose flour
½ cup tapioca flour
1 teaspoon baking powder
½ cup water
1 pound small okra, trimmed*

*1 cup vegetable oil
1 recipe chili dipping sauce of
  your choice (see recipes in
  Chapter 2)*

Yields approx. 20

If ever there was a way to eat okra, this is it. The tapioca flour creates a batter that fries up superlight. This dish make a fun appetizer or snack.

1. In a medium-sized mixing bowl, combine the flours, the baking soda, and water to form a batter. Add the okra pieces.
2. Heat the vegetable oil in a frying pan or wok over high heat. (It should be hot enough that a test piece of batter puffs up immediately.)
3. Add the battered okra, a few at a time, and fry until golden.
4. Using a slotted spoon, remove the okra to paper towels to drain.
5. Serve hot with your favorite chili dipping sauce.

Tropical Vegetables

1 teaspoon vegetable oil
1 shallot, minced
1 tablespoon sesame seeds
1 tablespoon Red Curry Paste (see recipes in Chapter 1)
½ cup coconut milk
1 tablespoon Tamarind Concentrate (see recipe on page 18)
2 tablespoons brown sugar
1 tablespoon fish sauce

2½ cups green beans, trimmed and cut into 1-inch lengths
1 yellow or red bell pepper, seeded and julienned
2 cups bamboo shoots
2½ cups baby spinach leaves
2 cups bean sprouts

1. To make the sauce, heat the vegetable oil in a small sauté pan on medium-high. Add the minced shallot and fry until golden. Transfer the fried shallot to paper towels to drain.
2. Using a mortar and pestle, crush half of the sesame seeds and half of the fried shallots together; set aside.
3. In a small saucepan, combine the Red Curry Paste and the coconut milk, and bring to a simmer over medium-low heat. Add the tamarind, brown sugar, fish sauce, and the reserved sesame seed–shallot mixture. Reduce heat to low and keep warm.
4. Bring a large saucepan of water to a boil. Add the green beans, the bell pepper pieces, and the bamboo shoots to the water and blanch for 30 seconds to 1 minute or until done to your liking. Using a slotted spoon, remove the vegetables from the water to a colander to drain.
5. Let the water return to boiling and add the spinach leaves and the bean sprouts. Immediately remove them from the water to drain.
6. Toss all of the vegetables together.
7. To serve, place the vegetables in the center of a serving plate. Pour some of the sauce over the vegetables. Pass additional sauce separately.

Thai-Style Bean Sprouts and Snap Peas

2 tablespoons vegetable oil
1 small onion, thinly sliced
1 (1-inch) piece ginger, peeled
   and minced
Pinch of white pepper
1 tablespoon soy sauce
½ pound sugar snap peas,
   trimmed

1 pound bean sprouts, rinsed
   thoroughly and trimmed if
   necessary
Salt and sugar to taste

Serves 4–6

This recipe lets the peas shine without overpowering their sweet, delicate flavor with anything heavy or overly spicy. The bean sprouts add a nice contrast.

1. Heat the vegetable oil over medium-high heat in a large skillet.
2. Add the onion and the ginger and sauté for 1 minute.
3. Stir in the white pepper and the soy sauce.
4. Add the sugar snap peas and cook, stirring constantly, for 1 minute.
5. Add the bean sprouts and cook for 1 more minute while stirring constantly.
6. Add up to ½ teaspoon of salt and a large pinch of sugar to adjust the balance of the sauce. Serve immediately.

CHAPTER 10
Noodle Dishes

Pad Thai	150
Fire Noodles	151
Rice Stick Noodles with Chicken and Vegetables	152
Chiang Mai Curried Noodles	154
Pan-Fried Noodles	155
Clear Noodles with Baked Shrimp	156
Sesame Noodles with Veggies	157
Panang Mussels with Noodles	158
Flowered Lime Noodles	158
Poached Chicken Breast with Peanut Sauce and Noodles	159
Thai Noodles with Chicken and Pork	160
Spicy Egg Noodles with Sliced Pork	161
Curried Rice Noodles with Tofu and Egg	162
Broccoli Noodles with Garlic and Soy	163

Pad Thai

8 ounces rice noodles

2 tablespoons vegetable oil

5–6 cloves garlic, finely chopped

2 tablespoons chopped shallots

½ cup cooked salad shrimp

¼ cup fish sauce

¼ cup brown sugar

6–8 teaspoons Tamarind Concentrate (see recipe on page 18)

¼ cup chopped chives

½ cup chopped roasted peanuts

1 medium egg, beaten

1 cup bean sprouts

Garnish:

1 tablespoon lime juice

1 tablespoon Tamarind Concentrate

1 tablespoon fish sauce

½ cup bean sprouts

½ cup chopped chives

½ cup coarsely ground roasted peanuts

1 lime cut into wedges

1. Soak the noodles in water at room temperature for 30 minutes or until soft. Drain and set aside.
2. Heat the vegetable oil in a wok or skillet over medium-high heat. Add the garlic and shallots, and briefly stir-fry until they begin to change color.
3. Add the reserved noodles and all the remaining ingredients except the egg and the bean sprouts, and stir-fry until hot.
4. While constantly stirring, slowly drizzle in the beaten egg.
5. Add the bean sprouts and cook for no more than another 30 seconds.
6. In a small bowl mix together all of the garnish ingredients except the lime wedges.
7. To serve, arrange the Pad Thai on a serving platter. Top with the garnish and surround with lime wedges.

Fire Noodles

15–20 (or to taste) Thai bird
   chilies, stemmed and seeded
5–10 (or to taste) cloves garlic
1 pound presliced fresh rice
   noodles (available at Asian
   grocery stores and on the
   Internet)
2 tablespoons vegetable oil
2 whole boneless, skinless
   chicken breasts, cut into
   bite-sized pieces

2 tablespoons fish sauce
2 tablespoons sweet black soy
   sauce
1 tablespoon oyster sauce
1 teaspoon white pepper
1½ tablespoons sugar
1 (8-ounce) can bamboo
   shoots, drained
1½ cups loose-packed basil
   and/or mint

Serves 4–6

These noodles live up their name—they are not for the faint of heart! The thick, lush noodles somehow have the ability to stand up to the power of the superhot Thai bird chilies and their garlic sidekick.

1. Place the chilies and garlic cloves in a food processor and process until thoroughly mashed together; set aside.
2. Bring a kettle of water to a boil. Place the noodles in a large colander and pour the hot water over them. Carefully unfold and separate the noodles; set aside.
3. Heat the oil in a wok or large skillet over medium-high heat. When it is quite hot, carefully add the reserved chili-garlic mixture and stir-fry for 15 seconds to release the aromas.
4. Raise the heat to high, add the chicken, and stir-fry until it begins to lose its color, about 30 seconds.
5. Stir in the fish sauce, soy sauce, oyster sauce, white pepper, and sugar.
6. Add the noodles and continue to stir-fry for 30 seconds, tossing them with the other ingredients.
7. Add the bamboo shoots and cook for another minute.
8. Turn off the heat and add the basil.

Cooling Down

If you bite into a chili that is just too hot to handle, try sucking on a spoonful of sugar or sucking on a hard candy.

Rice Stick Noodles
with Chicken and Vegetables

Serves 2–4

Rice noodles don't really have a Western equivalent. Silky smooth and a bit chewy, these rather flavorless delights absorb the flavors of the other ingredients, becoming one with the dish.

Noodles:

8 ounces rice stick noodles

2 tablespoons vegetable oil

1 tablespoon sweet black soy sauce

Chicken and vegetables:

2 tablespoons vegetable oil

4 cloves garlic, chopped

1 large whole boneless, skinless chicken breast,
     cut into bite-sized strips

¼ pound broccoli, chopped

1 small onion, finely sliced

1½ cups sliced Japanese eggplant

½ teaspoon Tabasco

2 tablespoons fish sauce

2 tablespoons Yellow Bean Sauce
     (see recipe on page 9)

3 tablespoons brown sugar

¼ cup chicken broth

1 tablespoon cornstarch mixed with
     1 tablespoon water

1 cup bean sprouts

¼–⅓ cup sliced green onions

1 small red bell pepper, seeded
     and cut into strips

(recipe continues on the next page)

Rice Stick Noodles
with Chicken and Vegetables (continued)

Noodles:

1. Soak the noodles in warm water for 15 minutes or until soft; drain.
2. Place a wok over medium-high heat and add the vegetable oil. When the oil is hot, add the noodles and stir-fry vigorously until they are heated through, about 45 seconds to 1 minute.
3. Add the soy sauce and continue to stir-fry for 1 more minute.
4. Place the noodles on a serving platter, covered in foil, in a warm oven until ready to serve.

Chicken and vegetables:

1. Place a wok over medium-high heat and add the vegetable oil. When the oil is hot, add the garlic and stir-fry briefly to release its aroma.
2. Add the chicken and cook until it starts to become opaque.
3. Add the broccoli and stir-fry for 30 seconds.
4. Add the onion and eggplant and stir-fry for 2 minutes.
5. Add the Tabasco, fish sauce, yellow bean sauce, and sugar. Stir-fry for 1 minute.
6. Add the broth, cornstarch mixture, bean sprouts, green onions, and red bell pepper; cook until vegetables are tender-crisp.
7. To serve, ladle the chicken and vegetable mixture over the reserved noodles.

 Thai Rice Noodles

Thai rice stick noodles have a transparent appearance, a slightly chewy texture, and almost no flavor, which makes them great for absorbing dressings and sauces. They are also known as rice vermicelli. Cellophane noodles look similar to rice sticks, but are made of mung bean flour. They are also known as bean threads, silver threads, and shining noodles. Before boiling or stir-frying either cellophane or rice stick noodles, they are first soaked in hot water for a few minutes and then cut to the desired length with scissors. Both products can also be fried without soaking, creating a crunchy topping or snack.

Chiang Mai Curried Noodles

½ cup coconut milk
1 tablespoon Red Curry Paste (see recipes in Chapter 1)
1 tablespoon chopped garlic
1 tablespoon curry powder
Pinch of turmeric powder
2 tablespoons fish sauce
Pinch of sugar
1 teaspoon lime juice

¼ pound ground pork
4 ounces rice noodles, soaked in water for 20 to 30 minutes or until soft
Lime wedges, for garnish

1. Heat the coconut milk in a wok or heavy skillet over medium heat. Stir in the curry paste and cook until aromatic and a thin film of oil separates out.
2. Add the garlic and cook for about 30 seconds. Add the remaining ingredients except the pork, noodles, and limes, and cook until the sauce thickens slightly, stirring constantly.
3. Add the pork and continue to stir until the meat is cooked through. Reduce heat and keep the sauce warm.
4. Bring a pan of water to a rolling boil. Place the noodles in a wire basket or strainer and dip the noodles in the water for 10 to 20 seconds. Drain the noodles and transfer to serving plate.
5. Pour the sauce over the noodles. Serve with lime wedges.

Thai Noodle Meals
Ground meat is commonly used in Thai noodle dishes, not only for flavor, but for textural contrast with the noodles.

Pan-Fried Noodles

¾ pound fresh lo mein noodles or angel hair pasta

¼ cup minced chives

2 tablespoons (or to taste) prepared chili-garlic paste

3 tablespoons vegetable oil, divided

Salt to taste

Serves 6–8

People are always amazed when I tell them that the wedge on their plate is noodles! They are crispy on the outside and still noodlelike inside. I like to serve this with anything grilled or roasted.

1. Boil the noodles in a large pot for no more than 2 to 3 minutes. Drain, rinse under cold water, and drain again.
2. Add the chives, chili paste, 1 tablespoon of the oil, and salt to the noodles; toss to coat, and adjust seasonings.
3. In a heavy-bottomed 10-inch skillet, heat the remaining oil over medium-high heat. When it is hot, add the noodle mixture, spreading evenly. Press the noodles into the pan with the back of a spatula. Cook for approximately 2 minutes. Reduce heat and continue to cook until the noodles are nicely browned. Flip the noodles over in 1 piece. Continue cooking until browned, adding additional oil if necessary.
4. To serve, cut the noodles into wedges.

Noodles of Fun

Other Asian noodles include mein, which are Chinese in origin and are similar to Western egg noodles. They are made with wheat flour, water, and egg, and come fresh, dried, or frozen. Japan also has a variety of noodles, including buckwheat Soba, thin wheat Somen, and thicker, rounder Udon, to name a few.

Clear Noodles
with Baked Shrimp

Serves 2

Traditionally, this
Chinese-inspired dish
would be baked in
a clay pot, making
for a spectacular
presentation.

1 7-ounce package rice noodles
2 cloves garlic, chopped
¼ cup chopped cilantro
20–30 black peppercorns
1 tablespoon vegetable oil
1 medium onion, thinly sliced
1 teaspoon sugar

1 tablespoon soy or fish sauce
Sesame oil to taste
6 large shrimp, shell on, rinsed
    and patted dry

1. Soak the noodles in hot water until soft, about 10 minutes. Drain and
   set aside.
2. Using a mortar and pestle or a food processor, thoroughly combine
   the garlic, cilantro, and peppercorns.
3. Add the vegetable oil to a wok or large skillet over low heat. Add the
   garlic mixture and stir-fry for 1 minute. Add the sliced onion and continue cooking until the onion is tender, then turn off the heat.
4. Add the sugar, soy sauce, and a few drops of sesame oil to the wok;
   stir to combine. Add the noodles and toss to coat. Pour the noodle
   mixture into an ovenproof baking dish. Place the whole shrimp on
   top of the noodles, cover the dish, and bake for 20 minutes in a
   400-degree oven. Serve immediately.

Thai Table Setting
*A traditional Thai table setting includes only a fork and spoon.
The fork is used to push the food onto the spoon, not to place
food into the mouth. Only a spoon is used for this.*

Sesame Noodles with Veggies

2 tablespoons vegetable oil
2 cloves garlic, minced
2 cups broccoli, cut into
   bite-sized pieces
1 red bell pepper, seeded and
   cut into strips
2 tablespoons water
8 ounces egg noodles
4 ounces tofu, cut into bite-
   sized cubes

1 tablespoon sesame oil
2–3 tablespoons soy sauce
2–3 tablespoons prepared
   chili sauce
3 tablespoons sesame seeds

Serves 2–4

Sesame oil is a standard ingredient in most Asian cuisines but is not as common in Thai cooking. However, here it pairs well with the other ingredients to create a subtle perfumed quality.

1. Heat the oil in a large sauté pan or wok over medium heat. Add the garlic and sauté until golden, approximately 2 minutes.
2. Add the broccoli and red bell pepper, and stir-fry for 2 to 3 minutes. Add the water, cover, and let the vegetables steam until tender, approximately 5 minutes.
3. Bring a large pot of water to boil. Add the noodles and cook until al dente; drain.
4. While the noodles are cooking, add the remaining ingredients to the broccoli mixture. Remove from heat, add the noodles, and toss to combine.

Panang Mussels and Noodles

1 pound Asian egg noodles
2 tablespoons vegetable oil
1 teaspoon Black Bean Paste
  (see recipe on page 10)
1 medium onion, chopped

6–8 stalks celery, chopped
¼ cup white wine
2 cups chicken broth
1 pound mussels, washed and
  debearded

1. Bring a large pot of water to a boil over high heat. Add the noodles and cook until al dente. Rinse the noodles under cold water and set aside.
2. Heat the oil in a large sauté pan over medium heat. Add the Black Bean Paste, onion, and celery, and sauté for 5 minutes.
3. Add the wine and chicken broth, and bring to a boil.
4. Add the mussels and reduce heat to low; cover and steam for 5 minutes.
5. To serve, divide the noodles between 4 soup plates. Divide the mussels between the plates (discarding any that have not opened) and pour the broth over the top.

Flowered Lime Noodles

8 ounces angel hair pasta
1 tablespoon salted butter
2–3 tablespoons lime juice
4 ounces grated Parmesan cheese

Rose petals or other organic
  edible flowers
Lime slices
Black pepper

1. Bring a large pot of water to a boil over high heat. Add pasta and cook according to package instructions; drain.
2. Toss the pasta with butter, lime juice, and parmesan.
3. To serve, top with rose or flower petals and lime slices. Pass black pepper at the table.

Poached Chicken Breast with Peanut Sauce and Noodles

⅔ cup crunchy peanut butter

1½ cups coconut milk

2 tablespoons fish sauce

¼ cup lime juice

2 teaspoons brown sugar

4 cloves garlic, minced

Salt and pepper to taste

¼ cup chicken stock

¼ cup half-and-half

1 pound Chinese egg noodles (mein)

1 tablespoon peanut oil

1 tablespoon sesame oil

6–8 green onions, trimmed and thinly sliced

3 whole boneless, skinless chicken breasts, halved and poached

1 pound snow peas, trimmed and blanched

> **Serves 6**
>
> Using chicken satay as a starting point, this dish is a bit more upscale. It's a great luncheon or brunch item because it's not heavy or overpowering, but still rich in flavor.

1. Combine the peanut butter, coconut milk, fish sauce, lime juice, brown sugar, garlic, salt, and pepper in a small saucepan over low heat. Cook until smooth and thick, stirring frequently.
2. Transfer to a blender and purée.
3. Add the chicken stock and half-and-half, and blend; set aside.
4. Bring a large pot of water to a boil. Add the noodles and cook until al dente. Drain, rinse under cold water, and drain again.
5. Toss the noodles with the peanut and sesame oils.
6. To serve, place some pasta in the middle of each serving plate. Spoon some of the peanut sauce over the pasta. Slice each chicken breast on the diagonal. Transfer 1 sliced breast to the top of each portion of noodles. Spoon some additional peanut sauce over the chicken. Surround the noodles with the snow peas. Garnish with the sliced green onions.

Thai Noodles with Chicken and Pork

For the sauce:

½ cup peanut butter
½ cup soy sauce
1 teaspoon minced garlic
3 tablespoons sesame oil
3 tablespoons honey
1 teaspoon hot chili oil
¼ teaspoon white pepper

For the noodles:

1 pound dry flat Asian noodles
1 tablespoon vegetable oil
1 teaspoon sesame oil
½ teaspoon minced garlic
½ pound boneless, skinless chicken breast, sliced thin
½ pound boneless pork tenderloin, cut into thin strips
1 large yellow onion, diced
6 ounces salad shrimp
6–8 green onions, trimmed, white portions sliced, green portions julienned

1. Place all of the sauce ingredients in a blender and process until smooth; set aside.
2. Bring a large pot of water to boil over high heat. Prepare the noodles according to package directions, drain, and stir in the sauce mixture, reserving ¼ cup; set aside.
3. Heat the oils in a large sauté pan over high heat. Add the garlic and sauté briefly.
4. Add the chicken, pork, and onion, and sauté for 5 to 6 minutes or until the meats are cooked through.
5. Add the white portion of the green onion and the shrimp and sauté for 2 more minutes.
6. Add the green parts of the onions and the remaining sauce, stirring until everything is well coated.
7. To serve, place the noodles on a large platter and top with the meat sauté. Pass additional hot chili oil separately.

Spicy Egg Noodles with Sliced Pork

1 small cabbage, shredded
1 cup bean sprouts
1 package fresh angel hair pasta
½ teaspoon vegetable oil
4 tablespoons minced garlic
2 tablespoons fish sauce
2 tablespoons sugar
4–6 tablespoons rice vinegar
2 teaspoons ground dried red chili pepper (or to taste)

1 small Barbecued Pork Tenderloin (see recipe on page 94), thinly sliced
Freshly ground black pepper to taste
2 scallions, trimmed and thinly sliced
2 teaspoons chopped cilantro

> **Serves 2 as a main course or 4 as an appetizer.**
>
> If you don't have left-over pork, but still want to make a quick version of this dish, slice some store-bought roast chicken over the top.

1. Bring a large pot of water to a boil over high heat. Add the cabbage and blanch about 30 seconds. Using a slotted spoon, remove the cabbage from the boiling water; set aside.
2. Let the water return to boiling. Add the bean sprouts and blanch for 10 seconds. Using a slotted spoon, remove the sprouts from the water; set aside.
3. Return the water to boiling. Add the fresh angel hair pasta and cook according to package directions. Drain the pasta and place it in a large mixing bowl.
4. In a small sauté pan, heat the vegetable oil over medium heat. Add the garlic and sauté until golden. Remove from heat. Stir in the fish sauce, sugar, rice vinegar, and dried chili pepper.
5. Pour the sauce over the pasta and toss to coat.
6. To serve, divide the cabbage and the bean sprouts into 2 to 4 portions and place in the center of serving plates. Divide the noodles into 2 to 4 portions and place over the cabbage and sprouts. Divide the pork slices over the noodles. Grind black pepper to taste over the noodles and top with the sliced scallions and chopped cilantro.

Curried Rice Noodles
with Tofu and Egg

½ teaspoon ground coriander
½ teaspoon ground cumin
1 teaspoon curry powder
1 tablespoon Red Curry Paste
   (see recipes in Chapter 1)
1 cup coconut milk
2–3 cups water
2 tablespoons minced shallots
2 tablespoons sugar
2 tablespoons fish sauce

½ of a 7-ounce package
   rice noodles
1 hard-boiled egg, sliced
⅓ cup cubed extra-firm tofu
⅓ cup bean sprouts
1 green onion, trimmed and
   thinly sliced
2 tablespoons chopped cilantro

1. In a small bowl, thoroughly combine the coriander, cumin, curry powder, and curry paste.
2. Pour the coconut milk into a medium-sized saucepan. Stir in the curry paste mixture and place over medium heat. Bring to a simmer and cook for about 5 minutes or until a thin layer of yellow oil begins to form on the surface of the sauce.
3. Stir in 2 cups of the water, the shallots, sugar, and fish sauce. Return the sauce to a simmer and let cook 30 minutes, stirring occasionally and adding additional water if necessary.
4. Meanwhile, soak the noodles in hot water for 10 minutes or until soft.
5. To serve, mound the noodles into serving bowls. Top the noodles with the sliced egg, tofu, and bean sprouts. Ladle some of the curry sauce over top. Sprinkle with green onion slices and chopped cilantro.

Broccoli Noodles
with Garlic and Soy

*1 pound broccoli, trimmed into
   bite-sized florets*
16 ounces rice noodles
1–2 tablespoons vegetable oil
2 cloves garlic, minced
2 tablespoons soy sauce
1 tablespoon sweet soy sauce

1 tablespoon sugar
Hot sauce
Fish sauce
Lime wedges

Serves 2–4
Try substituting other sturdy green vegetables such as asparagus, quartered Brussels sprouts, or green beans.

1. Bring a pot of water to boil over high heat. Drop in the broccoli and blanch until tender-crisp or to your liking. Drain and set aside.
2. Soak the rice noodles in hot water until soft, about 10 minutes.
3. In a large sauté pan, heat the vegetable oil on medium. Add the garlic and stir-fry until golden. Add the soy sauces and the sugar, stirring until the sugar has completely dissolved.
4. Add the reserved noodles, tossing until well coated with the sauce. Add the broccoli and toss to coat.
5. Serve immediately with hot sauce, fish sauce, and lime wedges on the side.

CHAPTER 11
Rice Dishes

Basic White Rice	166
Basic Sticky Rice	167
Sweet-Spiced Fried Rice	168
Fried Rice with Pineapple and Shrimp	169
Vegetarian Fried Rice	170
Chicken Fried Rice	171
Far East Fried Rice	172
Fried Rice with Tomatoes	173
Fried Rice with Chinese Olives	174
Ginger Rice	175
Curried Rice	176
Lemon Rice	177
Dill Rice	178
Fragrant White Rice	178
Shrimp Rice	179
Flavorful Steamed Rice	180
Fragrant Brown Rice	181

Basic White Rice

Serves 2–4

If you take only one thing away from this book, it should be how to make great rice from scratch. No parboiled, precooked, or dehydrated rice would ever find its way into a true Thai cook's kitchen.

1 cup long-grain rice   *2 cups water*
(such as Jasmine)

1. Place the rice in a colander and run under cool water.*
2. Place the rice and the water in a medium-sized pot. Stir briefly. Bring to a rolling boil over medium-high heat. Reduce heat to low, cover, and simmer for 18 to 20 minutes.
3. Remove the rice from the heat, keeping it covered, and let it rest for at least 10 minutes.
4. Fluff the rice just before serving.

* Washing rice is completely optional. By rinsing the rice, you remove some of the starch. The end result will be slightly whiter rice, but rice with a little less nutritional value.

Can I Use a Cooking Liquid Other Than Water?
Traditionally, Thai meals call for white rice that has been steamed in water. However, rice is terrific when a low-salt stock such as chicken or vegetable is used in place of the water. Another flavorful liquid substitution is a combination of half water and half coconut milk.

Basic Sticky Rice

1 cup glutinous rice
Water

1. Place the rice in a bowl, completely cover it with water, and let soak overnight. Drain before using.
2. Line a steamer basket or colander with moistened cheesecloth. (This prevents the grains of rice from falling through the holes in the colander.)
3. Spread the rice over the cheesecloth as evenly as you can.
4. Bring a pan of water with a cover to a rolling boil. Place the basket over the boiling water, making sure that the bottom of it does not touch the water. Cover tightly and let steam for 25 minutes.

Sticky Rice Varieties

Sticky rice comes in white, red, and black varieties. If you choose either red or black, you will need to increase the steaming time to at least 1 hour.

Serves 2–4

Sticky rice takes a little more practice to master (well, at least it did for me), but this, too, is a staple in the Thai kitchen. Take the time to get it right and don't get upset if it takes you a few tries to get it exactly right.

Sweet-Spiced Fried Rice

Makes approx. 4 cups

Although sweet spiced, this is still a savory side dish, great alongside grilled meat or fish.

*1½ cups long-grained rice
    (such as Jasmine)
3 tablespoons vegetable oil
½ onion, sliced into rings
1 (1–inch) cinnamon stick
1 bay leaf
3 cloves*

*½ teaspoon mace
1 tablespoon brown sugar
Salt
2¼ cups water*

1. Soak the rice in cold water for 20 minutes.
2. Meanwhile, heat the oil in a medium-sized pot over medium heat. Add the onions and sauté until golden, approximately 10 to 15 minutes.
3. Add the spices and sauté for an additional 2 minutes. Sprinkle the brown sugar over the onion mixture and caramelize for 1 to 2 minutes, stirring constantly. Add the rice and sauté for an additional 3 minutes, stirring constantly.
4. Add the salt and the water to the pot and bring to a boil. Reduce heat, cover, and simmer until the rice is tender, approximately 10 to 15 minutes.
5. Remove the cinnamon stick and cloves before serving.

Rice Nutrition

Rice's nutritional value is dependent on its processing method, not just its variety. Modern polishing methods, which produce gleaming white kernels, remove most of the minerals and vitamins, leaving only carbohydrates. More traditional polishing methods retain vitamins A, B, C, D, and E and protease inhibitors, which are all cancer retardants.

Fried Rice
with Pineapple and Shrimp

1 ripe whole pineapple
4 tablespoons vegetable oil
1/3 cup finely chopped onion
2 garlic cloves, finely minced
10 ounces peeled shrimp,
    deveined and cut into 1/2-inch
    pieces
1/2 teaspoon turmeric

1/2 teaspoon curry powder
1/2 teaspoon shrimp paste
2 1/4 cups day-old, cooked
    Jasmine or other
    long-grained rice
Salt to taste
Sugar to taste

> **Serves 2–4**
>
> This dish makes a great presentation and the fruit and spices complements the shrimp perfectly. Make some extra— this dish reheats in a microwave perfectly, as do almost all fried rice dishes.

1. To prepare the pineapple, cut it in half lengthwise, leaving the leaves intact on 1 side. Scoop out the pineapple flesh of both halves, leaving a 1/2-inch edge on the half with the leaves. Reserve the hollowed-out half to use as a serving bowl. Dice the pineapple fruit and set aside.
2. Preheat the oven to 350 degrees.
3. In a wok or heavy sauté pan, heat the oil on medium. Add the onion and garlic, and sauté until the onion is translucent. Using a slotted spoon, remove the onions and garlic from the wok and set aside.
4. Add the shrimp and sauté approximately 1 minute; remove and set aside.
5. Add the turmeric, curry powder, and shrimp paste to the wok; stir-fry briefly. Add the rice and stir-fry for 2 to 3 minutes. Add the pineapple and continue to cook. Add the reserved shrimp, onions, and garlic. Season to taste with salt and sugar.
6. Mound the fried rice into the pineapple "serving bowl." Place the pineapple on a baking sheet and bake for approximately 10 minutes. Serve immediately.

Vegetarian Fried Rice

Serves 4–6

Yes, this fried rice is vegetarian, but it's certainly not boring. It's chock full of flavorful veggies and gets a flavor boost from both lime juice and brown sugar, ingredients not too common in fried rice.

3 tablespoons vegetable oil, divided

3 cups day-old long-grained rice

½ cup finely diced onion

2 garlic cloves, finely chopped

1 tablespoon finely chopped fresh gingerroot

2 red chili peppers, seeded, veined, and thinly sliced

4 scallions, sliced

7 ounces green beans, trimmed and cut into 1-inch pieces

2 medium carrots, peeled and julienned into 1-inch pieces

2 stalks of celery, sliced

½ cup vegetable stock

9 ounces tomatoes, peeled, seeded, and diced

2 tablespoons vegetarian "oyster" sauce

3 tablespoons soy sauce

½ teaspoon ground turmeric

Salt and freshly ground pepper to taste

Grated zest and juice of ½ of a lime

½ teaspoon brown sugar

1. In a wok or large sauté pan, heat 2 tablespoons of the vegetable oil over medium-high heat. Add the rice and stir-fry for 2 to 3 minutes. Remove the rice from the wok and set aside.
2. Add the remaining tablespoon of oil to the wok. Add the onion, garlic, and ginger; sauté for 1 minute.
3. Add the chilies, scallions, green beans, carrots, and celery; stir-fry for 3 minutes.
4. Add the stock and bring to a boil; reduce heat and simmer for 5 minutes.
5. Add the tomatoes and simmer for an additional 2 minutes.
6. Add the "oyster" and soy sauces and turmeric. Season to taste with salt and pepper.
7. Stir in the lime zest, lime juice, brown sugar, and rice. Mix until combined.

Chicken Fried Rice

1 tablespoon vegetable oil
1 tablespoon minced garlic
1 tablespoon minced ginger
1 medium onion, sliced
½ medium head Chinese
    cabbage, coarsely chopped
3 cups cooked long-grain
    white rice
¼ cup fish sauce
¼ cup dry sherry

¼ cup chicken stock
1 cup snow peas, trimmed
    and cut into bite-sized pieces
1 cup shredded, cooked
    chicken
2 eggs, beaten

1. In a large skillet or wok, heat the oil over medium-low heat. Add the garlic, ginger, and onion, and stir-fry for 5 minutes or until the onion becomes translucent.
2. Add the cabbage, increase the heat to medium, and stir-fry for 10 minutes.
3. Add the rice and stir-fry for 2 minutes.
4. Combine the fish sauce, sherry, and stock in a small bowl; add to the wok and stir to combine.
5. Add the snow peas and chicken; stir-fry for 2 minutes more.
6. Move the rice to the sides of the wok, forming a hole in the middle. Pour the eggs into the hole and cook for about 1 minute, stirring the eggs with a fork. Fold the cooked eggs into the fried rice.

Serving Rice

In Southeast Asia, baskets are lined with banana leaves or lettuce and used as serving dishes for rice.

Far East Fried Rice

Serves 4–6

This fried rice dish uses fish sauce, rice vinegar, and red pepper flakes to add spark. The recipe does not call for any meat, but if you have any left over by all means use it here!

2 tablespoons fish sauce
1½ tablespoons rice vinegar
2 tablespoons sugar
2½ tablespoons vegetable oil
2 eggs, beaten
1 bunch green onions, trimmed and thinly sliced
2 tablespoons minced garlic
1 teaspoon dried red chili pepper flakes

2 large carrots, peeled and coarsely shredded
2 cups bean sprouts, trimmed if necessary
5 cups day-old long-grain white rice, clumps broken up
¼ cup chopped mint or cilantro leaves
¼ cup roasted peanuts, chopped

1. Combine the fish sauce, rice vinegar, and sugar in a small bowl; set aside.
2. In a wok or large skillet, heat the oil over medium-high heat. Add the eggs and stir-fry until scrambled.
3. Add the green onions, garlic, and pepper flakes and continue to stir-fry for 15 seconds or until fragrant.
4. Add the carrots and bean sprouts; stir-fry until the carrots begin to soften, about 2 minutes.
5. Add the rice and cook for 2 to 3 minutes or until heated through.
6. Stir in the fish sauce mixture and add the fried rice, tossing until evenly coated.
7. To serve, garnish the rice with chopped mint, or cilantro, and chopped peanuts.

Fried Rice with Tomatoes

3 tablespoons vegetable oil
1 whole boneless, skinless
   chicken breast, cut into bite-
   sized pieces
1 clove garlic, minced
1 medium onion, slivered
2 eggs
4 cups cooked rice
1 tomato, cut into 8–10
   wedges

1 green onion, trimmed
   and sliced
2 teaspoons soy sauce
1 teaspoon fish sauce
1 teaspoon sugar
1 teaspoon ground white
   pepper

> **Serves 2–4**
>
> You don't see tomatoes used very often in Thai cooking, so they are definitely a surprise in this fried rice recipe. I like the color and the flavor they add to an otherwise basic dish.

1. In a large skillet or wok, heat the vegetable oil on medium-high. Add the chicken pieces and the garlic, and stir-fry 1 minute.
2. Add the onion and continue to stir-fry for an additional minute.
3. Break in the eggs, mixing well.
4. Stir in all the remaining ingredients; stir-fry for 2 more minutes.
5. Serve immediately.

Storing Cooked Rice

Cooked rice is very susceptible to spoilage. It should not be left at room temperature longer than it needs to be for serving, and should not be stored in the fridge for more than 3 days (in an airtight container). Rice can also be frozen in an airtight container for up to 6 months.

Fried Rice with Chinese Olives

Serves 2–3

Here's another ingredient you probably don't associate with Asian food—olives. Chinese olives are rather small and quite salty. They aren't the easiest thing to find: check a local Asian market.

3 tablespoons vegetable oil
3 cloves garlic, minced
½ cup ground pork or chicken
10 Chinese olives, pitted and chopped
3 cups day-old cooked rice
Fish sauce (optional)

Cucumber slices
Lime wedges
Chopped cilantro
Hot sauce

1. Heat the oil in a wok or large skillet on medium. Add the garlic and stir-fry briefly. Add the pork and olives. Stir-fry until the pork is cooked through and any juices that have accumulated have cooked off.
2. Add the rice, breaking up any clumps, and stir-fry until the rice is hot. Adjust the saltiness with a bit of fish sauce if necessary.
3. Serve accompanied by cucumber slices, lime wedges, chopped cilantro, and hot sauce.

Cilantro
It is a proven fact that some people cannot stand the taste of cilantro—it is like an allergy of the tastebuds! If you or someone you're cooking for falls into this category, fresh parsley makes an acceptable—if not dull—substitute.

Ginger Rice

2 tablespoons vegetable oil
1 (½-inch) piece of gingerroot,
  peeled and thinly sliced
1 stalk lemongrass, sliced
  into rings (tender inner
  portion only)
2–3 green onions, sliced into
  rings

1 red chili pepper, seeded
  and minced
1½ cups long-grained rice
Pinch of brown sugar
Pinch of salt
Juice of ½ lime
2¾ cups water

1. In a medium-sized pot, heat the oil over medium heat. Add the gingerroot, lemongrass, green onions, and chili pepper; sauté for 2 to 3 minutes.
2. Add the rice, brown sugar, salt, and lime juice, and continue to sauté for an additional 2 minutes. Add the water to the pot and bring to a boil.
3. Reduce the heat, cover with a tight-fitting lid, and simmer for 15 to 20 minutes, until the liquid is absorbed.

Do Not Disturb

As a general rule, do not stir simmering rice—as it causes the grains to break, resulting in a gummy end product.

Serves 4–6

It may take a few extra minutes to prep the flavoring agents in this rice side dish, but it's well worth the effort. I like it so much that sometimes I eat the leftovers for lunch without anything else

---

Curried Rice

Serves 4–6

This rice dish shines with the flavors of India. Curry powder, golden raisins, and mango chutney give the rice a slightly sweet, slightly spicy taste that works really well with grilled chicken.

2 tablespoons vegetable oil
½ cup finely chopped onion
1½ cups long-grained rice
1 teaspoon curry powder
2¾ cups vegetable stock
Salt to taste

¼ cup golden raisins (regular raisins can be substituted)
2 teaspoons Mango Chutney (see recipe on page 274)

1. In a medium-sized pot, heat the oil over medium heat. Add the onions and sauté for 2 minutes, until the onions are soft but not browned.
2. Add the rice and continue to sauté for an additional 2 minutes. Add the curry powder and sauté for 1 more minute.
3. Pour in the vegetable stock and season with salt. Bring to a boil, then reduce heat and cover. Simmer the rice for 15 to 20 minutes, stirring occasionally.
4. Add the raisins and the chutney. Continue to simmer for an additional 5 minutes or until tender.

Chutney Convenience
Chutneys are one of those few blessings that are almost better in preserved jar form. However, a good jarred chutney can be pricey, and it isn't so hard to make!

Lemon Rice

1⅓ cups water
Pinch of salt
1 cup basmati rice, soaked in
　cold water for 30 minutes
½ teaspoon turmeric
1 tablespoon vegetable oil
1 green chili pepper, seeded
　and minced

¼ cup cashew nuts, soaked in
　cold water for 5 minutes
¼ teaspoon mustard seed
8 fresh curry leaves
Juice of ½ lemon

Serves 2–4

Fresh curry leaves add
a delightful flavor and
aroma to this dish.
The leaves are edible,
but you will be
chewing for a long
time if you try.

---

1. In a medium-sized pan, bring the water to a boil. Add the salt, rice, and turmeric; reduce heat, cover, and simmer for 10 minutes. (At the end of the 10 minutes, the rice will have absorbed all of the liquid.) Remove from heat and let cool.

2. In a wok, heat the oil and stir-fry the chili pepper. Add the nuts, mustard seed, and curry leaves; continue to cook for an additional 30 seconds. Stir in the lemon juice. Add the cooled rice to the wok and toss until heated.

Chili Safety

The oils in chilies are very caustic. Wear gloves while you work with them and make sure not to touch your eyes.

Dill Rice

Serves 2–4

I like to add fresh dill to everything, especially when it's growing like a weed in my garden. I throw it in soups, tuna or chicken salad, or use it as a green in a tossed salad.

2 tablespoons vegetable oil
2 green cardamom pods
4 tablespoons chopped fresh dill
1 cup long-grained rice (such as Jasmine)
1 green chili pepper, seeded and minced
Salt
1½ cups water

1. In a medium-sized pot, heat the vegetable oil over medium heat. Add the cardamom pods and sauté for 1 minute. Add the chili and sauté briefly. Stir in the salt and the dill and cook for an additional 2 to 3 minutes. Add the rice and sauté for 3 more minutes.
2. Stir in the water and bring the mixture to a boil. Reduce heat, cover, and simmer for 20 to 25 minutes or until the liquid has been absorbed.
3. Remove the cardamom pods and fluff the rice before serving.

Fragrant White Rice

Serves 6–8

Fresh aromatic herbs and spices flavor this sublime side dish. The rice is cooked in a combination of coconut milk and water, which gives it a richer consistency than if it were only cooked with water.

2 tablespoons vegetable oil
10 fresh curry leaves
1 stalk lemongrass, cut into thin rings (inner tender potion only)
Zest of ½ kaffir lime
2 mace blades
6 cloves
2½ cups Jasmine rice
1¾ cups water
1¼ cups coconut milk
Salt and freshly ground pepper to taste

1. In a medium-large saucepan, heat the oil on medium. Add the curry leaves and sauté until you can begin to smell the aroma. Add the lime zest and the remaining spices and sauté for an additional 2 to 3 minutes, stirring constantly.
2. Add the rice to the pot and stir to combine with the spice mixture. Add the water, coconut milk, and salt and pepper. Bring to a boil; reduce heat, cover, and simmer for 15 to 20 minutes or until the liquids have been absorbed. Adjust seasoning.

Shrimp Rice

5 tablespoons dried shrimp,
   soaked in cold water for
   10 minutes
2 red chili peppers, seeded,
   veined, and finely minced
1 medium to large onion,
   finely chopped
2 cloves garlic, finely chopped
5 tablespoons vegetable oil
4 tablespoons fish sauce

1 tablespoon lime juice
Salt to taste
1¾ cups long-grained rice
1 stalk lemongrass, halved
   and crushed (inner white
   potion only)
1 quart water

Serves 4–6

This is not shrimp
fried rice, but rather
shrimp-flavored rice.
In fact, there are no
fresh shrimp in it at
all. The rice gets its
shrimp overtones
from the combination
of dried shrimp and
fish sauce.

1. Make a shrimp paste by combining the dried shrimp, chili peppers, onion, and garlic in a blender or food processor and processing until smooth.
2. In a medium-sized saucepan, warm the oil over medium heat. Add the shrimp paste and cook for 3 to 4 minutes, stirring constantly.
3. Add the fish sauce, lime juice, and salt to the paste and stir until well blended; set aside.
4. Pour the rice into a large pot and place the lemongrass on top. Add the water and bring to a boil; reduce heat, cover, and simmer for 15 minutes.
5. Remove the lemongrass stalk and stir in the shrimp paste. Continue cooking for 5 to 10 minutes or until the rice is done.

Flavorful Steamed Rice

¾ cup long-grained rice
2 cloves garlic, minced
1 teaspoon salt
¼ cup chicken or vegetable
  broth
1 tablespoon minced gingerroot
2 green onions, trimmed and
  thinly sliced

2 teaspoons lime juice
1 teaspoon fish sauce
½ cup finely chopped cilantro

1. Bring a pot of water to a rolling boil. Add the rice, let the water return to a boil, and cook for 10 minutes. Drain in a sieve, rinse, and set aside. (Leave the rice in the sieve.)
2. Add 1 inch of water to the pot and bring to a boil. Set the sieve over the boiling water, cover it with a clean kitchen towel and a lid, and let steam for about 20 minutes. (Check occasionally, adding more water if necessary.)
3. Mash together the garlic and the salt to form a paste.
4. In a large bowl, combine the garlic paste, broth, gingerroot, green onions, lime juice, and fish sauce.
5. Add the steamed rice and toss until well combined. Let cool to room temperature.
6. Stir the cilantro into the rice.

Fragrant Brown Rice

2 tablespoons vegetable oil
2 garlic cloves, minced
4 green onions, trimmed and
    thinly sliced
1½ stalks celery, trimmed and
    thinly sliced
1 medium carrot, peeled and
    julienned
2 red chili peppers, seeded
    and minced
1 tablespoon finely chopped
    gingerroot

1⅔ cups brown rice (white
    rice can be substituted)
4½–5½ cups vegetable stock
1 kaffir lime leaf or 2
    (2-inch-long, ½-inch-wide)
    pieces of lime zest
1 tablespoon lime juice
Salt and freshly ground pepper
    to taste

Serves 4–6

Just because this dish is extra healthy, that doesn't mean it doesn't taste terrific. Brown rice is more nutritious than white because the nutrient-rich outer layer is not rubbed off in the polishing process.

1. In a medium to large saucepan, heat the vegetable oil on medium. Add the garlic and green onions, and cook for 2 minutes. Add the celery, carrots, chilies, and ginger, and cook for an additional 2 minutes.
2. Add the rice and stir until well combined. Add half of the vegetable stock, the kaffir lime leaf, lime juice, and salt and pepper. Bring to a boil; reduce heat and simmer, uncovered, for 45 to 50 minutes, adding additional stock as needed.

CHAPTER 12

Desserts

Sweet Sticky Rice	184
Tropical Coconut Rice	184
Sticky Rice with Coconut Cream Sauce	185
Pineapple Rice	186
Crispy Crepes with Fresh Fruit	187
Tropical Fruit with Ginger Crème Anglaise	188
Fresh Oranges in Rose Water	189
Banana Coconut Soup	190
Lemongrass Custard	191
Coconut Custard	192
Steamed Coconut Cakes	193
Coconut-Pineapple Soufflé for 2	194
Mango Fool	195
Citrus Fool	195
Pineapple-Mango Sherbet	196
Mango Sauce over Ice Cream	197
Pumpkin Custard	197
Watermelon Ice	198
Taro Balls Poached in Coconut Milk	199
Bananas Poached in Coconut Milk	200
Tofu with Sweet Ginger	200
Pumpkin Simmered in Coconut Milk	201

Sweet Sticky Rice

Serves 6

There is not much to this dessert, but it's delicious. I love the somewhat gelatinous quality this rice takes on. The rice is intended to be eaten alongside fresh fruits, but I think it's pretty tasty all by itself.

1 1/2 cups white glutinous rice
1 1/3 cups canned coconut milk
1/2 cup granulated sugar
1/2 teaspoon salt

1. Place the rice in a bowl and add enough water to completely cover the rice. Soak for at least 4 hours or overnight. Drain.
2. Line a steamer basket with wet cheesecloth. Spread the rice evenly over the cheesecloth. Place the container over rapidly boiling water. Cover and steam until tender, about 25 minutes; set aside.
3. In a medium-sized saucepan, combine the coconut milk, sugar, and salt and heat on medium-high. Stir until the sugar is completely dissolved. Pour over the rice, stir to combine, and let rest for 30 minutes.
4. To serve, place in small bowls or on plates. Garnish with mangoes, papayas, or other tropical fruit.

Tropical Coconut Rice

Serves 6–8

Coconut and rice are the most typical ingredients found in Thai desserts. This one calls for coconut, not only coconut in a semiliquid form but also toasted.

2 cups short-grained rice
2 cups water
1 cup coconut cream
1/4 cup toasted coconut (see "Toasted Coconut" on page 16)
1/2 cup finely chopped tropical fruits of your choice

1. Put the rice, water, and coconut cream in a medium-sized saucepan and mix well. Bring to a boil over medium-high heat. Reduce heat and cover with a tight-fitting lid. Cook for 15 to 20 minutes or until all of the liquid has been absorbed.
2. Let the rice rest off the heat for 5 minutes.
3. Fluff the rice and stir in the toasted coconut and fruit.

Sticky Rice
with Coconut Cream Sauce

1 cup coconut cream
4 tablespoons sugar
1 teaspoon salt
4 ripe mangoes, thinly sliced
   (or other tropical fruits)

3 cups cooked Sweet Sticky
   Rice (see recipe on
   page 184)

Serves 6

Here the coconut is not cooked into the sticky rice, but makes its way into the sauce. Tropical fruit is served alongside.

1. For the sauce, place the coconut cream, sugar, and salt in a small saucepan. Stir to combine and bring to a boil over medium-high heat. Reduce heat and simmer for 5 minutes.
2. To serve, arrange mango slices on each plate. Place a mound of rice next to the fruit. Top the rice with some of the sauce.

Peeling, Pitting, and Slicing a Mango
Cut the skin off the mango lengthwise on both sides and peel back the skin. Cut the flesh off the mango pit in long vertical strips. Slice or dice as desired.

Pineapple Rice

Serves 4–6

As you have probably noticed, rice is used in every Thai meal—breakfast, lunch, and dinner.

1 ripe pineapple
¼ cup sugar
Pinch of salt
½ cup short-grained rice
Zest and juice of 1 lemon

2 teaspoons chopped crystallized ginger, divided
3 tablespoons roasted cashew
  nuts, chopped

1. Cut the pineapple in half lengthwise, leaving the leaves intact on 1 side. Scoop out the pineapple flesh of both halves, leaving a ½-inch edge on the half with the leaves. Dice the pineapple fruit from 1 half and purée the fruit from the other half in a food processor along with the sugar and salt; set aside.
2. Strain the fruit purée through a fine-mesh sieve into a measuring cup. Add enough water to make 1¾ cups. Transfer to a small saucepan and bring to a boil over medium-high heat.
3. Rinse and drain the rice. Stir the rice into the pineapple purée. Stir in the lemon zest, lemon juice, and 1 teaspoon of the ginger. Bring to a boil; reduce heat, cover, and simmer until the liquid has been absorbed, about 20 minutes.
4. Mix the reserved pineapple cubes into the rice.
5. To serve, spoon the rice into the hollowed out pineapple that has the leaves. Garnish with the remaining ginger and the roasted cashews.

 Crystallized Ginger
Crystallized ginger is small ginger pieces, usually about ¼-inch dice, that has been simmered in syrup and then dried. The result is a slightly chewy, spicy-sweet candylike condiment. It can be found in specialty grocery stores.

Crispy Crepes with Fresh Fruit

1 package frozen puff pastry
  sheets, thawed according to
  package instructions
2 tablespoons confectioner's
  sugar, divided
2 cups raspberries, blueberries,
  or other fresh fruit, the
  best 12 berries reserved
  for garnish

1 cup heavy cream
¼ cup shredded, unsweetened
  coconut
1 tablespoon unflavored rum
  or coconut-flavored rum

Serves 4

If you want to substitute a mixture of tropical fruits for the berries, feel free.

---

1. Preheat oven to 400 degrees.
2. Place the puff pastry sheet on a work surface and cut into 12 equal-sized pieces. Place the pastry pieces on a baking sheet.
3. Bake the pastry approximately 10 minutes. Remove from the oven and use a sifter to shake a bit of the confectioner's sugar over the puff pastry. Return to the oven and continue baking for approximately 5 minutes or until golden. Place the puff pastry on a wire rack and let cool to room temperature.
4. Place the berries in a food processor and briefly process to form a rough purée.
5. Whip the cream with the remaining confectioner's sugar until thick, but not stiff. Stir in the coconut and the rum.
6. To serve, place 1 piece of puff pastry in the middle of each serving plate, spoon some cream over the pastry, and then top with some purée. Place another pastry on top, garnish with some of the remaining berries, any leftover juice from the purée, and a sprinkle of confectioner's sugar.

Tropical Fruit
with Ginger Crème Anglaise

Yields 1½ cups

Here I've taken a standard crème anglaise and infused it with fresh ginger, giving the sauce a slightly piquant flavor. This sauce is equally tasty over gingerbread or sponge cake.

4 (1-inch) pieces peeled gingerroot, slightly mashed
1 cup half-and-half
3 egg yolks
2 tablespoons sugar
A variety of tropical fruits,
  sliced

1. In a small heavy saucepan over medium-low heat, bring the ginger and the half-and-half to a slight simmer. Do not boil.
2. In the meantime, whisk together the eggs yolks and the sugar.
3. Slowly pour the hot half-and-half into the egg mixture, stirring constantly so that the eggs do not cook.
4. Pour the custard back into the saucepan and cook over medium-low heat, stirring constantly with a wooden spoon for 5 minutes or until slightly thickened.
5. Pour the crème anglaise through a mesh strainer into a clean bowl and let cool to room temperature.
6. Pour over slices of your favorite tropical fruits.

 Freezing Ginger
Ginger freezes fantastically. However, you may want to peel it, cut it into 1-inch pieces, and then wrap it tightly before doing so.

Fresh Oranges in Rose Water

8 oranges
3 cups water

1½ cups sugar
4–6 teaspoons rose water

1. Peel and segment the oranges. Place them in a bowl, cover, and set aside in the refrigerator.
2. In a saucepan, bring the water and the sugar to a boil over medium-high heat. Boil gently for 15 to 20 or until the mixture becomes syrupy. Remove from heat and stir in the rose water. Let cool to room temperature and then refrigerate.
3. To serve, place orange segments in individual dessert cups. Pour rose water syrup over the top.

Rose Water

Rose water is a subtle flavoring agent made from distilling the oil of rose petals. The oil is then infused into water. It can be found in specialty food shops.

Banana Coconut Soup

Serves 6–8

This is such an incredibly soothing soup. It reminds me of eating warm pudding, only it's a lot better!

4 cups canned coconut milk
4 cups banana slices, plus
    extra for garnish
2 tablespoons minced
    gingerroot
1 cinnamon stick
1 tablespoon lemon juice

Salt to taste
(see "Toasted Coconut" on
    page 16)

1. In a large saucepan, bring the coconut milk to a boil. Add the banana, ginger, cinnamon stick, lemon juice, and a pinch of salt. Reduce heat and simmer for 10 to 15 minutes or until the banana is very soft.
2. Remove the cinnamon stick and allow to cool slightly.
3. Using a handheld blender (or a blender or food processor), purée the soup until smooth.
4. Serve the soup in preheated bowls, garnished with banana slices and coconut.

Thai Dessert Origins

Many of the desserts in this chapter are not of pure Thai origin. Some are derived from traditional Portuguese recipes since they were the first Westerners to reach the area. Soon after, eggs became an important ingredient in Thai desserts along with flour, sugar, fruit, and coconut ingredients which were already used extensively.

Lemongrass Custard

2 stalks fresh lemongrass,
    finely chopped (tender inner
    portion only)
2 cups whole milk

6 egg yolks
½ cup sugar

Serves 6

This is a standard custard that has simply been infused with lemongrass and it is nothing short of divine. It can be served warm or chilled.

1. Preheat oven to 275 degrees.
2. In a medium-sized saucepan, over medium-high heat, bring the milk and the lemongrass to a boil. Reduce the heat and simmer for 5 minutes. Cover the milk mixture, turn off the heat, and let sit for 10 minutes on the burner.
3. In a mixing bowl, beat the egg yolks with the sugar until thick.
4. Strain the milk mixture through a fine-mesh sieve, then slowly pour it into the egg yolks, whisking constantly.
5. Divide the mixture between 6 small custard cups and place the cups in a high-sided baking or roasting pan. Add warm water to the pan so that it reaches to approximately 1 inch below the top of the custard cups. Cover the pan tightly with foil.
6. Place the pan in the oven and bake for approximately 20 minutes or until the custards are set on the sides but still slightly wobbly in the center.

Coconut Custard

Serves 6

This coconut custard uses coconut milk in place of whole milk. Melted butter brings the fat content up to where it needs to be in order for the custards to set.

1 (16-ounce) can coconut cream
2/3 cup fine granulated sugar
6 large eggs, lightly beaten

3 tablespoons butter
Fresh tropical fruit (optional)

1. In a large, heavy-bottomed saucepan, stir together the coconut cream and the sugar.
2. Over medium heat, cook and stir the mixture until the sugar is completely dissolved.
3. Reduce the heat to low and stir in the eggs. Cook, stirring occasionally, until the mixture is thick and coats the back of a spoon, about 10 to 12 minutes.
4. Remove the pan from the heat and add the butter. Stir until the butter is completely melted and incorporated.
5. Pour the custard into six 4-ounce custard cups. Place the cups in a baking pan. Pour boiling water into the baking pan until it comes halfway up the sides of the custard cups.
6. Carefully transfer the baking pan to a preheated 325-degree oven. Bake the custards for 30 to 40 minutes until set. (The tip of a knife should come out clean when inserted into the middle of the custard.)
7. Serve warm or at room temperature. Garnish with chopped tropical fruit, if desired.

Steamed Coconut Cakes

5 eggs
4 tablespoons finely granulated
* sugar*
½ cup rice flour
¼ cup all-purpose flour

Pinch of salt
½ cup coconut milk
½ cup grated sweet coconut

1. In a large mixing bowl, beat the eggs and the sugar together until thick and pale in color.
2. Add the rice flours and salt.
3. Beating constantly, slowly pour in the coconut milk. Beat the batter for 3 more minutes.
4. Bring some water to boil in a steamer large enough to hold 10 small ramekins. When the water begins to boil, place the ramekins in the steamer to heat for 2 minutes.
5. Divide the shredded coconut evenly between all of the ramekins and use a spoon to compact it in the bottom of the cups.
6. Pour the batter evenly between the cups. Steam for 10 minutes.
7. Remove the cakes from the cups as soon as they are cool enough to handle.
8. Serve warm or at room temperature.

Coconut-Pineapple Soufflé for 2

Softened butter for the molds
Sugar for the molds
½ cup (½-inch) cubes ladyfingers or sponge cake
2 tablespoons dark rum
2 tablespoons finely chopped fresh pineapple
1 egg yolk

2½ tablespoons grated sweetened coconut
2 egg whites
Lemon juice
2 tablespoons sugar

1. Preheat oven to 400 degrees.
2. Butter 2¾- or 1-cup soufflé molds and then sprinkle them with sugar. Refrigerate the molds until ready to use.
3. Place the ladyfinger cubes in a small bowl. Pour the rum over the cubes and let soak for 5 minutes.
4. Squeeze the juice from the pineapple, saving both the pulp and 1 tablespoon of the juice.
5. In a small bowl, beat the egg yolk with the pineapple juice until very thick. Fold in the cake cubes, pineapple pulp, and coconut.
6. In another small bowl, beat the egg whites with a few drops of lemon juice until foamy. Gradually add the 2 tablespoons of sugar, while continuing to beat until the whites are stiff and glossy.
7. Gently fold the pineapple mixture into the egg whites.
8. Spoon the batter into the prepared molds and bake for 8 to 10 minutes or until puffy and lightly browned.

Mango Fool

2 ripe mangoes, peeled and
   flesh cut from the pits
2 tablespoons lime juice
¼ cup sugar

1 cup heavy cream
1 tablespoon confectioners' sugar
Crystallized ginger (optional)
Mint leaves (optional)

1. Place the mangoes in a food processor with the lime juice and sugar. Purée until smooth.
2. In a large bowl beat the heavy cream with the confectioners' sugar until stiff.
3. Thoroughly fold the mango purée into the heavy cream.
4. Serve in goblets garnished with crystallized ginger or sprigs of mint, if desired.

Serves 4–6

A fool is usually a combination of heavy whipped cream and a fruit purée. The fruit is just barely folded into the cream, leaving slight stripes. This grown-up "pudding" is simple, light, and a true delight

Citrus Fool

½ cup orange, lime, or lemon juice
3 tablespoons sugar
3 tablespoons unsalted butter
1 large egg, beaten

2 (3-inch-long, ½-inch wide)
   strips of citrus zest, minced
½ cup heavy cream

1. Place the juice in a small saucepan. Over medium-high heat, reduce the liquid by half.
2. Remove the pan from the heat and stir in the sugar and butter. Stir in the egg until well combined.
3. Return the pan to the burner and cook on medium-low heat for 3 to 5 minutes or until bubbles just begin to form.
4. Remove the pan from the heat and stir in the citrus zest. Place the pan in a bowl of ice and stir the mixture until it is cold.
5. In another bowl, whip the cream until stiff. Fold the citrus mixture thoroughly into the cream.

Serves 4

Make sure that you remove the pan from the heat source before you stir in the egg or it will scramble right before your eyes and the recipe will be ruined.

Pineapple-Mango Sherbet

Serves 4–6

You can try different varieties of this same concept. How about Grapefruit-Papaya?

1 large orange, peeled and
  segmented
2 mangoes, peeled, pitted, and
  cut into 1-inch cubes
1 cup pineapple pieces
1 tablespoon lime zest
⅓ cup sugar

½ cup plain yogurt
1 teaspoon orange-flavored
  liqueur (optional)

1. Place the orange segments, mango cubes, and pineapple pieces on a baking sheet lined with waxed paper; place in the freezer for 30 to 45 minutes or until just frozen.
2. Transfer the fruit to a food processor. Add the lime zest and sugar, and process until well combined.
3. With the machine running, add the yogurt and liqueur. Process for an additional 3 minutes or until the mixture is fluffy.
4. Pour the mixture into an 8" × 8" pan, cover with foil, and freeze overnight.
5. To serve, let the sherbet temper at room temperature for 10 to 15 minutes, then scoop into glass dishes.

Sherbet versus Sorbet

Sherbet differs from sorbet in that the latter is dairy-free. In this sherbet the dairy is provided by plain yogurt, which adds creaminess and a bit of bite.

Mango Sauce over Ice Cream

*2 mangoes, peeled, pitted,
    and diced*
1 banana, peeled and chopped
²/₃ cup (or to taste) sugar

*Juice of 2 large limes
    (or to taste)*
1 tablespoon brandy (optional)
Vanilla ice cream

1. In a medium-sized saucepan over low heat, simmer the mangoes, banana, sugar, and lime juice for 30 minutes, stirring frequently.
2. Add the brandy and simmer 5 more minutes.
3. Remove from heat and allow to cool slightly or to room temperature.
4. To serve, scoop ice cream into individual serving bowls. Spoon sauce over top.

> **Yields 2 cups**
>
> This outstanding mango, banana, and lime sauce is great over ice cream, pound cake, or angel food cake. You might even try it spooned over some grilled fish!

Pumpkin Custard

1 small cooking pumpkin
5 eggs
¹/₃ cup brown sugar

Pinch of salt
1 cup coconut cream

1. With a small sharp knife, carefully cut the top off of the pumpkin.
2. Using a spoon, remove and discard the seeds and most of the soft flesh; set the pumpkin aside.
3. In a medium-sized mixing bowl, whisk the eggs together. Stir in the brown sugar, salt, and coconut cream until well combined.
4. Pour the mixture into the pumpkin.
5. Place the pumpkin in a steamer and let steam for approximately 20 minutes or until the custard is set.

> **Serves 4**
>
> This custard variation uses pumpkin, brown sugar, and coconut cream to create a rich, autumnal dessert. It is steamed right in the pumpkin shell, so not only does it taste delicious, it makes a great presentation, too.

Watermelon Ice

⅓ cup water
½ cup sugar
1 (3-pound) piece of watermelon, rind cut away, seeded, and cut into small chunks (reserve a bit for garnish if desired)

1 tablespoon lime juice
Mint sprigs (optional)

1. Place the water and sugar in a small saucepan and bring to a boil. Remove from heat and allow to cool to room temperature, stirring frequently. Set the pan in a bowl of ice and continue to stir the syrup until cold.
2. Place the watermelon, syrup, and lime juice in a blender and purée until smooth.
3. Pour the purée through a sieve into a 9-inch baking pan. Cover the pan with foil.
4. Freeze the purée for 8 hours or until frozen.
5. To serve, scrape the frozen purée with the tines of a fork. Spoon the scrapings into pretty glass goblets and garnish with a small piece of watermelon or mint sprigs.

Taro Balls Poached in Coconut Milk

2 cups glutinous rice flour
1 cup corn flour
1 cup cooked taro, mashed
4 cups coconut milk
1 cup brown sugar

⅛ teaspoon salt
Fresh tropical fruit (optional)

1. In a large mixing bowl, combine the rice and the flours.
2. Add the mashed taro and knead to form a soft dough.
3. Roll into small bite-sized balls and set aside.
4. In a medium to large saucepan, heat the coconut milk over low heat.
5. Add the brown sugar and the salt, stirring until dissolved.
6. Bring the mixture to a low boil and add the taro balls.
7. Poach the balls for 5 to 10 minutes or until done to your liking.
8. Serve hot in small glass bowls, garnished with tropical fruit.

Serves 6–12

Here we have a dessert that is unfamiliar to most Americans. The balls have a texture unlike anything else I know, but are a little reminiscent of dumplings or a stiff pudding.

What Is Taro?

Taro is a large tropical plant, also known as "the elephant ear." It has very large, broad leaves (hence the name) and a big, thick, starchy root. "Taro" in ingredients lists refers to the root. Taro is very similar to an Irish potato in texture and taste, but is healthier and easier to digest. Taro is a very important crop to many people living in tropical climates.

Bananas Poached in Coconut Milk

Serves 2–3

The sugar in this recipe makes for a really sweet dessert, and the Thai love it. If you would prefer to let the banana flavor stand more on its own, add less sugar.

2–3 small, slightly green bananas
4 cups coconut milk
1 cup sugar
¼ teaspoon salt

Fresh coconut wedges (optional)
Fresh pineapple wedges (optional)

1. Peel the bananas and slice them in half lengthwise.
2. Pour the coconut milk into a pan large enough to hold the bananas laid flat in a single layer. Add the sugar and salt and bring to a boil.
3. Reduce the heat, add the bananas, and simmer until the bananas are just warmed through, about 3 to 5 minutes.
4. Serve the bananas warm on small plates garnished with fresh coconut and pineapple wedges.

Tofu with Sweet Ginger

Yields 3 cups of sauce

Soft tofu has the texture of a very thick yogurt. If you're lactose intolerant, it's the way to go. Plus it's high in protein and low in fat. Even the sugar content in this recipe is relatively low.

3 cups water
1 (2- to 3-inch) piece of ginger, peeled and smashed with the back of a knife

⅓ cup brown sugar
1 12-ounce package soft tofu

1. Place the water, ginger, and brown sugar in a small saucepan. Bring to a boil over high heat. Reduce the heat to a simmer and let the sauce cook for at least 10 minutes. (The longer you let the mixture cook, the spicier it will get.)
2. To serve, spoon some of the tofu into dessert bowls and pour some sauce over the top. (This sauce is equally good over plain yogurt.)

Pumpkin Simmered in Coconut Milk

1 cup water
½ teaspoon salt
⅓ cup brown sugar
2 cups fresh pumpkin meat cut
*   into large julienned pieces*

(acorn squash is a good
*   substitute)*
½ cup coconut milk

Serves 4
The trick to this simple recipe is using a flavorful pumpkin. I've found that pumpkins straight from the patch are the best. They seems to be left on the vine longer, which allows their flavor to develop.

1. Put the water and the coconut milk in a medium-sized pan over low heat. Add the salt and half of the sugar; stir until well combined. Adjust the sweetness to your liking by add more water or sugar if necessary.

2. Add the julienned pumpkin to the pan and bring to a boil over medium heat. Reduce to a simmer and cook until soft, about 5 to 10 minutes depending on both the texture of the pumpkin and your own preference.

3. The pumpkin may be served hot, warm, or cold.

CHAPTER 13
Drinks and Teas

Ginger Tea	204
Lemongrass Tea	204
Thai Limeade	205
Iced Sweet Tea	205
Thai Iced Tea	206
Super-Simple Thai Iced Tea	206
Fresh Coconut Juice	207
Thai-Inspired Singapore Sling	207
Tom's Thai "Martinis"	208
Tropical Fruit Cocktail	209
Mango Bellini	209
Royal Thai Kir	210

Ginger Tea

Yields 8 cups

Although not really a tea, this ginger infusion is refreshing no matter what it's called.

8 cups water
1 large branch (approximately
  ⅓ pound) of ginger, cut
  into long pieces

½–¾ cup sugar

1. Bring the water to a boil in a large pan. Add the ginger, reduce heat, and simmer for 10 to 20 minutes, depending on how strong you like your tea.
2. Remove the ginger and add the sugar to taste, stirring until it is completely dissolved.
3. Serve hot or over ice.

Lemongrass Tea

Yields 8 cups

Another infusion, this "tea" is light, flavorful, and oh-so Thai. A 50–50 mix of this tea with Ginger Tea is also great!

8 cups water
1 cup lemongrass stalks,
  chopped

¼–⅓ cup sugar

1. Bring the water to a boil in a large pan. Add the lemongrass, remove from heat, and let steep for 10 to 20 minutes, depending on how strong you like your tea.
2. Remove the lemongrass and add the sugar to taste, stirring until it is completely dissolved.
3. Serve hot or over ice.

Thai Limeade

*1 cup lime juice, lime rinds
    reserved*
8 cups water

⅓–½ cup sugar
Salt to taste (optional)

1. Combine the lime juice and the sugar; set aside.
2. Bring the water to boil in a large pot. Add the lime rinds and remove from heat. Let steep for 10 to 15 minutes. Remove the lime rinds.
3. Add the lime juice mixture to the hot water, stirring to completely dissolve the sugar. Add salt if desired.
4. Serve over ice.

> **Yields 9 cups**
>
> Do you remember Lemon Shakeups from the county fair? This is sort of the Thai version of a shakeup without the shaking!

Iced Sweet Tea

1 tablespoon sugar
*1 tablespoon sweetened
    condensed milk*
1–2 tablespoons Thai tea leaves

1 cup hot water
Ice
1 teaspoon milk

1. Put the sugar and sweetened condensed milk into a large glass.
2. Place the tea leaves into a tea ball and place it in the glass.
3. Add the hot water. Let steep until done to your preferred strength.
4. Stir to dissolve the sugar and sweetened condensed milk.
5. Add ice and top with milk.

> **Yields slightly more than 1 cup.**
>
> Thai like their tea milky and super sweet. If you prefer your tea hot, reduce the sugar and sweetened condensed milk by half. And, of course, don't add the ice!

Thai Iced Tea

Yields approx. 8 cups

Similar to the previous recipe but without the condensed milk, this tea is slightly less rich, but certainly no less sweet.

6 cups water
1 cup Thai tea leaves
1 cup sugar

Ice
1–1½ cups half-and-half

1. Bring the water to boil in a medium-sized pot. Remove from heat and add the tea leaves, pushing them into the water until they are completely submerged. Steep approximately 5 minutes or until the liquid is a bright orange.
2. Strain through a fine-mesh sieve or coffee strainer.
3. Stir in the sugar until completely dissolved.
4. Allow the tea to reach room temperature and then refrigerate.
5. To serve, pour the tea over ice cubes, leaving room at the top of the glass to pour in 3 to 4 tablespoons of half-and-half; stir briefly to combine.

Super-Simple Thai Iced Tea

Yields approx. 1 cup

After you have become addicted to tea Thai-style but you are rushing to that morning meeting, here is the brew for you. Add milk or condensed milk if you like.

2 tablespoons sugar
1–2 tablespoons Thai tea leaves

1 cup hot water
Ice

1. Put the sugar into a large glass.
2. Place the tea leaves in a tea ball and place it in the glass.
3. Add the hot water. Let steep until done to your preferred strength.
4. Stir to dissolve the sugar and add ice.

Fresh Coconut Juice

1 young coconut   *Sprig of mint for garnish*
Ice

1. Using a meat cleaver, make a V-shaped slice on the top of the coconut.
2. Pour the juice over a glass of ice.
3. Garnish with a mint sprig.

> **Serves 1–2, depending on the size of the coconut.**
>
> Exactly what the recipe title says, this recipe calls for whacking open a coconut and drinking the juice. Remember Gilligan's Island?

Thai-Inspired Singapore Sling

2 tablespoons whiskey   *1 teaspoon brown sugar*
1 tablespoon cherry brandy   *Dash of bitters*
1 tablespoon orange liqueur   *¼–⅓ cup pineapple juice*
1 tablespoon lime juice   *Mint sprig (optional)*

1. Place all of the ingredients into a cocktail shaker and shake well to combine.
2. Serve over crushed ice and garnish with a sprig of mint if desired.

Pass on the Wine

Beer is the most popular alcoholic beverage served with Thai food. Three brands are domestically brewed—Singha, Amarit, and Kloster. In each case, the barley is homegrown, but the hops come from Germany.

> **Yields 1 cocktail**
>
> Created in 1915 by a Raffles Hotel bartender, the Singapore Sling was originally meant to be a woman's drink. Nowadays, no trip to Singapore, is complete without sipping this classic at Raffles's famous Long Bar.

Tom's Thai "Martinis"

1 whole ripe pineapple
1 bottle dark rum
1 bottle light rum
1 bottle coconut rum

3 stalks lemongrass, trimmed, cut into 3-inch lengths and tied in a bundle

1. Remove the pineapple greens and then quarter the remaining fruit. Place the pineapple quarters and the lemongrass bundle in a container large enough to hold all of the liquor.
2. Pour the rums over the fruit and stir to combine. Cover the container and let infuse for at least 1 week at room temperature.
3. Remove the lemongrass bundle and discard.
4. Remove the pineapple quarters and cut into slices for garnish.
5. To serve, pour some of the rum into a martini shaker filled with ice; shake well. Pour into martini glasses and garnish with a pineapple slice.

What Not to Eat
Lime leaves, lemongrass, and Siamese ginger are all great flavoring agents, but they are really difficult to chew. Don't eat them.

Tropical Fruit Cocktail

*1 small mango, papaya, banana,
or other tropical fruit, peeled
and roughly chopped (reserve
a bit for garnish if desired)*
4 tablespoons lime or lemon juice
1 teaspoon grated ginger

1 tablespoon brown sugar
1¼ cups orange or grapefruit juice
1¼ cups pineapple juice
⅓–½ cup (or to taste) rum

1. Place the chopped fruit, lime juice, ginger, and sugar in a blender and process until smooth.
2. Add the remaining ingredients to the blender and process until well combined.
3. To serve, pour over crushed ice and decorate with fruit slices of your choice.

Yields 3–4 cups

When you think of fruit cocktail, you probably think of either the canned fruit you ate as a child or some kiddie cocktail. Well, this is neither. It is sophisticated, not too sweet, and very adult thanks to the rum.

Mango Bellini

2 tablespoons puréed mango
*1 teaspoon mango schnapps
(optional)*

½ teaspoon lemon juice
Chilled champagne

Place the mango purée, mango schnapps, and lemon juice in a champagne flute. Fill the flute with champagne and stir.

Yields 1 glass

Similar to the Royal Thai Kir, this Mango Bellini is a bit fruitier. The lemon juice helps to balance the fruit. Whichever cocktail you choose, you can't go wrong with a combination of mango and champagne!

Royal Thai Kir

1–2 teaspoons crème de
    mango or mango schnapps

Chilled dry champagne

Pour the crème into a champagne flute and fill with champagne.

Wine Choices

Pairing wine with Thai food is not an easy endeavor because
of the complexity of flavors that appear in a single dish. Sparkling
wine or champagne act to quell a bit of the fire. (As does a cold
glass of beer!) Slightly chilled Alsacian-style Rieslings, Pinot Gris, and
Pinot Blanc can also do the trick. If you are absolutely set on
drinking red, please do. Try a full-flavored, yet fruity, wine such as
a Zinfandel. Or if you want a cold glass of red, chill a bottle of
Beaujolais. Its low tannins help offset the heat of the chilies.

CHAPTER 14

Thai-Inspired Cooking

Asian Carrot Sticks	212
Spicy Shrimp Dip	213
Cream of Coconut Crabmeat Dip	214
Marinated Mushrooms	214
Thai-Spiced Guacamole	215
Asian-Inspired Chicken and Wild Rice Soup	216
Chicken Salad—1	217
Chicken Salad—2	218
Chicken Salad—3	219
Jicama, Carrot, and Chinese Cabbage Salad	219
Peanut Potato Salad	220
Asian Couscous Salad	221
Asian 3-Bean Salad	222
Crunchy Sprout Salad	222
Many Peas Asian-Style Salad	223
Thai Pasta Salad	224
Thai Chicken Pizza	225
Grilled Steak with Peanut Sauce	226
Asian Marinara Sauce	226
Thai-Style Grilled Pork Chops	227
Southeast Asian Burgers	228
Grilled Lobster Tails with a Lemongrass Smoke	229
Thai-Flavored Green Beans	230
Southeast Asian Asparagus	230
Asian Ratatouille	231
Pickled Chinese Cabbage	232
Crazy Coconut Pie	232
Lime Butter Cake	233
Meringues with Tropical Fruit	234

Asian Carrot Sticks

1 pound thin carrots, peeled and cut into quarters lengthwise
4 tablespoons water
4 tablespoons olive oil
2 cloves garlic, minced
2 tablespoons rice vinegar
⅛–¼ teaspoon cayenne pepper
½–1½ teaspoons paprika
½–1 teaspoon Chinese 5-spice powder
3 tablespoons chopped cilantro
Salt and pepper to taste

1. Place the carrots in a pan large enough to hold them comfortably. Cover the carrots with water and bring to a boil over high heat. Drain the carrots and return them to the pan.
2. Add the 4 tablespoons of water, the olive oil, and the garlic; bring to a boil, reduce to a simmer, and cook until just tender. Drain.
3. In a small bowl, stir together remaining ingredients; pour over the carrots, tossing to coat.
4. Season to taste with salt and pepper.
5. The carrots may be eaten immediately, but develop a richer flavor if allowed to marinate for a few hours.

Spicy Shrimp Dip

5 tablespoons butter
1 tablespoon minced chives
½ teaspoon salt
½ serrano chili, seeded and
 minced
½ teaspoon grated lemon zest

8 ounces shrimp, cleaned and
 chopped
Salt and freshly ground black
 pepper to taste

1. In a medium-sized sauté pan, melt the butter over medium heat. Stir in the chives, salt, chili pepper, and lemon zest; sauté for 2 minutes.
2. Reduce the heat to low and add the shrimp; sauté for 3 minutes or until opaque.
3. Transfer the mixture to a food processor and coarsely purée. Season with salt and pepper.
4. Firmly pack the purée into a small bowl. Cover with plastic wrap, and refrigerate for 4 hours or overnight.
5. To serve, remove the shrimp dip from the refrigerator and allow it to sit for 5 to 10 minutes. Serve the dip with an assortment of crackers and toast points or some favorite veggies.

Cream of Coconut Crabmeat Dip

¾ cup cream of coconut
1¼ pounds (10 ounces) crab-meat, picked over to remove shell pieces
¼ teaspoon salt
2 green onions, trimmed and thinly sliced

2 tablespoons chopped cilantro
1 tablespoon lemon or lime juice
1 jalapeño, seeded and minced
Ground white pepper to taste

1. In a small saucepan, combine the cream of coconut, crabmeat, and salt; bring to a simmer over medium-low heat. Simmer for 5 minutes.
2. Stir in the green onions, cilantro, lemon juice, jalapeño, and pepper. Pour into a serving dish and let stand at room temperature until cool.
3. Serve with fresh vegetables and crackers.

Marinated Mushrooms

¾ cup olive oil
½ cup water
¼ cup rice wine vinegar
Juice of 1 lime
3 cloves garlic

1 whole serrano or jalapeño pepper
2 stalks lemongrass
3 (½-inch) pieces gingerroot
1½ pounds whole small white mushrooms

1. Place all of the ingredients except the mushrooms in a large pot; bring to a boil, reduce heat, and simmer for 10 to 15 minutes.
2. Add the mushrooms to the pot, stirring to coat.
3. Remove the pot from the heat and let cool to room temperature, about 1 hour.
4. Refrigerate for at least 2 hours, preferably overnight.

Thai-Spiced Guacamole

2 ripe avocados, pitted and
   chopped
4 teaspoons lime juice
1 large plum tomato, seeded
   and chopped
1 tablespoon chopped onion
1 small garlic clove, minced
1 teaspoon grated lime zest

1 teaspoon grated gingerroot
1 teaspoon chopped serrano
   or jalapeño chili
1–2 tablespoons chopped
   cilantro
Salt and freshly ground black
   pepper to taste

> **Yields 2 cups**
>
> This recipe is a great example of how lime zest and ginger can give a Mexican favorite a Southeast Asian twist. Try serving the guacamole with some rice chips alongside the tortillas chips.

1. Place the avocado in a medium-sized bowl. Add the lemon juice and coarsely mash.
2. Add the remaining ingredients and gently mix together.
3. Serve within 2 hours.

 Thai Mexican Similarities
If you look through a Mexican cookbook, you'll find many typical Mexican ingredients that are also Thai staples—lime juice, chilies, cilantro, garlic, and onion.

Asian-Inspired Chicken and Wild Rice Soup

Serves 6–8

The chewy quality of the rice in this soup complements the crispy pea pods and delicate chicken, and its nutty flavor substitutes for peanuts.

1 tablespoon vegetable oil
2 whole boneless, skinless
   chicken breasts, trimmed
   and cut into thin strips
1–2 garlic cloves, minced
2–3 teaspoons minced ginger
2 tablespoons fish sauce
6 cups low-fat, low-salt chicken
   broth

2 cups cooked wild rice
½ cup sliced green onions
½ pound snow peas, trimmed
   and diagonally sliced
Salt and freshly ground white
   pepper

1. In a large soup pot, heat the oil on medium-high. Add the chicken strips and sauté for 2 to 3 minutes.
2. Add the garlic and gingerroot and sauté for another minute.
3. Stir in the fish sauce, broth, and rice. Bring to a boil; reduce heat, cover, and simmer for 10 minutes.
4. Add the green onions and snow peas; simmer to heat through.
5. Adjust seasoning with salt and freshly ground white pepper to taste.

Wild Rice

Wild rice isn't rice at all, but the seed of a native American grass. Processed white rice typically needs less water added than long-grain brown rice or wild rice, which can take up to 6 cups of water per cup of dry rice. Unlike its white and brown counterparts, wild rice is a very heavy and filling dish.

Chicken Salad—1

For the dressing:

¼ cup vegetable oil
2 tablespoons rice wine
    vinegar
1 tablespoon soy sauce
2 teaspoons grated gingerroot
Pinch of sugar
¼ teaspoon (or to taste) salt

For the salad:

2 cups chopped cooked
    chicken
4 ounces snow peas, trimmed
3 green onions, trimmed and
    sliced
1 cup bean sprouts
1 medium head of Chinese
    cabbage, shredded
1 tablespoon toasted sesame
    seeds

Serves 4

This light, flavorful chicken salad is great for a summer lunch. Serve it with some slices of mango and papaya, some great bread, and a glass of Vouvray—and you are ready to go.

1. Place the salad dressing ingredients in a small bowl and whisk vigorously to combine.
2. In a medium-sized bowl, combine the chicken, snow peas, green onions, and bean sprouts. Add the dressing and toss to coat.
3. To serve, arrange the cabbage on a serving platter. Mound the chicken salad over the cabbage. Garnish with the sesame seeds.

Chicken Salad—2

3 tablespoons hoisin sauce, divided
1 tablespoon soy sauce
1 tablespoon dry sherry
2 whole boneless, skinless chicken breasts
1 tablespoon vegetable oil
4 tablespoons lime juice
1 teaspoon sesame oil
3 tablespoons sesame seeds, toasted
3 tablespoons peanuts, chopped
⅓ cup sliced scallions
¼ cup chopped cilantro, plus extra for garnish
Peanut oil for frying
¼ pound rice sticks
Bibb or romaine lettuce leaves

1. Combine 1 tablespoon of the hoisin sauce, the soy sauce, and the sherry in a medium-sized bowl. Add the chicken breasts and marinate for 20 to 30 minutes.
2. Heat the vegetable oil in a large skillet over medium-high heat. Add the chicken breasts, reserving the marinade. Brown the breasts on both sides. Add the reserved marinade to the skillet, cover, and cook over medium-low heat until tender, about 20 minutes.
3. Let the chicken cool to room temperature, then shred it into bite-sized pieces; set aside.
4. In a medium-sized bowl, combine the shredded chicken with the remaining hoisin sauce, the lime juice, sesame oil, sesame seeds, peanuts, scallions, and cilantro. Add the shredded chicken and stir to coat.
5. Add approximately 1 inch of peanut oil to a large skillet and heat on high until the oil is very hot, but not smoking.
6. Add the rice sticks carefully and fry for approximately 6 to 8 seconds or until puffed and golden; turn the rice sticks with tongs and fry for another 6 to 8 seconds. Remove the rice sticks to a stack of paper towels to drain.
7. Toss about ⅔ of the rice sticks with the chicken mixture.
8. To serve, place a mound of salad on a lettuce leaf on the center of each plate. Top with the remaining rice sticks and garnish with additional cilantro.

Chicken Salad—3

1 cup cooked chicken meat
2 cups shredded bok choy
½ cup very thinly sliced celery
1 scallion, thinly sliced
1 teaspoon vegetable oil
1 clove garlic, minced

1 (¼-inch) piece ginger, peeled
*   and minced*
¼ cup soy sauce
2 tablespoons rice vinegar
1 tablespoon sugar
¼ teaspoon sesame oil (optional)

1. In a medium-sized bowl, toss together the chicken, bok choy, celery, and scallion.
2. In a small bowl, thoroughly whisk together the remaining ingredients. Pour over the salad and toss well to combine.

> **Makes 3–4 cups**
>
> This salad makes a great packed lunch, because the salad holds up pretty well at room temperature and the dressing doesn't require refrigeration. Keep the salad and dressing in separate containers.

Jicama, Carrot, and Chinese Cabbage Salad

1 teaspoon ground anise
½ cup chopped cilantro
⅓ cup vegetable oil
2 tablespoons lime juice
½ teaspoon prepared chili-garlic
*   sauce*
2 pounds jicama, peeled and
*   finely julienned*

2 large carrots, peeled and
*   finely julienned*
¾ pound Chinese cabbage,
*   thinly shredded*
Salt and black pepper to taste

1. Thoroughly combine the ground anise, cilantro, vegetable oil, lime juice, and chili-garlic sauce in a large mixing bowl.
2. Add the vegetables and toss to coat.
3. Season with salt and pepper.

> **Serves 6–8**
>
> This crunchy salad reminds me of coleslaw. All of the vegetables are cut in a fine julienne and then tossed in a dressing. Serve it as a side dish, a salad, or as a topping for sandwiches.

Peanut-Potato Salad

3 pounds peeled boiling potatoes
1 cup salted peanuts, coarsely chopped, divided
1 medium-sized red bell pepper, cored and chopped
2 stalks celery, sliced
4 green onions, trimmed and sliced

¼ cup chopped cilantro
¼ cup chopped mint
¾ cup mayonnaise
¼ cup peanut butter
3 tablespoons rice vinegar
Salt and pepper to taste

1. Bring a large pot of water to a boil over high heat. Add the potatoes and cook until tender. Drain and cool. Cut into ½-inch cubes.
2. In a large bowl, combine the potato cubes, ¾ cup of peanuts, red bell pepper, celery, green onion, cilantro, and mint.
3. In a small bowl, whisk together the mayonnaise, peanut butter, and vinegar. Season to taste with salt and pepper.
4. Pour the dressing over the potato mixture and toss to coat. Refrigerate for at least 1 hour. Garnish with the remaining peanuts before serving.

Thai Potatoes?

Potatoes were originally cultivated by South American native populations, but then spread throughout the world. Potatoes have yet to be infused too deeply into Thai cuisine, with most recipes involving potatoes originating from a taro recipe, or a different potato recipe is given a Thai kick.

Asian Couscous Salad

¾ *pound snow peas, trimmed*

1 red bell pepper, cored,
   seeded, and chopped

1 yellow bell pepper, cored,
   seeded, and chopped

5–7 green onions, trimmed and
   thinly sliced

1 medium-sized red onion,
   chopped

1–2 jalapeño chilies, seeded
   and finely chopped

1 clove garlic, minced

2¾ cups couscous

3½ cups boiling water, divided

1 packed cup basil

1 packed cup mint

1 packed cup cilantro

½ cup vegetable oil

2 tablespoons lemon juice

3 tablespoons lime juice

Salt and freshly ground black
   pepper to taste

Serves 8–10

Serve this easy-to-make and healthy salad as a snack, a side dish, or as a light lunch. It is also super picnic fare.

1. Place the snow peas, peppers, onions, chilies, garlic, and couscous in a large bowl; toss to blend.
2. Pour 3 cups of the boiling water over the couscous mixture, cover tightly, and let stand at room temperature for 1 hour.
3. Add the remaining ½ cup boiling water and all the remaining ingredients to the couscous; toss together, cover, and let stand for at least 30 more minutes.
4. Season with salt and freshly ground black pepper.

Asian 3-Bean Salad

Serves 4–6

This 3-bean salad is inspired by the ones from the 1950s, but is jazzed up with Asian spices and rice vinegar.

1 (14-ounce) can garbanzo beans
1 (14-ounce) can black beans
1 (14-ounce) can red kidney beans
1 medium-sized red onion, chopped
⅓ cup chopped cilantro
4 tablespoons olive oil
3 tablespoons rice vinegar
3 cloves garlic, minced
1 teaspoon minced jalapeño
½ teaspoon lime zest
Salt and pepper to taste

1. Place all the beans in a colander. Thoroughly rinse under cool running water. Drain and set aside.
2. Stir together all the remaining ingredients and pour over beans; stir to combine.
3. Refrigerate overnight, stirring occasionally. Season with salt and pepper.

Crunchy Sprout Salad

Serves 4

Think spring! The dressing in this salad is fresh and lively, but not overpowering. This salad is also nice with a drained can of mandarin orange segments tossed in.

¼ cup rice vinegar
2 tablespoons fish or soy sauce
2 tablespoons vegetable oil
1 tablespoon sugar
2 teaspoons grated gingerroot
2 cups sprouts of your choice
6 cups baby greens (preferably an Asian mix)

1. In a large bowl whisk together the vinegar, fish sauce, vegetable oil, sugar, and gingerroot.
2. Add the sprouts, toss to coat, and let marinate for 30 minutes.
3. Add the greens and toss until well combined.

Many Peas Asian-Style Salad

1 cup sugar snap peas
½ cup snow peas
½ cup fresh green peas
2 teaspoons sesame seeds, toasted
1 tablespoon rice vinegar
1 tablespoon sesame oil

1 tablespoon brown sugar
2 teaspoons soy sauce
6 cups pea shoots or other sweet baby lettuce

Serves 4

Pea lovers rejoice—this recipe is for you. It goes without saying (even though I am), the fresher the ingredients the better. No compromising!

1. Bring a large pot of water to a boil. Add the sugar snap peas and boil for 2 minutes. Add the snow peas and green peas and boil for 1 minute more. Drain and rinse in cold water. Pat dry with paper towels.
2. In a large bowl, thoroughly combine the sesame seeds, vinegar, oil, sugar, and soy sauce. Add the peas and the greens and toss to coat.

Substituting Dried Lemongrass for Fresh
If you can't find lemongrass, substitute 1 tablespoon of dried lemongrass per stalk of fresh or several strips of peel from a lemon or lime.

Thai Pasta Salad

Serves 8–12

Salads made with pasta always used to have an Italian dressing or mayonnaise base. A great update to a concept that has been around for a long while, this salad features a spicy peanut dressing.

8 ounces dried bow tie or
  other bite-sized pasta
3 green onions, trimmed and
  thinly sliced
2 medium carrots, shredded
1½ cups thinly sliced Napa
  cabbage or bok choy
1½ cups thinly sliced red
  cabbage
1 tablespoon brown sugar
1 clove garlic, minced

2 tablespoons vegetable oil
⅓ cup rice wine vinegar
¼ teaspoon ground ginger
½ teaspoon red pepper flakes
3 tablespoons smooth
  peanut butter
2 tablespoons water
1 tablespoon soy sauce
1 cup bean sprouts

1. Cook the pasta according to package directions. Drain and rinse under cold water. Place the pasta in a large mixing bowl and add the green onions, carrots, and cabbage.
2. In a small mixing bowl, thoroughly combine all the remaining ingredients except the sprouts.
3. Pour the dressing over the pasta and vegetables; cover and refrigerate for at least 2 hours or overnight.
4. Just before serving, toss in the bean sprouts.

Thai Chicken Pizza

2 whole boneless, skinless
    chicken breasts, cut in half
1 recipe Asian or Thai
    Marinade (see recipes in
    Chapter 1)
1 unbaked pizza crust
¼–⅓ cup peanut or
    hot chili oil
1½ cups fontina cheese
1½ cups mozzarella cheese

4 green onions, trimmed and
    thinly sliced
1 medium carrot, peeled and
    coarsely grated
1½ cups bean sprouts
½ cup coarsely chopped
    dry-roasted peanuts
⅓ cup chopped cilantro leaves

> **Yields 1 large pizza**
>
> This is a great recipe to use up leftover Siamese Roast Chicken (see recipe on page 102). Simply chop up the leftover meat and proceed with step 3.

1. Place the chicken breasts in an ovenproof dish. Pour the marinade over the chicken, turning to coat thoroughly. Cover and refrigerate for at least 8 hours. Let the chicken return to room temperature before proceeding.
2. Preheat oven to 325 degrees. Bake the chicken for 30 to 40 minutes or until cooked through. Remove the chicken from the oven and let cool to room temperature. Shred the chicken into very small pieces; set aside.
3. Prepare the pizza dough according to package directions.
4. Brush the dough with some of the oil. Top the oil with the cheeses, leaving a ½-inch rim. Evenly spread the chicken, green onions, carrot, bean sprouts, and peanuts on top of the cheese. Drizzle a little oil over the top.
5. Bake according to package directions for the crust. Remove from oven, sprinkle with cilantro, and serve.

Grilled Steak with Peanut Sauce

*1 recipe of Thai Marinade
  (see recipes in Chapter 1)
1 (2-pound) flank steak, trimmed*

*1 recipe of Peanut Dipping Sauce
  (see recipes in Chapter 2)*

1. Quickly rinse the steak under cold water and pat dry. Place the steak in a large Ziplock bag along with the marinade. Turn the meat until it is well coated with the marinade on all sides. Refrigerate overnight. (Let the steak return to room temperature before cooking.)
2. Preheat a broiler or grill. Cook the steak, turning once and basting with the remaining marinade, until done to your preference
3. Remove the meat from the grill, cover it with foil, and let it rest for 5 minutes to let some of the juices reabsorb. To serve, thinly slice the steak across the grain. Pass the peanut sauce separately.

Asian Marinara Sauce

*2 tablespoons vegetable oil
1 medium onion, chopped
1 (1-inch) piece of ginger,
  peeled and minced
1–3 serrano chilies, seeded
  and minced*

*1 cup water
1 pound chopped canned
  tomatoes with the juice
1 teaspoon salt
1 teaspoon sugar*

1. In a large saucepan, heat the oil over medium heat.
2. Add the onion and ginger and sauté for 2 minutes.
3. Add the chilies and continue cooking 1 minute more.
4. Stir in the water, tomatoes, salt, and sugar. Reduce heat to low and simmer for at least 30 minutes.

Thai-Style Grilled Pork Chops

1 garlic clove, minced
⅓ cup fish sauce
2 tablespoons cream sherry
3 tablespoons rice vinegar
2 teaspoons brown sugar

2 teaspoons minced gingerroot
2 (1-inch-thick) pork chops

Serves 2

The sugar and the sherry in this marinade help the chops develop a nicely charred crust. But pay attention while you are grilling. These same ingredients can cause brief fire flare-ups.

1. In a small saucepan, over medium heat, bring the garlic, fish sauce, sherry, vinegar, brown sugar, and gingerroot to a boil. Remove from heat and allow to cool to room temperature. (You can also put the marinade in the refrigerator to cool it.)
2. Place the pork chops in a plastic bag and pour in the marinade, making sure to coat both sides of the chops. Let the chops marinate at room temperature for 15 minutes.
3. Pour the marinade into a small saucepan and bring to a simmer over medium-low heat. Cook for 5 minutes.
4. Grill the chops on a hot grill for 5 to 6 minutes per side for medium.
5. Serve the chops with the marinade drizzled over the top.

Southeast Asian Burgers

<table>
<tr><td>

Serves 4

These burgers are great topped with Pickled Chinese Cabbage (see recipe on page 232).

</td><td>

1 clove garlic, minced
3 tablespoons bread crumbs
1 pound ground beef or
ground turkey
¼ cup chopped cilantro
¼ cup chopped basil
¼ cup chopped mint

</td><td>

2 tablespoons lime juice
1 teaspoon sugar (optional)
3 shakes Tabasco

</td></tr>
</table>

1. In a medium-sized mixing bowl, combine all the remaining ingredients.
2. Using your hands, gently mix the ingredients together and form 4 patties. Season each patty with salt and pepper.
3. Grill the patties to your liking, about 5 minutes per side for medium.

Serving Marinades

If you are going to use a marinade as a sauce, make sure to bring it to a boil after the marinating foods have been removed. Otherwise, reusing the marinade can make you sick (e.g., food poisoning).

Grilled Lobster Tails
with a Lemongrass Smoke

6 (4–6 ounce) lobster tails
Olive oil
Cracked black pepper

3–4 whole lemongrass stalks,
bruised
Salt to taste

1. To prepare the lobster tails, lay each tail flat-side down (shell up). Using a sharp knife, cut through the shell and halfway through the meat lengthwise. Use your fingers to pull the meat away from the membranes and the inner shell, then invert the meat until it sits on top of the shell instead of being surrounded by it.
2. Brush the lobster generously with olive oil and sprinkle with black pepper. Place the lemongrass stalks in a Tuscan herb grill.
3. Heat grill to medium-high heat. Place the herb grill on the main grill grate and place the lobster tails on top, meat side up. Close the lid of the grill and cook for 7 to 8 minutes. (The shells should be bright red and the meat quite firm.)
4. Turn the lobster tails over and continue cooking for 2 to 3 minutes.
5. Sprinkle with salt and serve.

What is a Tuscan Herb Grill?

A Tuscan herb grill is a flat, hinged grate that looks similar to a screen. The 2 sides fit closely together and hold fresh herbs, such as fennel or basil, which smoke during the grilling process, imparting a smoky, herbal note to grilled meats or fish.

Thai-Flavored Green Beans

2 pounds French or regular green beans, trimmed and cut into bite-sized pieces
1 rounded tablespoon shrimp paste
2 tablespoons vegetable oil
3 tablespoons unsalted butter
2 teaspoons minced garlic
½ cup chopped cilantro

1. In a pot large enough to hold all of the beans, steam them until tender-crisp.
2. Drain the beans, reserving cooking liquid. Cover the beans with foil to keep warm.
3. In a small bowl, whisk together the shrimp paste and vegetable oil.
4. In a large skillet, melt the butter over medium-high heat. Add the garlic and sauté until golden. Stir in the shrimp paste mixture and 1 tablespoon of the reserved cooking liquid.
5. Add the reserved green beans, stirring to coat. Cook until heated through.
6. Remove the pan from the heat and toss in the cilantro.

Southeast Asian Asparagus

1 tablespoon sesame oil
1 pound asparagus, trimmed and cut into 2-inch pieces
1 teaspoon fish sauce
1 teaspoon toasted sesame seeds
⅛ cup toasted peanuts

1. Heat the sesame oil in a large skillet over medium-high heat. Add the asparagus and sauté for 3 minutes.
2. Add the fish sauce, sesame seeds, and peanuts. Sauté for 2 more minutes or until the asparagus is done to your liking.

Asian Ratatouille

2 Japanese eggplants
(about 1 pound), cut into
½-inch cubes
½ teaspoon salt
3 tablespoons sesame oil
2 ribs of celery, sliced
1 onion, slivered
1 red bell pepper, cored,
seeded, and julienned
3 tablespoons vegetable oil
2 small zucchini, halved lengthwise and sliced

1 cup sliced mushrooms
¾ cup vegetable stock
2 tablespoons soy sauce
1 tablespoon dry sherry
1 tablespoon cornstarch
1 teaspoon minced garlic
1 teaspoon minced ginger
2 teaspoons Plum Dipping
Sauce (see recipe on
page 25)
1 tablespoon chopped cilantro

Serves 6–8

The similarity between this Asian version and the French classic is evident. But instead of seasoning the dish with herbs de Provence, this ratatouille gets its zip from ginger, plum sauce, and soy.

1. Place the eggplant in a colander and sprinkle with the salt. Let rest for 30 minutes.
2. In a large ovenproof pot, heat the sesame oil on medium. Add the celery, onion, and red bell pepper; sauté for 5 minutes. Remove the vegetables from the pan and set aside.
3. Add the vegetable oil to the pot. Sauté the zucchini, mushrooms, and eggplant for 5 minutes. Stir in the celery, onion, and bell pepper and set aside.
4. In a small mixing bowl, whisk together the stock, soy sauce, sherry, and cornstarch. Pour over the vegetables and stir to combine.
5. Bake, covered, in a 350-degree oven for 40 minutes.
6. Stir in the garlic, ginger, and plum sauce. Cover and continue to bake for an additional 10 minutes.

Pickled Chinese Cabbage

4 cups water
6 cups rice vinegar
1 tablespoon chopped garlic
1 tablespoon chopped cilantro
2 large shallots or 1 medium
   onion, chopped

3 pounds Chinese cabbage,
   cored, halved, and thinly
   sliced
Salt and white pepper

1. Place all of the ingredients except the cabbage in a large stew pot and bring to a boil. Reduce heat and simmer for 5 minutes.
2. Bring the cooking liquid back to a boil and stir in the cabbage. Cover and cook the cabbage for 3 to 5 minutes.
3. Remove the pot from heat and let cool to room temperature. Season to taste with salt and white pepper.
4. Refrigerate for at least 8 hours before serving.

Crazy Coconut Pie

¾ stick of butter, melted
4 eggs
2 cups milk
½ cup flour

¾ cup sugar
1½ teaspoons vanilla
1 cup sweetened shredded
   coconut

1. Preheat oven to 350 degrees. Grease and flour a 10-inch pie plate.
2. Place all of the ingredients in a blender and blend for 1 minute. Pour the batter into the prepared pan.
3. Bake for 45 minutes or until golden on top.

Lime Butter Cake

3 cups cake flour
3 teaspoons baking powder
¼ teaspoon salt
2 sticks unsalted butter
1½ cups sugar

4 eggs, lightly beaten
1 cup milk
Grated peel of 1 lime
3 tablespoons lime juice
Powdered sugar (optional)

1. Preheat oven to 325 degrees.
2. Sift together the cake flour, baking powder, and salt 3 times; set aside.
3. In the bowl of an electric mixer, beat the butter until creamy.
4. Gradually add in the sugar, then beat at medium speed for 5 minutes, scraping down the sides of the bowl every so often.
5. Add the beaten eggs slowly and continue to beat for 5 more minutes. (The mixture will be thick and double in volume.)
6. Using a rubber spatula, gradually fold in ¼ of the flour mixture into the batter. Then fold in ⅓ of the milk. Repeat this process until all of the flour and the milk have been incorporated. (You will add flour last.)
7. Fold in the lime peel and lime juice.
8. Pour the batter into a greased molded cake pan, smoothing the surface and slightly building up the sides.
9. Bake the cake for 45 to 55 minutes or until the top is golden and the sides are beginning to pull away from the pan.
10. Remove from the oven and let cool for 1 to 2 minutes. Carefully unmold.
11. Let cool to room temperature. Dust with powdered sugar or serve with Ginger Anglaise Sauce (see recipe on page 188).

Yields 1 (12–inch) cake

This cake is so moist and flavorful, I simply dust it with powdered sugar. If you want to frost it, go with something light and not too sweet. A crème anglaise or vanilla ice cream goes nicely with it, too.

Meringues with Tropical Fruit

My friend, Leslie Kowitz, hosted an afternoon tea a while back, which included a plethora of teas and sweets. My favorite was a meringue shell filled with berries. Here it is with a tropical twist.

Butter at room temperature to prepare baking dishes
6 egg whites
2 cups superfine sugar
2 cups heavy cream, whipped

2 cups mixed fresh tropical fruit, cut into bite-sized pieces

1. Preheat oven to 200 degrees. Butter pieces of parchment paper cut to line 2 baking sheets.
2. Place the egg whites in a cold bowl. Beat until soft peaks form. Add the sugar and continue to beat until stiff.
3. Using a pastry bag, pipe 3- to 4-inch circles of meringue onto the prepared baking sheets.
4. Bake for 90 to 120 minutes or until they are dry, taking care not to let the meringues turn color. If the meringues aren't dry after 2 hours of baking, turn the oven off and let the meringues sit in the oven overnight.
5. Allow the meringues to cool completely. Fill a pastry bag with the whipped heavy cream. Pipe cream into the center of the meringues. Top with tropical fruit and serve.

Singapore Shellfish Soup	236
Roasted Duck, Melon, and Mango Salad	238
Spice-Poached Chicken	239
Tea-Smoked Chicken	240
Pork Medallions in a Clay Pot	241
Singapore Shrimp	242
5-Spiced Vegetables	243
Peninsula Sweet Potatoes	244
Beef Cambogee	244
Hot Noodles with Tofu	245
Singapore Noodles	246
Oyster Mushroom Soup	246
Sweet Cambodian Broth with Pork and Eggs	247
Cambodian-Style Pan-Fried Chicken and Mushrooms	248
Cambodian Beef with Lime Sauce	249
Red Curry Cambogee	250
Lemongrass Curry Sauce	250
Sweet-and-Sour Vegetables	251
Minted Vegetables	252
Shrimp "Pâté"	253

Vietnamese Pork Sticks	254
Happy Pancakes	256
Honeyed Chicken	257
Vietnamese Oxtail Soup	258
Fruit in Sherried Syrup	260
Banana Brown Rice Pudding	260
Vietnamese Bananas	261
Basic Vietnamese Chili Sauce	262
Chilied Coconut Dipping Sauce	262
Tropical Fruits with Cinnamon and Lime	263
Potato Samosas	264
Chapati	266
Mulligatawny Soup	267
Tandoori Chicken	268
Punjab Fish	269
Indian-Scented Cauliflower	270
Cardamom Cookies	271
Almond "Tea"	272
Cucumber Raita	272
Tamarind Dipping Sauce	273
Garam Masala	273
Mango Chutney	274

Singapore Shellfish Soup

Serves 6–8

Singapore sits at the southern end of the Malay Peninsula, surrounded by the Strait of Malacca, the South China Sea, and the Java Sea. No wonder seafood is a Singaporean mainstay.

2 tablespoons vegetable oil, divided

1 pound large raw shrimp, peeled, shells reserved

1 pound mussels, cleaned and debearded

3 stalks lemongrass, outer layers removed, inner core thinly sliced

3 serrano chilies, seeded and chopped

2 cloves garlic, minced

1 (1-inch) piece ginger, peeled and chopped

4 small shallots, peeled and sliced

1 tablespoon anchovy paste

1 teaspoon turmeric

1 tablespoon ground coriander

1 (14-ounce) can coconut milk

1–2 tablespoons fish sauce

1 7-ounce package of rice noodles, soaked in hot water until soft

1 tablespoon lime zest

6 large scallops, sliced horizontally into 2–3 pieces, depending on their size

1 cup bean sprouts

¼ cup chopped cilantro

Lime wedges

(recipe continues on the next page)

Singapore Shellfish Soup (continued)

1. In a medium-sized saucepan heat 1 tablespoon of the oil over medium-high heat and fry the shrimp shells until pink.
2. Add 3 cups of water to the pan and bring to a boil; reduce the heat and simmer for 30 minutes. Strain the shells from the broth, then boil the broth until it is reduced to 2 cups.
3. In a large skillet, bring ½ cup of water to a boil. Add the mussels, cover, and let steam until opened, about 5 minutes. Discard any mussels that have not opened. Strain the cooking liquid and reserve. Shell all but about ⅓ of the mussels; set the mussels aside.
4. Place the lemongrass, chilies, garlic, ginger, shallots, anchovy paste, and 2 tablespoons of water in a food processor. Process to form a thick paste, adding more water if needed.
5. Heat the remaining vegetable oil in a large soup pot over medium heat. Add the lemongrass paste and fry, stirring continuously, until lightly browned, about 10 minutes. Stir in the turmeric and ground coriander and cook for 1 minute more.
6. Add the shrimp broth and mussel cooking liquid to the pot, stirring to dissolve the paste. Bring to a boil, reduce heat, and simmer for 10 to 15 minutes.
7. Add the coconut milk and fish sauce; return to a boil. Add the noodles and lime zest; simmer for 2 minutes. Add the shrimp and simmer for 2 minutes more. Add the scallop slices. After 30 seconds or so, add the shelled mussels and bean sprouts. Gently stir to combine.
8. To serve, ladle the soup into deep soup bowls. Garnish with the mussels in their shells, sprinkle with chopped cilantro and the juice from a lime wedge over the top of each bowl.

Roasted Duck, Melon, and Mango Salad

Serves 4–6

You can roast the duck yourself, or order either roast duck or duck confit from a gourmet shop. You can also substitute chicken if you prefer. Feel free to try other fruits in this salad, too.

1 teaspoon soy sauce
2 teaspoons fine sugar
1 teaspoon oyster sauce
1 tablespoon plus 2 teaspoons
  vegetable oil
½ roast duck, meat removed
  and shredded
3 tablespoons water
½ teaspoon granulated salt
1 teaspoon sugar
½ teaspoon sesame oil
1 teaspoon ketchup
1 teaspoon bottled chili sauce
1½ teaspoons cornstarch
1½ teaspoons apricot jam
1 cup cubed honeydew melon
1 cup cubed cantaloupe
½ large cucumber, seeded and
  sliced
1 cup cubed jicama
1 mango, cut into bite-sized
  pieces
1 pear, cut into bite-sized pieces
3 tablespoons ground peanuts
2 tablespoons toasted sesame
  seeds

1. In a medium-sized mixing bowl, combine the soy sauce, fine sugar, oyster sauce, and 1 tablespoon of the vegetable oil. Add the shredded duck to the bowl and toss to coat; set aside.
2. In a small bowl, whisk together the 3 tablespoons of water, salt, 1 teaspoon of sugar, sesame oil, ketchup, chili sauce, and cornstarch; set aside.
3. In a small saucepan, heat the remaining vegetable oil over medium heat. Add the sauce mixture to the pan and cook until it thickens. Stir in the apricot jam and remove the pan from the heat. Cool the sauce in the refrigerator. Stir before using.
4. Mound the duck in the center of a large serving platter. Arrange the fruits and vegetables around the duck. Spoon the sauce over the duck, fruits, and vegetables. Sprinkle the salad with chopped peanuts and sesame seeds. Serve at once.

Duck Confit
Duck confit is a lusciously moist and intensely flavored treat. The duck is cured in spices and then slowly braised in its own fat. It is delicious and surprisingly not greasy!

Spice-Poached Chicken

1 whole star anise
½ teaspoon whole black
    peppercorns
½ teaspoon whole cloves
1 (2-inch) cinnamon stick
1 cardamom pod
¼ teaspoon dried tangerine
    peel (dried orange peel
    can be substituted)
5 cups water

¼ cup light soy sauce
2 tablespoons sugar
4–6 boneless, skinless chicken
    breasts

Serves 4–6
I like to use this chicken as a base for chicken salad. The subtle spices impart a terrific flavor that turns a standby into a stand-up! Serve the chicken salad on a whole-grain roll with lettuce and apple slices.

1. Place the star anise, peppercorns, cloves, cinnamon stick, cardamom pod, tangerine peel, and water in a stew pot. Bring the mixture to a boil over high heat. Let boil until the poaching liquid is reduced to 4 cups.
2. Stir in the soy sauce and the sugar. Return the liquid to a boil.
3. Add the chicken breasts and reduce to a simmer. Poach the breasts until done, about 20 minutes.

Tangerines and Mandarin Oranges
Tangerines and mardarin oranges are the same thing! The name just tells you where they were grown. If they are from the United States, they are tangerines. If not, they're called mandarins.

Tea-Smoked Chicken

Serves 6–8

Make sure your stove's ventilation hood works before you start this recipe. The smoke stays mostly in the wok while the chicken is cooking, but it comes out in a big poof when you remove the lid.

6–8 boneless, skinless chicken breasts
½ teaspoon salt
2 teaspoons rice wine
½ cup green tea leaves
½ cup brown sugar
½ cup cooked rice
1 teaspoon sesame oil

1. Quickly rinse the chicken breasts under cold water and pat dry. Sprinkle with the salt and rice wine. Set aside in the refrigerator for 30 minutes.
2. Meanwhile, prepare the wok: Line the bottom with a sheet of aluminum foil. Place the tea leaves, brown sugar, and rice in the bottom of the wok and toss to combine. Put a wire grill rack on the wok.
3. Heat the wok over medium-high heat. Put the chicken on the rack and cover with a tight-fitting lid. Turn off the heat after smoke begins to emit from the wok, but leave it on the burner for 10 minutes or until the chicken is cooked through.
4. Brush the chicken with the sesame oil. Serve at once.

Thai Asian Fusion

Blending Chinese ingredients with local spices creates a type of fusion cooking that is unique to Singapore, called Nonya. These dishes are a specialty of "Hawker Centers," open-air centers with fast-food street stalls selling everything from satay to stir-fried noodles to spicy crab. Don't miss them if you travel to Singapore.

Pork Medallions in a Clay Pot

2 tablespoons oyster sauce

2 tablespoons light soy sauce

2 tablespoons sweet (dark) soy sauce

1 tablespoon Black Bean Paste (see recipe on page 10)

1 teaspoon sesame oil

1 teaspoon rice wine

½ teaspoon ground black pepper

1 clove garlic, minced

1 tablespoon cornstarch

2 pork tenderloins, trimmed and cut into ½-inch slices

2 tablespoons vegetable oil

1 tablespoon Tamarind Concentrate (see recipe on page 18)

1 cup water

Serves 4

Soy sauce, black bean paste, sesame oil, and rice wine are all traditional Chinese ingredients. The Chinese use clay pots over an open heat source as a type of oven, an appliance still not used much in Asia.

1. Prepare the marinade by combining the oyster sauce, light and dark soy sauces, Black Bean Paste, sesame oil, rice wine, black pepper, garlic, and cornstarch in a medium bowl.

2. Add the pork slices to the bowl of marinade and toss to coat thoroughly. Cover the pork and let marinate at room temperature for 30 minutes.

3. Heat the vegetable oil in a wok over medium-high heat. Add the marinated pork and stir-fry for 3 to 4 minutes.

4. Transfer the pork to a clay pot or other ovenproof braising vessel.

5. Stir together the tamarind and water; pour over the pork.

6. Bake the pork in a 350-degree oven for 1½ hours, until very tender.

Singapore Shrimp

2 tablespoons vegetable oil
1 cup sliced domestic
   mushrooms
¼ cup green onion slices
1 clove garlic, minced
1 teaspoon minced ginger
2 teaspoons hoisin sauce
2 teaspoons oyster sauce
2 teaspoons Red Curry Paste
   (see recipes in Chapter 1)

¼ teaspoon Chinese 5-spice
   powder
1 can coconut milk
Salt and pepper to taste
1½ pounds cooked shrimp

1. In a wok or large sauté pan, heat the vegetable oil on medium-high.
2. Add the mushrooms, green onions, garlic, and ginger; stir-fry for 2 to 3 minutes.
3. Stir together the hoisin sauce, oyster sauce, and curry paste, and 5-spice powder until well combined. Add the mixture to the wok.
4. Stir in the coconut milk and adjust seasoning to taste with the salt and pepper. Add the shrimp and bring to a simmer. Cook for 1 to 2 minutes until the shrimp are heated through.

5-Spiced Vegetables

½ cup orange juice
1 tablespoon cornstarch
½ – ¾ teaspoon Chinese
    5-spice powder
¼ teaspoon crushed red
    pepper flakes
2 tablespoons soy sauce
2 teaspoons honey
1 tablespoon vegetable oil

1 pound mushrooms, sliced
1 cup carrot slices
1 small onion, halved and
    thinly sliced
1–2 cloves garlic, minced
3 cups broccoli florets

Serves 4

Here the 5 flavors of Asia—salty, hot, sweet, sour, and bitter—are found in the sauce. Add a little more honey if you prefer a sweeter sauce and fewer red pepper flakes if you don't want as much heat.

1. In a small bowl, combine the orange juice, cornstarch, 5-spice powder, red pepper flakes, soy sauce, and honey; set aside.
2. Heat the vegetable oil in a wok or skillet over medium-high heat. Add the mushrooms, carrots, onion, and garlic. Stir-fry for approximately 4 minutes.
3. Add the broccoli and continue cooking another 2 to 4 minutes.
4. Stir in the sauce. Cook until the vegetables are done to your liking and the sauce is thick, approximately 2 minutes.
5. Serve over rice noodles, pasta, or rice.

Peninsula Sweet Potatoes

Serves 4

To really give your Thanksgiving guests something to talk about, try serving this version of sweet potatoes.

1 pound sweet potatoes or yams of varying varieties, peeled and cut into bite-sized pieces

1 bay leaf
1 teaspoon sugar
¼ teaspoon salt
1 (14-ounce) can coconut milk

1. Place the sweet potato pieces in a large saucepan. Add just enough water to cover them, and bring to a boil. Add the bay leaf and cook until the potatoes are soft. Remove the bay leaf and discard.
2. Stir in the sugar and salt. After the sugar has dissolved, remove the pan from the heat and stir in the coconut milk. Adjust the seasonings by adding salt and/or sugar if necessary. Adjust the consistency by adding more water and/or coconut milk.

Beef Cambogee

Serves 4–6

Meat and potatoes, Cambodian style. As the meat and potatoes simmer in the curry, they become tender and deeply flavored. The peanuts and bean sprouts add snap.

5 cups Red Curry Cambogee (recipe on page 250)
1 pound sirloin, trimmed, and cut into bite-sized pieces

2–3 medium-sized russet potatoes, peeled and cut into bite-sized pieces
½ cup chopped peanuts
2 cups bean sprouts

1. In a large saucepan, bring the curry sauce to a simmer.
2. Add the meat and potatoes and simmer until done to your liking, about 20 to 30 minutes.
3. Garnish with the peanuts and bean sprouts.

Hot Noodles with Tofu

*½ pound Chinese wheat
    noodles*
Vegetable oil for frying
*½ pound firm tofu, cut into
    1-inch cubes*
*½ pound dried tofu, soaked in
    hot water for 15 minutes
    and cut into 1-inch cubes*
3 tablespoons sesame oil
3 tablespoons minced ginger

*½ teaspoon yellow asafetida
    powder*
*1 bunch choy sum, chopped
    into 1-inch pieces*
3 tablespoons soy sauce
3 tablespoons sambal oelek
3 tablespoons lemon juice
*2 cups mung bean shoots or
    bean sprouts*

Serves 4
To serve this dish, mound the noodles on the center of four plates. Generously top with fresh shoots or sprouts.

1. Cook the noodles al dente according to package directions. Rinse under cold water and drain; set aside.
2. Heat about 2 inches of vegetable oil in a wok or large skillet over medium high heat. Add the firm tofu cubes and deep-fry until golden. Using a slotted spoon, remove the tofu cubes to paper towels to drain; set aside.
3. Add the dried tofu pieces and deep-fry them until they blister. Remove and drain on paper towels; set aside.
4. In another wok or skillet heat the sesame oil over high heat. Add the ginger and stir-fry 1 minute.
5. Add the asafetida and choy sum, and stir-fry until soft.
6. Stir in the soy sauce, sambal oelek, and lemon juice. Add the noodles and tofu pieces. Stir-fry until hot, about 2 minutes more.

Singapore Noodles

Serves 2–3

Do you have 5 minutes and some leftover chicken, beef, pork, shrimp, or a combination thereof? If so, this is the meal for you. It's satisfying, it's easy, and it's foolproof!

2 tablespoons vegetable oil
4 cloves garlic, minced
2 tablespoons minced ginger
2 cups cooked meat or shrimp in bite-sized pieces
2 green onions, trimmed and thinly sliced

1–2 teaspoons red pepper flakes
¼ cup oyster sauce
3 tablespoons curry powder
2 teaspoons soy sauce
1 package rice sticks, soaked in hot water until soft and drained

1. Heat the vegetable oil in a wok or large skillet over medium-high heat. Add the garlic and the ginger. Stir-fry until soft.
2. Add the cooked meat or shrimp, green onion, and red pepper flakes to the wok; stir-fry until hot.
3. Stir in the oyster sauce, curry powder, and soy sauce. Add the rice noodles and toss. Serve immediately.

Oyster Mushroom Soup

Serves 4

Oyster mushrooms are fan-shaped mushrooms with a mild flavor and a tender bite. In this Cambodian-style soup they add texture to a complex, yet simple-to-make broth.

4 cups vegetable broth
1 tablespoon Tabasco
2–3 serrano chilies
½ stalk lemongrass, outer leaves removed, inner core finely chopped

3 (2-inch-long, ½-inch wide) pieces lime zest
1 teaspoon sugar
2 tablespoons lemon juice
½ pound oyster mushrooms, cleaned and separated if large

1. In a large saucepan, bring the vegetable broth and the Tabasco to a boil. Meanwhile, crush the chilies with a mallet to break them slightly open: A good whack will do it.
2. Add all of the remaining ingredients to the boiling broth, reduce the heat, and simmer until the mushrooms are cooked to your liking. Remove the chilies before serving.

Sweet Cambodian Broth
with Pork and Eggs

4 cups water
5 tablespoons soy sauce
½ teaspoon freshly ground
*   black pepper*
½ teaspoon salt
1 cup sugar
1 cup fish sauce
6–8 hard-boiled eggs
1 large pork tenderloin, cut
*   into bite-sized cubes*

1 cup thinly sliced bamboo
*   shoots*
Rice, cooked according to
*   package directions*

Serves 4–6
When I say sweet, I mean sweet. As the sugar cooks, it gives a syrupy consistency to this very traditional dish. Luckily the sweetness is counter-acted somewhat by a good amount of salty ingredients.

1. Bring the water to a boil in a large saucepan. Add the soy sauce, black pepper, salt, sugar, fish sauce, and hard-boiled eggs; simmer for 15 minutes.
2. Add the cubed pork and the bamboo shoots and simmer for an additional 30 minutes.
3. Reduce the heat to low, cover, and let simmer for 2 to 3 hours. Adjust seasonings to taste.
4. To serve, mound some rice in the bottom of soup bowls. Ladle soup over the rice.

Cambodian-Style Pan-Fried Chicken and Mushrooms

Serves 4–6

Spoon the seasoned mushrooms and a bit of the pan drippings over the chicken. Serve noodles on the side.

6 ounces dried Chinese
   mushrooms
2 tablespoons vegetable oil
4 cloves garlic, crushed
½ teaspoon grated ginger
1½ pounds chicken breasts
   and legs

1 cup water
2 teaspoons sugar

1. Place the dried mushrooms in a bowl, cover with boiling water, and let soak for 30 minutes. Drain the mushrooms and rinse under cold water; drain again and squeeze dry. Remove any tough stems. Cut the mushrooms into bite-sized pieces; set aside.
2. Place the vegetable oil in a wok or large skillet over medium-high heat. Add the garlic and the ginger and stir-fry briefly.
3. Add the chicken and fry until the skin turns golden.
4. Stir in the water and the sugar. Add the mushrooms.
5. Reduce the heat to low, cover, and cook until the chicken is tender, about 30 minutes.

Cambodian Beef with Lime Sauce

1 tablespoon sugar
2 teaspoons freshly ground
   black pepper, divided
2 tablespoons soy sauce
5–7 cloves garlic, crushed
1½ pounds sirloin, trimmed
   and cut into bite-sized cubes

2 tablespoons lime juice
1 teaspoon water
2 tablespoons vegetable oil

Serves 4

This simple marinade is so good that even though the lime sauce is a breeze, the meat is equally good without it. If you don't have any beef on hand, use pork tenderloin instead.

1. In a bowl large enough to hold the beef, combine the sugar, 1 teaspoon of black pepper, soy sauce, and garlic. Add the beef and toss to coat. Cover and let marinate for 30 minutes.
2. In a small serving dish, combine the remaining black pepper, the lime juice, and the water; set aside.
3. In a large sauté pan, heat the vegetable oil over medium-high heat. Add the beef cubes and sauté for 4 minutes for medium-rare.
4. This dish may be served either as an appetizer or a main dish. For the appetizer, mound the beef on a plate lined with lettuce leaves with the lime sauce on the side. Use toothpicks or small forks to dip the beef into the lime sauce. For a main dish, toss the beef with the lime sauce to taste. Serve with Jasmine rice.

Red Curry Cambogee

4 dried Thai bird chilies, stemmed and seeded
1 cup boiling water
4 tablespoons sweet paprika

2 tablespoons vegetable oil
4 cups Lemongrass Curry Sauce (recipe follows)

1. Break the dried chilies into pieces and place them in a small bowl. Cover with the boiling water and let sit until soft, about 15 minutes.
2. Place the chilies, their steeping water, and the paprika in a blender. Process to form a thin paste.
3. Heat the vegetable oil over medium-high heat in a wok. Add the chili paste and stir-fry until it begins to darken. Remove from heat and set aside.
4. Place the Lemongrass Curry Sauce in a medium-sized saucepan. Stir in half of the chili paste and bring to a boil. Reduce the heat and let simmer for 5 to 10 minutes. Check the flavor of the sauce, adding more chili paste if needed.

Lemongrass Curry Sauce

⅓ cup chopped lemongrass, inner core only
4–5 cloves garlic, chopped
1 teaspoon minced ginger
1 teaspoon turmeric
1 jalapeño chili, stemmed and seeded

3 small shallots, coarsely chopped
3 (14-ounce) cans coconut milk
3 (2-inch-long, ½-inch wide) pieces lime peel
¼ teaspoon salt

1. Place the lemongrass, garlic, ginger, turmeric, chili, and shallots in a food processor; process to form a paste.
2. Bring the coconut milk to a boil and add the lemongrass paste, lime peel, and salt. Reduce heat and let simmer for 30 to 45 minutes. Remove the lime peel.

Sweet-and-Sour Vegetables

1 cup sliced carrots
1 large green pepper, seeded
    and cut into bite-sized pieces
1 onion, sliced
2 cloves garlic, crushed
1 teaspoon grated ginger
1 cup water, divided
4 cups broccoli
6 green onions, trimmed and
    cut into 1-inch lengths

1 cup unsweetened pineapple
    juice
¼ cup rice vinegar
2 tablespoons soy sauce
⅓ cup brown sugar
2 tablespoons cornstarch
1 cup fresh pineapple chunks

Serves 6

A medley of vegetables, this dish is heavily influenced by Cambodia's northern neighbor, China. You can serve these as an accompaniment or as a main dish over rice.

1. Place the carrots, onion, green pepper, garlic, and ginger in a large saucepan with ½ cup of the water. Bring the water to a boil and let cook for 5 minutes, stirring frequently.
2. Add the broccoli, green onions, and the remaining ½ cup of water. Bring the water to a boil; reduce the heat, cover, and let simmer for 5 minutes.
3. Meanwhile, in a small bowl, thoroughly combine the pineapple juice, rice vinegar, soy sauce, brown sugar, and cornstarch.
4. Add the pineapple juice mixture and the pineapple chunks to the wok. Increase the heat to medium and cook, stirring constantly, until the sauce thickens.

Minted Vegetables

2 teaspoons vegetable oil, divided
4 medium carrots, peeled and cut into thin slices
1 medium onion, cut into 1-inch pieces
1 red bell pepper, seeded and cut into 1-inch pieces
3 cups broccoli pieces
3 cups thinly sliced red cabbage
½ cup vegetable broth
Salt and pepper to taste
3–4 tablespoons chopped mint

1. In a large skillet, heat 1 teaspoon of vegetable oil over medium-high heat. Add the carrot slices, onion, and bell pepper; sauté for 5 minutes.
2. Add the remaining teaspoon of oil, the broccoli, the cabbage, and the vegetable broth. Continue to sauté until the vegetables are done to your liking, about 10 minutes for tender-crisp.
3. Season to taste with salt and pepper. Stir in the chopped mint.

Shrimp "Pâté"

1¼ cups minced shrimp
½ teaspoon salt
1 teaspoon sugar
¼ teaspoon white pepper
1 red chili, seeded and finely
    minced (optional)
2 tablespoons vegetable oil

8 (4-inch) pieces sugarcane
Sweet-and-sour or other favorite
    dipping sauce

Serves 4

Although not really a pâté in the traditional sense, you can still see the French influences in this dish. The ground shrimp is made into an almost mousse-like concoction that is slow-roasted—perfect with a glass of Chablis.

1. Preheat oven to 375 degrees.
2. Place the shrimp, salt, sugar, white pepper, and chili in a food processor; process until smooth.
3. Drizzle in 1 to 2 tablespoons of the vegetable oil. Process the shrimp mixture until it reaches the consistency necessary to make a meatball, using more or less oil.
4. Divide the shrimp mixture into 4 equal parts.
5. Using your hands, mold a "shrimp ball" around the center of each of the sugarcane pieces.
6. Place the "skewers" on a baking sheet and roast for approximately 20 minutes. If you prefer them a bit more browned, broil them (after they are done baking) until the desired color is reached.
7. To serve, spoon some of the sweet-and-sour sauce into the middle of 4 plates. Place the sugarcane "skewer" on top of the sauce.

Vietnamese Pork Sticks

For the pork:

1 pound lean ground pork
6 large water chestnuts, minced
1 clove garlic, minced
1 green onion, trimmed and minced
1 tablespoon soy sauce
2 teaspoons vegetable oil
1¼ teaspoons lemon juice
1 (½-inch) piece ginger, peeled and minced
¼ teaspoon sugar
¼ teaspoon Chinese hot chili oil
⅛ teaspoon salt
12 bamboo skewers, soaked in water
12 Boston or leaf lettuce leaves
½ cup chopped cilantro
½ cup chopped mint
½ cup chopped basil

For the dipping sauce:

½ cup soy sauce
5 tablespoons lemon juice
3 tablespoons water
2 garlic cloves, minced
1 (1-inch) piece ginger, minced
2 teaspoons sugar
1 teaspoon oyster sauce
Pinch of cayenne pepper

(recipe continues on the next page)

Vietnamese Pork Sticks (continued)

1. To prepare the pork: In a large bowl, use your hands to thoroughly combine the ground pork, water chestnuts, garlic, green onion, soy sauce, vegetable oil, lemon juice, ginger, sugar, chili oil, and salt.
2. Divide the mixture into 12 portions. Shape each portion into a cylinder about 3 inches by 1 inch. Carefully insert a bamboo skewer through each cylinder lengthwise. Set aside.
3. Place the lettuce leaves, cilantro, mint, and basil in 4 separate serving bowls. Refrigerate until ready to serve.
4. To prepare the dipping sauce: In a small saucepan combine all the sauce ingredients. Bring the mixture to a boil over medium-high heat. Reduce heat and simmer for 5 minutes. Remove the sauce from the heat and let cool.
5. Prepare a charcoal or gas grill. Place the skewers in a grill basket, making sure they are firmly held but not squashed. Grill the skewers until the pork is cooked through and the outside is crispy, about 10 to 15 minutes, turning the basket frequently.
6. To serve, pour each guest some of the dipping sauce into a small individual bowl. Place the bowls of cilantro, mint, and basil in the middle of the table. Place 2 lettuce leaves and 2 pork skewers on each guest's plate.
7. To assemble, have each guest slide the pork from the skewer onto a lettuce leaf. Sprinkle the pork with some of the herbs to taste. Roll the lettuce around the pork and dip in the sauce.

Happy Pancakes

Serves 4

Another example of French/Vietnamese fusion. The pancake is actually a version of a French crepe. The topping, on the other hand, is Vietnamese all the way.

1 cup rice flour
1½ cups water
2 eggs, lightly beaten
¼ teaspoon salt
1 teaspoon sugar
1 tablespoon vegetable oil
½ cup finely sliced straw
* mushrooms, rinsed and*
* patted dry*

3 ounces cooked salad shrimp,
* rinsed and patted dry*
½ cup bean sprouts
¼ cup mixed, chopped herbs
* (mint, cilantro, basil, etc.)*
Chili dipping sauce

1. In a medium-sized bowl, whisk together the rice flour, water, eggs, salt, and sugar. Set aside and let the batter rest for 10 minutes.
2. Strain the batter through a mesh sieve to remove any lumps.
3. Add the vegetable oil to a large sauté or omelet pan. Heat on high until very hot, but not smoking.
4. Pour the batter into the hot pan, swirling it so that it coats the bottom of the pan evenly. Sprinkle the mushrooms over the batter. Cover and let cook for 1 minute.
5. Sprinkle the shrimp and bean sprouts evenly over the pancake. Continue cooking until the bottom is crispy and browned.
6. To serve, cut the pancake into quarters. Sprinkle with the chopped herbs. Pass a favorite dipping sauce separately.

Honeyed Chicken

2 tablespoons honey
2 tablespoons fish sauce
2 tablespoons soy sauce
½ teaspoon Chinese
   5-spice powder
2 tablespoons vegetable oil
1 medium onion, peeled and
   cut into wedges

1 pound boneless, skinless
   chicken breasts, cut into
   bite-sized pieces
3–4 cloves garlic, thinly sliced
1 (1-inch) piece ginger, peeled
   and minced

Serves 3–4

This is a version of
a sweet-and-sour
chicken without the
bell peppers, fried
batter, or red food
coloring! The glaze is
multidimensional in its
flavor profile, and no
batter means a
healthier dish.

1. Combine the honey, fish sauce, soy sauce, and 5-spice powder in a small bowl; set aside.
2. Heat the oil in a wok on medium-high. Add the onion and cook until it just begins to brown.
3. Add the chicken; stir-fry for 3 to 4 minutes.
4. Add the garlic and ginger, and continue stir-frying for 30 more seconds.
5. Stir in the honey mixture and let cook for 3 to 4 minutes, until the chicken is glazed and done to your liking.

Vietnamese Oxtail Soup

Serves 6–8

Don't be afraid of eating tails! These inexpensive pieces of meat are extremely tender and flavorful when braised in this fashion. If you can't find oxtails, beef or veal shanks would be a great substitute.

2 medium onions

1 tablespoon vegetable oil

5 pounds meaty oxtails

4 (½-inch) pieces ginger, peeled

2 medium carrots, peeled and julienned

1 small cinnamon stick

1 whole star anise

1 tablespoon whole black peppercorns

2 garlic cloves, peeled and crushed

1 green onion, trimmed and thinly sliced

3 tablespoons fish sauce

Freshly ground black pepper to taste

½ pound bean sprouts

¼ cup chopped cilantro

4 serrano chilies, seeded and thinly sliced

2 limes, cut into wedges

1 (7-ounce) package rice sticks, soaked in hot water until soft and drained

(recipe continues on the next page)

Vietnamese Oxtail Soup (continued)

1. Cut 1 of the onions into ¼-inch slices. Heat the vegetable oil in a medium-sized sauté pan over medium-high heat. Add the onion slices and sauté until they just begin to brown. Drain the oil from the browned onion and set aside.
2. Slice the remaining onion into paper-thin slices. Cover with plastic wrap and set aside.
3. Rinse the oxtails in cold water and place them in a stock pot. Cover the tails with cold water and bring to a boil. Reduce the heat and skim any residue that has come to the surface. Let simmer for 15 minutes.
4. Add the browned onions, ginger, carrots, cinnamon, star anise, pepper-corns, and garlic. Return the stock to a simmer and cook for 6 to 8 hours, adding water if necessary.
5. When the broth is done, skim off any additional residue. Remove the oxtails from the pot and let cool until easy to handle. Remove the meat from the bones. Arrange the meat on a platter and garnish it with the sliced green onions. Discard the bones.
6. Strain the broth and return to the stove. Add the fish sauce and black pepper to taste. Keep warm.
7. On a second platter, arrange the bean sprouts, chopped cilantro, sliced chilies, and lime wedges.
8. Bring a pot of water to a boil. Plunge the softened rice noodles in the water to heat. Drain.
9. To serve, place a portion of the noodles in each bowl. Set a tureen of the broth on the table along with the platter of oxtail meat and the platter of accompaniments. Let your guests serve themselves.

Fruit in Sherried Syrup

Serves 4–6

This simple syrup can be made ahead of time and stored in the refrigerator for up to a week! Try it in some hot or iced tea!

2 tablespoons sugar
4 tablespoons water
2 tablespoons dry sherry
2 teaspoons lemon juice

1 orange, peeled and segmented
2 cups fresh pineapple chunks
1½ cups kiwi slices

1. In a small saucepan over high heat, boil the sugar and the water until syrupy. Remove from the heat and let cool to room temperature. Stir in the lemon juice and sherry; set aside.
2. In a serving bowl, combine the orange segments, the pineapple chunks, and the kiwi. Pour the syrup over the fruit and toss to combine. Refrigerate for at least 1 hour before serving.

Banana Brown Rice Pudding

Serves 4–6

This satisfying dessert requires no baking! It is also lacking eggs and cream, so it takes on the texture of porridge more than of custard. The banana and the fruit cocktail give the pudding flavor and structure.

1 medium banana, sliced
1 (15-ounce) can fruit cocktail, drained
¼ cup water
2 tablespoons honey

1 teaspoon vanilla extract
½ teaspoon cinnamon
½ teaspoon nutmeg
1 cup skim milk
1½ cups cooked brown rice

1. In a medium-sized saucepan, combine the banana, fruit cocktail, water, honey, vanilla, cinnamon, and nutmeg. Bring to a boil over medium-high heat. Reduce the heat and simmer for 10 minutes or until the bananas are tender.
2. Stir in the milk and the rice. Return the mixture to a boil, reduce heat again, and simmer for 10 more minutes. Serve warm.

Vietnamese Bananas

3 tablespoons shredded
   coconut (unsweetened)
3 tablespoons butter
3 tablespoons brown sugar
1 tablespoon grated ginger
Grated zest of 1 orange
6 bananas, peeled and sliced
   in half lengthwise

4 tablespoons lime juice
6 tablespoons orange liqueur
3 teaspoons toasted sesame
   seeds

Serves 6

This dessert is a take-off on Bananas Foster, the simple yet spectacular tableside dessert made famous in the 1960s and the 1970s along with cherries jubilee!

---

1. Heat a small nonstick pan over high heat. Add the coconut and cook, stirring constantly, until golden brown. Remove the coconut from the pan and set aside.
2. In a large sauté pan, melt the butter over medium-high heat. Stir in the brown sugar, the ginger, and orange zest. Place the bananas in the pan, cut-side down, and cook for 1 to 2 minutes or until the sauce starts to become sticky. Turn the bananas over to coat in the sauce. Place the bananas on a heated serving platter and cover with aluminum foil.
3. Return the pan to the heat and thoroughly stir in the lime juice and the orange liqueur. Using a long-handled match, ignite the sauce. Allow the flames to die down and then pour the sauce over the bananas.
4. Sprinkle the bananas with the toasted coconut and the sesame seeds. Serve immediately.

Basic Vietnamese Chili Sauce

Yields approx. ¼ cup

This Vietnamese chili sauce differs from most Thai hot sauces with its use of dried chilies instead of fresh, yielding a smokier, somewhat softer flavor. Brown sugar also has a mellowing effect.

2 dried red chilies, stemmed, seeded, and soaked in hot water until soft
2 cloves garlic, minced
½ teaspoon brown sugar

2 tablespoons fish sauce
1 tablespoon rice wine vinegar
1 tablespoon lemon juice

Using a mortar and pestle, grind together the dried chilies and the garlic to form a rough paste. Stir in the sugar until well incorporated. Stir in the remaining ingredients.

Chilied Coconut Dipping Sauce

Yields approx. ⅓ cup

This Vietnamese dipping sauce goes especially well with shrimp and fish.

¼ cup fresh coconut juice
1 teaspoon rice wine vinegar
1 teaspoon sugar
1 serrano chili, seeded and minced

2 cloves garlic, minced
1 tablespoon lime juice
2 tablespoons fish sauce

1. Bring the coconut juice, rice wine vinegar, and sugar to a boil in a small saucepan. Remove from heat and allow the mixture to cool to room temperature.
2. Stir in the remaining ingredients.

Tropical Fruits
with Cinnamon and Lime

Zest and juice of 6 limes
3 tablespoons honey
½ teaspoon sesame oil
½–1 teaspoon cinnamon
Pinch of salt

6 cups of tropical fruits,
* such as mango, papaya,*
* bananas, melons, star fruit,*
* kiwi, etc., (anything really)*
* cut into bite-sized pieces*

1. Combine the lime zest and all but about ⅓ of the lime juice in a small bowl. Slowly drizzle in the honey, whisking to form a smooth mixture. Whisk in the sesame oil, cinnamon, and salt. Adjust flavor to your liking with more lime juice if necessary.
2. Place the fruit in a large serving bowl. Pour the cinnamon-lime dressing over the fruit, toss to combine, and let rest in the refrigerator for 15 minutes before serving.

Serves 6–12

Typical in many Asian fruit concoctions, salt is added to this cinnamon-lime sauce to balance sweetness. If you can't adjust your Western palate to this juxtaposition of flavors, just leave out the salt.

Potato Samosas

Yields 20 samosas

Samosas are a good introduction to Indian cuisine, because although they are filled with unusual spices, their main ingredient is potato— a very comforting food no matter how it's prepared.

For the crust:

1½ cups all-purpose flour
½ teaspoon salt
4 tablespoons butter, at room temperature
Ice water
Vegetable oil for deep frying

For the filling:

1¼ pounds russet potatoes, peeled
1 tablespoon ghee (see note) or oil
2 teaspoons mustard seeds
½ teaspoon turmeric
½ teaspoon chili powder
¼ pound sweet peas, thawed if frozen
1 teaspoon salt
2 jalapeños, seeded and thinly sliced
3 tablespoons chopped mint
Lemon juice to taste

1. To make the pastry crust: In a large bowl, sift together the flour and the salt. Using a pastry cutter, cut the butter into the flour mixture.
2. Add the ice water, 1 tablespoon at a time, until a firm dough is achieved. You will probably use 5 to 6 tablespoons of water total. Knead the dough for approximately 5 minutes or until it is smooth and elastic. Place the dough in an oiled bowl, cover with plastic wrap, and set it aside while making the potato filling.

(recipe continues on the next page)

Potato Samosas (continued)

3. To make the filling: Bring a large pan of water to a boil. Add the potatoes and cook until quite tender. Drain the potatoes and allow them to cool until they are easy to handle. Cut them into a small dice; set aside.

4. In a large skillet, heat the ghee over medium-high heat. Add the mustard seeds and sauté until the seeds begin to pop. Stir in the turmeric and the chili powder; cook for 15 seconds. Stir in the potatoes, peas, salt, and jalapeño slices. (It is okay if the potatoes and the peas get a little smashed.) Remove from heat, stir in the mint and lemon juice to taste, and set aside.

5. Roll the pastry until it is quite thin (⅛-inch thick). Cut approximately ten 6-inch circles from the dough. Cut each circle in half. Place a heaping tablespoon of filling in the center of each half circle. Dampen the edges of the dough with cold water, fold the dough over on itself to form a triangle, and seal firmly.

6. To fry, add approximately 3 inches of vegetable oil to a large saucepan. Heat the oil over high heat until very hot, but not smoking. Add the samosas to the hot oil a few at a time and deep-fry until golden brown. Using a slotted spoon, remove the samosas to a stack of paper towels to drain.

7. Serve the samosas with Tamarind Dipping Sauce (see recipe on page 274).

 Ghee

Ghee is another name for clarified butter. It is simple to make. Simply melt a quantity of unsalted butter in a heavy saucepan. Bring it to a boil and let it simmer for 15 to 20 minutes or until the solid milk particles rise to the top and begin to brown. Remove the butter from the heat and strain it through cheesecloth. Ghee may be stored at room temperature for up to 1 week in an airtight container.

Chapati

Serves 6–8

Chapati is a simple griddle bread with a Muslim heritage.

3 cups whole-wheat flour
1½ teaspoons salt

1 tablespoon ghee or oil
1 cup lukewarm water

1. In a large mixing bowl, stir together 2½ cups of flour and the salt. Add the ghee and, using your fingers, rub it into the flour and salt mixture.
2. Add the lukewarm water and mix to form a dough. Knead the dough until it is smooth and elastic, about 10 minutes. (Don't skimp on the kneading; it is what makes the bread tender.)
3. Form the dough into a ball and place it in a small, oiled bowl. Cover tightly with plastic wrap and let it rest at room temperature for at least 1 hour.
4. Divide the dough into golf ball–sized pieces. Using a flour-covered rolling pin, roll each ball out on a flour-covered surface to approximately 6 to 8 inches in diameter and ⅛-inch thick.
5. Heat a large skillet or griddle over medium heat. Place a piece of dough on the hot surface. Using a towel or the edge of a spoon, carefully press down around the edges of the bread. (This will allow air pockets to form in the bread.) Cook for 1 minute. Carefully turn the chapati over and continue cooking for 1 more minute. Chapatis should be lightly browned and pliable, not crisp. Remove the bread to a basket and cover with a towel. Repeat until all of the rounds are cooked.

Asian Bread
Unlike in Thailand and most other Southeast Asian countries, bread is an integral part of the Indian diet. Most are not leavened and are made in individual servings, not in loaves.

Mulligatawny Soup

3 pounds chicken wings
4 whole cloves
2 medium onions, peeled
3 cloves garlic, peeled
1 jalapeño, seeded and sliced
1 (1½-inch) cinnamon stick
2 teaspoons whole peppercorns
5 cardamom pods, bruised
2 tablespoons ground coriander

1 tablespoon ground cumin
2 teaspoons salt
1 tablespoon vegetable oil
8–12 fresh curry leaves
6 cups chicken broth
1 (14-ounce) can coconut milk
Lemon juice to taste
4–5 cups cooked rice

> **Serves 8–10**
>
> I don't think you can find an Indian restaurant in the United States that doesn't serve this famous soup. It was first developed about 200 years ago in Madras and comes in vegetarian and meat versions.

1. Place the chicken wings in a large soup pot. Cover the chicken with cold water.
2. Stick the cloves into 1 of the onions and place the onion in the pot with the chicken.
3. Add the garlic, jalapeño, cinnamon stick, peppercorns, cardamom, coriander, cumin, and salt; bring the mixture to a boil, reduce to a simmer, and cook for 2 to 3 hours.
4. Let the stock come to room temperature. Remove the chicken pieces from the broth and cut the meat from the bones. Set aside the meat.
5. Strain the broth.
6. Thinly slice the remaining onion.
7. In a large sauté pan, heat the oil over medium-high heat. Add the onion slices and sauté until translucent. Add the curry leaves and the broth. Bring to a simmer and let cook for 5 minutes.
8. Add enough water to the coconut milk to make 3 cups of liquid. Add this and the reserved meat to the broth. Heat the soup, but do not let it boil. Season to taste with additional salt and a squeeze of lemon juice.
9. To serve, place approximately ½ cup of cooked rice in the bottom of each bowl. Ladle the soup over the rice.

Tandoori Chicken

4 skinless chicken breasts
4 skinless chicken legs
½ teaspoon saffron threads
½ cup plain yogurt
1 tablespoon grated ginger
2 small garlic cloves, minced
2 teaspoons salt
⅛ teaspoon chili powder

2 teaspoons paprika
1½ teaspoons Garam Masala
   (see recipe on page 273)
2 tablespoons ghee, melted

1. Using a small, sharp knife, make 3 to 4 (¼-inch-deep) slits in each piece of chicken. Set aside in a bowl large enough to hold all of the pieces.
2. Place the saffron in a small sauté pan over medium heat and toast for approximately 30 seconds. Place the saffron on a small plate and allow it to cool and crumble.
3. Stir the saffron into the yogurt.
4. Grind together the ginger, garlic, salt, chili pepper, paprika, and garam masala. Stir the spice mixture into the yogurt.
5. Pour the yogurt over the chicken, making sure that all of the pieces are coated. Cover and marinate overnight, turning the pieces in the marinade every so often.
6. Preheat the oven to 450 degrees.
7. Add the ghee to a roasting pan large enough to hold all of the chicken pieces. Add the chicken, breast side down. Spoon some of the ghee over the pieces. Roast for 10 minutes. Turn the pieces over, baste again, and continue roasting for 5 minutes. Turn them again and roast for an additional 5 minutes. Turn 1 last time (breasts should be up); baste and cook until done, about 5 more minutes.

Punjab Fish

4–6 firm-fleshed fish fillets, approximately 1-inch thick
Lemon juice
1 teaspoon salt
1 teaspoon black pepper
1 teaspoon turmeric
2–3 tablespoons vegetable oil
1 medium onion, thinly sliced
1 clove garlic, chopped
1 (1-inch) piece ginger, peeled and minced
2 serrano chilies, seeded and minced
2 tablespoons almond slivers
2 teaspoons cumin
2 teaspoons cardamom
¼ teaspoon cinnamon
⅛ teaspoon ground cloves
2 tablespoons boiling water
¼ teaspoon saffron strands, toasted and crushed
½ cup plain yogurt

> **Serves 4–6**
>
> Punjab, meaning "Five Rivers," is a state located in north-western India. It is known as a land of high spirits and pros-perity due to its fertile soil and many rivers.

1. Rinse the fish with cold water and pat dry. Rub the fish with lemon juice.
2. Combine the salt, pepper, and turmeric; sprinkle over the fish.
3. Heat 1 to 2 tablespoons of vegetable oil in a large frying pan over high heat. Brown the fish quickly on each side. Remove the fish to a plate, cover, and set aside.
4. Add the onion to the same pan and sauté until translucent and just beginning to brown.
5. Place the cooked onion in a food processor along with the garlic, ginger, chilies, and almonds. Process to form a paste, adding a bit of water if necessary. Add the cumin, cardamom, cinnamon, and clove; process to thoroughly blend.
6. If necessary, add additional vegetable oil to the frying pan to make about 2 tablespoons. Heat the oil over medium. Add the spice mixture and cook, stirring constantly, for about 2 minutes. Swirl a bit of water in the food processor to remove any remaining spices and pour it into the pan; stir to combine.
7. Pour 2 tablespoons of boiling water into a small cup. Add the toasted saffron and stir to combine. Pour the saffron water into the frying pan.
8. Stir in the yogurt. Bring to a simmer and let the sauce cook for 5 minutes.
9. Add the fish to the sauce, turning to coat. Cover and let simmer for approximately 10 minutes or until the fish is done to your liking.

Indian-Scented Cauliflower

3 tablespoons vegetable oil
1 teaspoon mustard seeds
1 clove garlic, minced
1 (2-inch) piece ginger, peeled and minced
½ teaspoon turmeric
½ medium to large head of cauliflower, separated into florets and cut into pieces
1 teaspoon salt
3 tablespoons water
½ teaspoon Garam Masala (see recipe on page 273)

1. In a saucepan large enough to easily hold the cauliflower, heat the vegetable oil over medium-high heat. Add the mustard seeds and fry until they pop. Add the garlic and the ginger; stirring constantly, cook until the garlic just begins to brown.
2. Stir in the turmeric. Add the cauliflower pieces and toss to coat with the spice mixture.
3. Add the water, cover, and let steam for 6 to 10 minutes or until done to your liking.
4. Pour off any excess water and sprinkle with the garam masala.

Cardamom Cookies

4 ounces ghee
½ cup fine sugar
1 cup fine semolina

3 tablespoons all-purpose flour
1½ teaspoons ground
  cardamom

1. Preheat oven to 300 degrees.
2. In a large mixing bowl, cream together the ghee and the sugar until light and fluffy.
3. Sift together the semolina, all-purpose flour, and cardamom.
4. Stir the dry ingredients into the ghee mixture; mix well.
5. Let the dough stand in a cool place for 30 minutes.
6. Form balls using approximately 1 tablespoon of dough for each. Place on an ungreased cookie sheet and flatten each ball slightly.
7. Bake for approximately 30 minutes or until pale brown.
8. Cool on a wire rack. Store in an airtight container.

Cardamom

The cardamom plant is a relative of ginger and grows in most tropical climates throughout the world. Cardamom pods have a very sweet-spicy smell and taste, similar to cinnamon. The spice refers to the seeds, which can be bought whole or ground.

Yields 2 dozen cookies

These cookies are reminiscent of short-bread in terms of texture and ingredients, but they are perfumed with a bit of ground cardamom. They're simply delicious with tea.

Almond "Tea"

3 ounces blanched almonds
2 ounces pumpkin seeds
½ teaspoon ground cardamom

3 cups water
2 cups milk
¼–½ cup sugar

1. Process the almonds, pumpkin seeds, cardamom, and half of the water in a blender or food processor until the solids are finely ground.
2. Strain the almond water through cheesecloth (or a clean Handi Wipe) into a container. Using the back of a spoon, press the solids to remove as much moisture as possible.
3. Return the almond mixture to the blender and add the remaining water. Process until thoroughly combined.
4. Strain this liquid into the container.
5. Stir the milk into the almond water. Add sugar to taste.
6. Serve over crushed ice.

Cucumber Raita

2 seedless cucumbers, peeled and cut into a small dice
1 teaspoon salt
1½ cups plain yogurt

1–2 green onions, trimmed and thinly sliced
2 tablespoons fresh mint
Lemon juice to taste

1. Place the diced cucumbers in a colander. Sprinkle with salt and let sit in the sink for 15 minutes to drain. Rinse the cucumber under cold water and drain again.
2. Combine the cucumber, yogurt, green onions, mint, and lemon juice to taste.
3. Cover and refrigerate for at least 30 minutes. Check seasoning, adding additional salt and/or lemon juice if necessary.

Tamarind Dipping Sauce

3 tablespoons tamarind pulp
1 cup hot water
1 teaspoon salt
2 teaspoons brown sugar
1 teaspoon ground cumin

½ teaspoon ground fennel
2 teaspoons grated ginger
Lemon juice to taste

1. Place the tamarind pulp in a small bowl. Pour boiling water over the pulp and let soak until soft, about 15 minutes.
2. Break up the pulp and then strain the tamarind water through a fine-mesh sieve, using the back of a spoon to push the pulp through, but leaving the tough fibers.
3. Stir in the remaining ingredients and let the tamarind sauce sit for at least 15 minutes before serving.

> **Makes about 1¼ cups**
>
> I love this dipping sauce. I spoon it over everything—samosas, papadam, all sorts of Indian breads, over rice, etc., etc. I promise you, once you try it you'll be hooked, too.

Garam Masala

4 tablespoons coriander seeds
2 tablespoons cumin seeds
1 tablespoon whole black peppercorns
2 teaspoons cardamom seeds

2 small cinnamon sticks, broken into pieces
1 teaspoon whole cloves

1. In a small heavy sauté pan, individually dry roast each spice over medium-high heat until they begin to release their aroma.
2. Allow the spices to cool to room temperature and then place them in a spice grinder and process to form a fairly fine powder.
3. Store in an airtight container.

> **Makes approx. ⅓ cup**
>
> The Indian spice mix you can't do without! If you always have a bit of this mixture on hand, you are just a step away from great Indian cuisine. I promise. (Garam masala is also available in specialty stores.)

Mango Chutney

**Makes approx.
5–6 cups**

In addition to serving
this condiment with
Indian food, I use it
to top broiled
salmon, as a spread
for scones, to mix
with white rice, or for
whatever takes my
fancy.

*2 large green mangoes, peeled
    and sliced*
*4 ounces dried apricots or
    cherries*
½ ounce golden raisins
1 tablespoon chopped ginger
1 tablespoon minced garlic
*1–2 red chili peppers, seeded
    and minced*
2 cups sugar
1 cup water

2 cups white vinegar
3 teaspoons salt
1 teaspoon cumin
*½ teaspoon black mustard
    seeds*
*2 teaspoons Garam Masala
    (see recipe on page 273)*

1. Place all of the ingredients in a heavy-bottomed saucepan. Bring to a
   simmer over medium heat, stirring until the sugar dissolves. Simmer
   for 30 minutes or until thick.
2. Seal in airtight jars.

Glossary:
Thai Flavors and Ingredients

BANANAS: Bananas are indigenous to Thailand, where over twenty-eight varieties are cultivated. The most common banana is the Cavendish, but don't be afraid to experiment with different varieties, especially in tropical fruit salads.

BASIL: Most commonly thought of as an Italian ingredient, basil is actually a key ingredient in cuisines from around the world. Basil comes in many varieties, including a Thai version, but any fresh basil works well in Thai cooking. Basil is quite delicate and is usually best added to dishes at the last possible moment.

BOK CHOY: Also known as Chinese cabbage, bok choy resembles Swiss chard in looks and regular green cabbage in taste. Stir-frying softens its flavor slightly.

CARDAMOM: This relative of ginger grows in most tropical environments. Its pods release a pungent, sweet-spicy flavor, somewhat similar to cinnamon.

CHILI PEPPERS: Chilies come in three basic forms: fresh, dried, and powdered. Botanists have named hundreds of different varieties, making chilies one of the most diverse plants on the planet. With that said, there are a few generalities that seem to hold true with all chilies. Chilies sweeten as they ripen, so a red chili (of the same variety) will be sweeter than a green one. And the bigger the chili pepper, the milder it usually is. So beware of chilies that come in small packages! The seeds and the veins pack the most punch, so to tone down your chili, don't use the seeds or veins.

CHILI SAUCE: Bottled chili sauce is a smooth combination of salted fish, red chilies, fish sauce, lime juice, and palm sugar. It is served with almost everything in Thailand. It comes in red and yellow varieties, and in various strengths.

CILANTRO: Cilantro is a pungent herb with a citruslike flavor, similar to parsley. It is also known as coriander.

COCONUT MILK: Coconut milk can be made fresh by grating and pressing fresh coconut meat, but the canned variety works just as well and is a lot less work! Coconut milk is not the same as coconut water, which is simply the liquid inside the coconut itself.

CORIANDER: Also known as cilantro, this herb is a cousin to parsley and is used as such. The seeds are also dried and ground and have a semisweet aroma.

CURRY: Curry powder is not a specific spice, but rather a combination of spices that vary depending on the desired effect. Some are sweet, while others are scorching hot. Basic commercial curry powders usually contain six to eight various ingredients.

CURRY LEAF: The leaves of an indigenous Southeast Asian plant that have no relation to curry powder or curry paste. The leaves do, however, release a curry-scented fragrance when crushed and are often added to various Asian dishes.

CURRY PASTE: Various combinations of spices and chilies, which can be either homemade or store-bought. They are super to keep on hand because they can be stored for long periods of time and help make quick, simple meals.

DRIED FISH: Crispy salt-preserved fish used as a snack and in soup.

DRIED SHRIMP: Tiny shrimp that are preserved in brine and then dried and used as a flavoring agent. Just a few go a long way. They are usually soaked in water for a few minutes before being added to a recipe, which both softens them and reduces their bite.

FISH SAUCE: Fish sauce or nan pla is one of the most used ingredients in Thai cuisine. It has a flavor similar to soy, although somewhat less salty. Salted, fermented fish, or shrimp gives the sauce its characteristic aroma and complex flavor. Beware—it doesn't smell very good to the Western nose, but is well worth getting used to.

FIVE-SPICE POWDER: A Chinese spice mixture that contains cinnamon, star anise, fennel, clove, ginger, peppercorns, and dried citrus peel.

GALANGAL: Galangal is a more pungent, fiery relative of ginger and is available both fresh and dried. If you can't find it, ginger is a perfectly acceptable substitute.

GARLIC: Garlic is a much-used relative of the onion with a sweet, pungent flavor. Pickled garlic is often used as a garnish.

GINGER: A rhizome that is now available in almost every supermarket, ginger adds a certain sweet-spicy component to dishes. It is available fresh, dried, crystallized, and preserved.

GUAVA: Also known as the tropical apple, the guava comes in two varieties—green and red. The green is native to Southeast Asia; the red is native to Hawaii. The fruit is especially high in vitamin C, iron, and calcium.

KAFFIR LIME: The juice, the zest, and the leaves of this thorny tropical tree are used extensively in southeast Asian cooking and impart a beautiful tropical fragrance and flavor.

LEMONGRASS: Lemongrass, or Citronella root, is an aromatic tropical grass with a flavor similar to lemon balm. It can be crushed whole or stripped of its fibrous outer leaves and chopped. Placed in a plastic bag, it will keep in the refrigerator for weeks.

LIME: A quintessential Thai ingredient; this citrus fruit is a great source of vitamin C.

MANGO: A kidney-shaped tropical fruit, mangoes are rich in vitamins A, B, and C. They are also high in sugar, sometimes 20 percent of their weight. Mangoes are used both fully ripe and green in some cases.

MINT: An herb used throughout the world to impart a refreshing, zesty aroma and flavor. Varieties include spearmint, peppermint, and lemon mint.

OYSTER SAUCE: Oyster sauce is made from oyster extracts, sugar, and other seasonings. It has a sweet-smoky flavor and is available in mild, hot, and "vegetarian" varieties.

PALM SUGAR: Palm sugar is a dark, unrefined sugar made from coconut palms. It is usually sold in blocks and must be crushed before it can be used. Dark brown sugar is a good and much easier-to-use substitute.

PAPAYA: This tropical fruit was introduced to Thailand by the Spanish after they conquered the Americas. Thai cooks use them both as a fruit and a vegetable.

RICE VINEGAR: Rice vinegar is milder and sweeter than regular white vinegar, but in a pinch white vinegar makes an acceptable substitute.

RICE WINE: Rice wine is a fermented concoction made from glutinous rice and millet and is used to add complexity and flavor. In Japan, it is known as mirin, which is a sweetish condiment used as a flavoring agent. If unavailable, dry sherry can be used as a substitute.

SHRIMP PASTE: A thick pungent paste made from salted fermented shrimp, which is often used in flavoring other curry pastes.

SOY SAUCE: Soy sauce is really not used very much in Thai cuisine. Instead, Thai cooks prefer fish sauce. However, soy can be used as a substitute for fish sauce and is specifically called for in some recipes. Soy sauce can be light or dark, which refers to flavor and color, not salt content. Tamari is a specific type of soy sauce that is strongly flavored, so use it sparingly.

SPRING ROLL WRAPPERS: Spring roll wrappers are similar to egg roll wrappers, but they are thinner and are made with only wheat flour and water. Egg roll wrappers also contain egg. When fried, spring roll wrappers are light and crisp.

STAR ANISE: The star anise is an inedible pod with a distinct licorice flavor that is infused into broths and sauces. Slightly crushing the pod helps to release its flavorful oils.

SWEET SOY SAUCE: This thick dark brown soy sauce is sweetened with palm sugar and star anise and is given piquant overtones with garlic. Sometimes the palm sugar is replaced with molasses.

TAMARIND: Tamarind is a large brown podlike fruit that contains both seeds and pulp, although the pulp is the only part used. It is usually sold in dried blocks of pulp, or in concentrates or pastes. If using pulp, soak it in hot water and then press it to release the thick sweet and sour juice. Concentrates and pastes are used straight from the jar. Tamarind has a flavor somewhat reminiscent of prunes and lemon.

TOFU: Tofu or bean curd is made from soybeans and water and is highly nutritious, due to its high plant proteins. It doesn't have much of a flavor on its own, but very quickly takes up the flavors of the dish it is in. It comes in a variety of textures ranging from soft to extra-firm. It is also available smoked.

YELLOW BEAN SAUCE: A sauce made from salted and fermented soybeans.

APPENDIX B
Thai Meals

All Seafood

Spicy Seafood Soup

Grilled Calamari Salad

Steamed Red Snapper

Shrimp Rice

Banana Coconut Soup

A Mild Thai Meal

Mee Grob

Asian Chicken Noodle Soup

Lime Ginger Fillets

Jasmine Rice

Mango Fool

Fiery Hot Summer Night

Spicy Shrimp Dip

Fiery Beef Salad

Fire Noodles

Thai Cashew Chicken

Sweet Sticky Rice

Vegetarian Dinner

Vegetarian Tom Yum Soup

Spicy Rice Salad

Sesame Noodles with Veggies

Meringues with Fresh Fruit

Southeast Asian Cocktail Party

Chicken, Shrimp, and Beef Satay

3-Flavor Rice Sticks

Asian Carrot Sticks

Thai Pickled Vegetables

Paper Rice Rolls

Marinated Mushrooms

Crab Spring Rolls

Various Dipping Sauces

Tom's Thai "Martinis"

Thai-Inspired Singapore Slings

Tropical Fruit Cocktails

Limeade

Weeknight Thai Dinner

Basil and Shrimp Wedges

Thai-Style Green Curry

Jasmine Rice

Sliced Mango and Coconut Ice Cream

Down Home Dinner in Thailand

Sweet-and-Sour Cucumber Salad

Chicken Fried Rice

Store-bought Coconut Ice Cream or Mango Sorbet

Sunny Summer Lunch

Chilled Mango Soup

Crunchy Coconut-Flavored Salad

Grilled Lobster with a Lemongrass Smoke

Ginger Rice

Crispy Crepes with Fresh Fruit

Thai-Inspired All-American

Thai Dinner Salad

Bangkok-Style Roasted Pork Tenderloin

Thai-Flavored Green Beans

Lemon Rice

Lime Butter Cake

A Salad Buffet

Shrimp and Noodle Salad

Cucumber Salad with Lemongrass

Chicken Salad—1

Jicama, Carrot, and Chinese Cabbage Salad

Asian Couscous Salad

Crunchy Sprout Salad

Fresh Oranges in Rose Water

Tropical Fruit with Ginger Crème Anglaise

A Backyard BBQ

Crudités with Mint Cilantro Chutney
and Sweet-and-Sour Dipping Sauce

Asian 3-Bean Salad

Cold Sesame Noodles

Peanut Potato Salad

Southeast Asian Burgers

Tropical Fruit Platter

Watermelon Ice

Thailand Resources

Sources for Thai Ingredients in the United States

THE SPICE HOUSE

1512 N. Wells St.
Chicago, IL
312-274-0378
Asian Spices

THE SPICE HOUSE

1048 N. Old World St.
Milwaukee, WI
414-272-0977
Asian Spices

KAM MAN FOOD PRODUCTS

200 Canal St.
New York, NY 10013
212-571-0330
Asian ingredients

DE WILDT IMPORTS

20 Compton Way
Hamilton Square, NJ 08969
800-338-3433
Asian ingredients

CASADOS FARMS

San Juan Pueblo, NM
505-852-2692
Fresh and dried chilies

DEAN & DELUCA

560 Broadway
New York, NY
800-221-7714
Asian ingredients

ETHNIC GROCER.COM

Thai produce, spices, prepared sauces, noodles, rice, and canned goods

IMPORTFOODS.COM

1-888-618-8424
Fresh Thai produce, cookware, spices, noodles, rice, sauces, and canned goods

PACIFICRIM-GOURMET.COM

Kitchenware, gourmet ingredients, garden seeds, cookbooks, and gifts

Great Thai Restaurants in the United States

Thai dining in the United States is becoming ever more popular, with storefront Thai restaurants almost as poplar as Chinese and Mexican. The following list offers a sampling of some of the best Thai restaurants in this country, all of them out of the ordinary and all of them worth a journey.

TAMARIND

80 14th St. NE
Atlanta, GA 30309
404-873-4888

THAI

3316 Greenmount Ave.
Baltimore, MD 21218
410-889-6002

BROWN SUGAR CAFÉ

129 Jersey St.
Boston, MA 02215
617-266-2928

BANGKOK 5

Rancho Mirage, California

ARUN'S

4156 N. Kedzie Ave.
Chicago, IL 60618
773-539-1909
Chef Arun Sampanthavivat

MEMA THAI CHINESE CUISINE

4-361 Kuhio Hwy.
Kapaa, HI 96746
808-823-0899

VONG

200 E. 54th St.
New York, NY
212-486-9592
Chef Jean Georges
Vongerichten

NAN

4000 Chestnut St.
Philadelphia, PA
215-382-0818
Chef Kamol Phutlek

LEMONGRASS THAI

1705 NE Couch St.
Portland, OR
503-231-5780
Chef Shelley Siripatrapa

THAI HOUSE CUISINE

4225 Convoy St.
Dan Diego, CA
858-278-1800

YUKOL PLACE THAI

2380 Lombard St.
San Francisco, CA
415-922-1599

KHAN TOKE THAI HOUSE

5937 Geary Blvd.
San Francisco, CA
415-668-6654

THEP PHANOM THAI CUISINE

400 Waller St.
San Francisco, CA
415-431-2526

DUANGRAT'S

5878 Leesburg Pike
Falls Church, VA
703-820-5775

Index

3-Bean Salad, 222
3-Flavor Rice Sticks, 44
5-Minute Dipping Sauce, 26
5-Spiced Vegetables, 243

A

Almond "Tea," 272
appetizers
  3-Flavor Rice Sticks, 44
  Asian Carrot Sticks, 212
  Basil and Shrimp Wedges, 36
  Chicken, Shrimp, and Beef Satay, 38–39
  Chinese-Style Dumplings, 53
  Cold Sesame Noodles, 52
  Crab Spring Rolls, 33
  Cream of Coconut Crabmeat Dip, 214
  Crispy Mussel Pancakes, 37
  Curried Fish Cakes, 47
  Fried Tofu with Dipping Sauces, 52
  Fried Won Tons, 51
  Marinated Mushrooms, 214
  Mee Krob, 42
  Omelet "Egg Rolls," 35
  Peanut Dipping Sauces, 22–23
  Pork, Carrot, and Celery Spring
    Rolls, 34
  Pork Toast Triangles, 41
  Rice Paper Rolls, 32
  Salt-Cured Eggs, 44
  Shrimp "Pâté," 253
  Shrimp Toast, 40
  Skewered Thai Pork, 50
  Son-in-Law Eggs, 43
  Spicy Coconut Bundles, 46
  Spicy Ground Pork in Basil Leaves, 49
  Spicy Scallops, 48
  Spicy Shrimp Dip, 213
  Thai Fries, 45
  Thai-Style Fried Okra, 145
  Vietnamese Pork Sticks, 254–255
apples, 77
arugula, 7
asparagus. See also vegetables/vegetarian
    dishes
  Asparagus (or Broccoli) Noodles with
    Garlic and Soy, 163
  Southeast Asian Asparagus, 230
  Stir-Fried Black Mushrooms and Asparagus,
    145

B

bamboo, 126
Bamboo Shoots (salad), 80
bamboo skewers, 50
Banana, Tamarind, and Mint Salsa, 27
Bangkok-Style Roasted Pork Tenderloin, 92
Barbecued Pork on Rice, 94

basil
  Basil and Shrimp Wedges, 36
  Basil Chicken, 108
  Basil Scallops, 132
  Clams with Hot Basil, 129
  Fire Noodles, 151
  Spicy Ground Pork in Basil Leaves, 49
Bean Sprouts and Snap Peas, 147
bean threads, 153
beef/beef dishes
  Beef Cambogee, 244
  Beef Satay, 39
  Beef with Rice Noodles, 87
  Cambodian Beef with Lime Sauce, 249
  Chiang Mai Beef, 93
  Chilied Beef, 89
  Cinnamon Stewed Beef, 99
  Curried Beef and Potato Stew, 83
  Fiery Beef Salad, 68
  Green Curry Beef, 82
  Grilled Ginger Beef, 86
  Grilled Steak with Peanut Sauce, 226
  Hot and Sour Beef, 85
  Lemongrass Marinade (for grilling), 16
  Minty Stir-Fried Beef, 88
  Peanut Dipping Sauce—2, 23
  Red Beef Curry, 84
  Red Curry Cambogee, 250
  Southeast Asian Burgers, 228
  Spicy Thai Dressing, grilling with, 28
  Thai Marinade—1, 11
  Thai-Spiced Beef Soup with Rice Noodles, 64
  Thai-Style Beef with Broccoli, 97
  Thai Vinegar Marinade, 15
beer, about Thai, 207
beverages. See drinks
Black Bean Paste, 11
blanching, xi
Brandied Chicken, 113
bread, Chapati, 266
broccoli. See also vegetables/vegetarian
    dishes
  Broccoli Noodles with Garlic and Soy, 163
  Thai-Style Beef with Broccoli, 97
broiling, x–xi
Brussels Sprout (or Broccoli) Noodles with
    Garlic and Soy, 163
Burgers, Southeast Asian, 228
butter/ghee, x, 265

C

cabbage. See vegetables/vegetarian dishes
Calamari Salad, Grilled, 74
Cambodian dishes
  Beef Cambogee, 244
  Beef with Lime Sauce, 249
  Lemongrass Curry Sauce, 250

  Oyster Mushroom Soup, 246
  Pan-Fried Chicken and Mushrooms, 248
  Red Curry Cambogee, 250
  Sweet Cambodian Broth with Pork and
    Eggs, 247
canola oil, x
Cardamom Cookies, 271
Cashew Chicken, 111
cauliflower. See also vegetables/vegetarian
    dishes
  Indian-Scented Cauliflower, 270
  Mint-Cilantro "Chutney" over Roasted
    Cauliflower, 30
  Roasted Asian Cauliflower, 143
Chapati (Indian bread), 266
Chiang Mai Beef, 93
Chiang Mai Curried Noodles, 154
chicken/chicken dishes. See also
    poultry/poultry dishes
  about handling chicken, x–xi, 106
  Asian Chicken Noodle Soup, 59
  Basil Chicken, 108
  Brandied Chicken, 113
  Cambodian-Style Pan-Fried Chicken and
    Mushrooms, 248
  Chicken and Noodle Salad, 71
  Chicken Fried Rice, 171
  Chicken Salads, 217–219
  Chicken Satay, 38
  Chicken Soup with Lemongrass, 58
  Chicken with Black Pepper and Garlic, 115
  Chili-Fried Chicken, 104
  Fire Noodles, 151
  Fragrant Roast Chicken, 109
  Fried Rice with Tomatoes, 173
  Ginger Chicken, 106
  Grilled Chicken with Mango-Pineapple
    Salsa, 26
  Grilling Rub, 19
  Honeyed Chicken, 257
  Jungle Chicken, 116
  Lemongrass Chicken Skewers, 112
  Lemony Chicken Soup, 60
  Peanut Dipping Sauces, 23
  Poached Chicken Breast with Peanut
    Sauce and Noodles, 159
  Red Chili Chicken, 107
  Rice Stick Noodles with Chicken and
    Vegetables, 152–153
  Siamese Roast Chicken, 102
  Spice-Poached Chicken, 239
  Spicy Egg Noodles with Sliced
    Chicken, 161
  Sweet-and-Sour Chicken, 110
  Tamarind Marinade, 13
  Tamarind Stir-Fried Chicken with
    Mushrooms, 103

Tandoori Chicken, 268
Tea-Smoked Chicken, 240
Thai Cashew Chicken, 111
Thai Chicken Pizza, 225
Thai Glazed Chicken, 114
Thai Marinade—1, 11
Thai Noodles with Chicken and Pork, 160
Thai-Style Green Curry Chicken, 105
Tom Ka Kai (soup), 57
Tom Yum (soup), 56
chili dishes
    Chilied Beef, 89
    Chilied Coconut Dipping Sauce, 262
    Chili-Fried Chicken, 104
    Chili Tamarind Paste, 8
    Chili Vinegar, 18
    Lemon Chili Vinegar, 17
    Red Chili Chicken, 107
    Vietnamese Chili Sauce, 262
chilies
    cooking with, 85
    dangers of, 82, 151, 177
    history of, 6
    nutritive value, 111
    roasting, 105
    types of, 84
Chinese-Style Dumplings, 53
chinois, xiii
chutneys
    about, 30, 176
    Mango Chutney, 274
    Mint-Cilantro Chutney, 30
cilantro, xiv, 174
Cinnamon Stewed Beef, 99
Clams with Hot Basil, 129
Clear Noodles with Baked Shrimp, 156
coconut. See also coconut milk; desserts
    about toasting, 16
    Chilied Coconut Dipping Sauce, 262
    Cream of Coconut Crabmeat Dip, 214
    Crunchy Coconut-Flavored Salad, 79
    Fresh Coconut Juice, 207
    Seared Coconut Scallops, 130
    Shredded Fresh Coconut, 17
    Spicy Coconut Bundles, 46
    Thai Fries, 45
coconut milk. See also coconut; desserts
    about poaching with, 2
    Chicken Soup with Lemongrass, 58
    Coconut Marinade, 14
    Curried Beef and Potato Stew, 83
    Fragrant White Rice, 178
    Green Curry Beef, 82
    Green Curry Chicken, 105
    Jungle Chicken, 116
    Lemony Chicken Soup, 60
    Mulligatawny Soup, 267
    Peanut Dipping Sauces, 22–23

Peninsula Sweet Potatoes, 244
Poached Chicken Breast with Peanut
    Sauce and Noodles, 159
Pork and Spinach Curry, 96
Pumpkin Soup, 62–63
Red Beef Curry, 84
Singapore Shellfish Soup, 236–237
Singapore Shrimp, 242
Thai Marinade—3, 12
Thai Vegetable Curry, 134
Tom Ka Kai (soup), 57
Vegetables Poached in Coconut Milk, 135
confit, duck, 238
cooking tips, viii–ix
corn. See also vegetables/vegetarian dishes
    Spicy Stir-Fried Corn, 143
crab. See seafood/seafood dishes
Crepes with Fresh Fruit, 187
crudités, Ginger-Lemongrass Vinaigrette for, 29
cucumbers
    about seeding, 76
    Crunchy Coconut-Flavored Salad, 79
    Cucumber Raita, 272
    Cucumber Salad with Lemongrass, 77
    Mango-Cucumber Salsa, 27
    Shrimp Toast, 40
    Sweet-and-Sour Cucumber Salad, 76
curry/curry dishes. See also pastes
    about, ix, xiv
    Chiang Mai Curried Noodles, 154
    Curried Beef and Potato Stew, 83
    Curried Fish Cakes, 47
    Curried Green Beans, 141
    Curried Mussels, 127
    Curried Rice, 176
    Curried Rice Noodles with Tofu and Egg, 162
    Curried Shrimp with Peas, 131
    Green Curry Beef, 82
    Green Curry Chicken, 105
    Lemongrass Curry Sauce, 250
    Pork and Spinach Curry, 96
    Red Beef Curry, 84
    Red Curry Cambogee, 250
    Thai Vegetable Curry, 134
custards. See also desserts
    Coconut Custard, 192
    Lemongrass Custard, 191
    Pumpkin Custard, 197

D
desserts. See also custards
    Banana Brown Rice Pudding, 260
    Banana Coconut Soup, 190
    Bananas Poached in Coconut Milk, 200
    Cardamom Cookies, 271
    Citrus Fool, 195
    Coconut-Pineapple Soufflé for 2, 194
    Crazy Coconut Pie, 232

Crispy Crepes with Fresh Fruit, 187
Fruit in Sherried Syrup, 260
Lime Butter Cake, 233
Mango Sauce over Ice Cream, 197
Meringues with Tropical Fruit, 234
Oranges in Rose Water, 189
Pineapple-Mango Sherbet, 196
Pineapple Rice, 186
Pumpkin Simmered in Coconut Milk, 201
Steamed Coconut Cakes, 193
Sticky Rice with Coconut Cream Sauce, 185
Sweet Sticky Rice, 184
Taro Balls Poached in Coconut Milk, 199
Tofu with Sweet Ginger, 200
Tropical Coconut Rice, 184
Tropical Fruit Cocktail (drink), 209
Tropical Fruits with Cinnamon and Lime, 263
Tropical Fruit with Ginger Crème Anglaise,
    188
Vietnamese Bananas, 261
Watermelon Ice, 198
Dill Rice, 178
dipping sauces. See sauces
drinks
    Almond "Tea," 272
    Fresh Coconut Juice, 207
    Mango Bellini, 209
    Royal Thai Kir, 210
    teas, 204–206
    Thai-Inspired Singapore Sling, 207
    Thai Limeade, 205
    Tom's Thai "Martinis," 208
    Tropical Fruit Cocktail, 209
Duck, Melon and Mango Salad, Roasted, 238
Dumplings, Chinese-Style, 53

E
eggplant. See also vegetables/vegetarian
    dishes
    about, xiv, 107
    Grilled Eggplant with an Asian Twist, 144
    Japanese Eggplant with Tofu, 144
    Pork and Eggplant Stir-Fry, 90
eggs/egg dishes
    Curried Rice Noodles with Tofu and Egg, 162
    hard-boiled eggs, 43
    Mee Krob, 42
    Omelet "Egg Rolls," 35
    Salt-Cured Eggs, 44
    Son-in-Law Eggs, 43
    Sweet Cambodian Broth with Pork and
        Eggs, 247

F
Fiery Beef Salad, 68
Fire Noodles, 151
fish/fish dishes. See also seafood/seafood
    dishes

about, 118–123
Baked Redfish with Lime Vinaigrette, 120
Broiled Salmon with 5-Spice Lime Butter, 121
Curried Fish Cakes, 47
Grilled Fish with Mango-Cucumber Salsa, 27
Grilled Fish with Mango-Pineapple Salsa, 26
Jalapeño-Lime Vinaigrette over Grilled Fish, 29
Lime-Ginger Fillets, 119
Marinated Steamed Fish, 124
Peanut Dipping Sauce–3, 23
Punjab Fish, 269
Quick Asian-Grilled Fish, 125
Roasted Southeast Asian Fish, 122
Snapper Baked with Fish Sauce and Garlic, 118
Steamed Red Snapper, 123
Flowered Lime Noodles, 158
food processors, xiii
food substitutions, xiv
Fragrant Brown Rice, 181
Fragrant Roast Chicken, 109
Fragrant White Rice, 178
fried rice. See also rice/rice dishes; stir-fries
Chicken Fried Rice, 171
Far East Fried Rice, 172
Fried Rice with Chinese Olives, 174
Fried Rice with Pineapple and Shrimp, 169
Fried Rice with Tomatoes, 173
Sweet-Spiced Fried Rice, 168
Vegetarian Fried Rice, 170
Fried Tofu with Dipping Sauces, 52
Fried Won Tons, 51
fruit(s). See also lemon(s); lime(s); mango(es); pineapple
apples, about, 77
Banana, Tamarind, and Mint Salsa, 27
mandarin oranges, about, 239
Papaya Salad, 78
Zesty Melon Salad, 79

G

Game with Banana, Tamarind, and Mint Salsa, 27
Garam Masala, 273
garlic, peeling, 88
ghee/butter, x, 265
ginger
about crystallized, 186
Ginger Chicken, 106
Gingered Green Beans, 141
Ginger-Lemongrass Vinaigrette, 29
Ginger Rice, 175
Ginger Tea, 204
Lime-Ginger Fillets, 119
Glazed Chicken, 114

green beans. See also vegetables/vegetarian dishes
about, xiv
Curried Green Beans, 141
Gingered Green Beans, 141
Green Bean (or Broccoli) Noodles with Garlic and Soy, 163
Green Beans with Macadamia Nut Sauce, 142
Stir-Fried Shrimp and Green Beans, 129
Thai-Flavored Green Beans, 230
Green Curry Pastes, 2–3
grilling
about, x–xi, 89, 139, 229
Asian Grilled Vegetables, 139
Chilied Beef, 89
Fiery Beef Salad, 68
Grilled Calamari Salad, 74
Grilled Eggplant with an Asian Twist, 144
Grilled Ginger Beef, 86
Grilled Lobster Tails with a Lemongrass Smoke, 229
Grilled Steak with Peanut Sauce, 226
Grilling Rub, 19
Quick Asian-Grilled Fish, 125
Shrimp (Chicken or Fish) with Mango-Pineapple Salsa, 26
Shrimp (Scallops, Chicken or Pork) and Noodle Salad, 71
Skewered Thai Pork, 50
Spicy Thai Dressing, 28
Thai-Style Grilled Pork Chops, 227
Guacamole, Thai-Spiced, 215

H, I

Happy Pancakes, 256
health foods, 56
herbs, grilling with, 229
Honeyed Chicken, 257
Hot and Sour Beef, 85
Iced Teas, 205–206
Indian dishes
Cucumber Raita, 272
Garam Masala, 273
Indian-Scented Cauliflower, 270
Mango Chutney, 274
Mulligatawny Soup, 267
Potato Samosas, 264–265
Punjab Fish, 269
Tamarind Dipping Sauce, 273
Tandoori Chicken, 268

J

Jalapeño-Lime Vinaigrette, 29
Japanese Eggplant with Tofu, 144
jicama, 79
Jicama, Carrot, and Chinese Cabbage Salad, 219

Jungle Chicken, 116
Jungle (or Northern) Curry Paste, 7

K, L

kaffir limes, xiv, 135
Lamb with Peanut Dipping Sauce–2, 23
lemongrass. See also desserts
about, xiv, 57, 109, 223
Chicken Soup with Lemongrass, 58
Cucumber Salad with Lemongrass, 77
Grilled Lobster Tails with a Lemongrass Smoke, 229
Lemongrass Chicken Skewers, 112
Lemongrass Curry Sauce, 250
Lemongrass Marinade, 16
Lemongrass Pork, 95
Lemongrass Tea, 204
Steamed Mussels with Lemongrass, 128
Vegetarian Lemongrass Soup, 65
lemon(s)
Lemon Chili Vinegar, 17
Lemon Rice, 177
Lemony Chicken Soup, 60
lime(s). See also desserts; drinks
about kaffir limes, xiv, 135
Baked Redfish with Lime Vinaigrette, 120
Broiled Salmon with 5-Spice Lime Butter, 121
Cambodian Beef with Lime Sauce, 249
Flowered Lime Noodles, 158
Jalapeño-Lime Vinaigrette, 29
Lime-Ginger Fillets, 119
Lobster Tails with a Lemongrass Smoke, Grilled, 229

M

Macadamia Nut Sauce, 142
Malaysian Marinade, 14
mandarin oranges, 239
mandoline, xiii
mango(es). See also desserts
about, 185
Chilled Mango Soup, 66
Mango Bellini (drink), 209
Mango Chutney, 274
Mango-Cucumber Salsa, 27
Mango-Pineapple Salsa, 26
Roasted Duck (or Chicken), Melon and Mango Salad, 238
marinades
about cooking with, 15, 124
about safety with, 10, 228
Asian Marinade, 12–13
Coconut Marinade, 14
Ginger-Lemongrass Vinaigrette, 29
Lemongrass Marinade, 16
Malaysian Marinade, 14
Tamarind Marinade, 13

Thai Marinades, 11–12, 15
Marinara Sauce, 226
Marinated Mushrooms, 214
Marinated Steamed Fish, 124
"Martinis," 208
Massaman (Muslim) Curry Paste, 6
meat. *See also* beef/beef dishes; pork/pork
    dishes
    about, ix, xii, 90, 91
    Peanut Dipping Sauce—2, 23
Mee Krob, 42
mint
    Banana, Tamarind, and Mint Salsa, 27
    Fire Noodles, 151
    Mint-Cilantro "Chutney," 30
    Minted Vegetables, 252
    Minty Dipping Sauce, 24
    Minty Stir-Fried Beef, 88
    Minty Tamarind Paste, 9
mortar and pestle, xiii, 115
Mulligatawny Soup, 267
mushrooms
    Cambodian-Style Pan-Fried Chicken and
        Mushrooms, 248
    Marinated Mushrooms, 214
    Oyster Mushroom Soup, 246
    Stir-Fried Black Mushrooms and
        Asparagus, 145
mussels. *See also* seafood/seafood dishes
    about, 127, 128
    Crispy Mussel Pancakes, 37
    Curried Mussels, 127
    Panang Mussels and Noodles, 158
    Steamed Mussels with Lemongrass, 128

N
noodles/noodle dishes
    about, 153, 154, 155
    Asian Chicken Noodle Soup, 59
    Asian Noodle and Vegetable Salad, 73
    Beef with Rice Noodles, 87
    Broccoli (Asparagus, Brussels Sprout, or
        Green Bean) Noodles with Garlic and
        Soy, 163
    Chiang Mai Curried Noodles, 154
    Clear Noodles with Baked Shrimp, 156
    Cold Sesame Noodles, 52
    Curried Rice Noodles with Tofu and Egg, 162
    Fire Noodles, 151
    Flowered Lime Noodles, 158
    Grilled Ginger Beef, 86
    Hot Noodles with Tofu, 245
    Macadamia Nut Sauce over Pasta, 142
    Northern (or Jungle) Curry Paste with
        Pasta, 7
    Pad Thai, 150
    Panang Mussels and Noodles, 158

Pan-Fried Noodles, 155
Peanut Dipping Sauce—3, 23
Peanut Pesto Pasta, 28
Poached Chicken Breast with Peanut
    Sauce and Noodles, 159
Rice Stick Noodles with Chicken and
    Vegetables, 152–153
Sesame Noodles with Veggies, 157
Shrimp (Scallops, Chicken or Pork) and
    Noodle Salad, 71
Singapore Noodles, 246
Spicy Egg Noodles with Sliced Pork (or
    Chicken), 161
Spicy Scallops over Pasta, 48
Thai Noodles with Chicken and Pork, 160
Thai Pasta Salad, 224
Thai-Spiced Beef Soup with Rice
    Noodles, 64
Thai-Style Beef with Broccoli, 97
Northern (or Jungle) Curry Paste, 7

O, P
Okra, Thai-Style Fried, 145
Olives, Fried Rice with Chinese, 174
Omelet "Egg Rolls," 35
Oranges in Rose Water, 189. *See also*
    desserts
Oxtail Soup, Vietnamese, 258–259
Oyster Mushroom Soup, 246
Pad Thai, 150
Panang Mussels and Noodles, 158
Pancakes, Happy, 256
Pan-Fried Noodles, 155
Papaya Salad, 78
pastes. *See also* curry/curry dishes
    about, 2–3, 5, 85
    Black Bean Paste, 10
    Chili Tamarind Paste, 8
    Green Curry Pastes, 2–3
    Minty Tamarind Paste, 9
    Northern (or Jungle) Curry Paste, 7
    Red Curry Pastes, 4–5
    Southern (or Massaman) Curry Paste, 6
peanuts/peanut sauces
    allergy to, 22
    Grilled Steak with Peanut Sauce, 226
    Peanut Dipping Sauces, 22–23
    Peanut Pesto, 28
    Peanut Potato Salad, 220
    Poached Chicken Breast with Peanut
        Sauce and Noodles, 159
Peninsula Sweet Potatoes, 244
pepper
    about, ix
    Chicken with Black Pepper and Garlic, 115
    Pumpkin with Peppercorns and Garlic, 140

Pesto, Peanut, 28
Pickled Chinese Cabbage, 232
Pickled Vegetables, 138
pineapple. *See also* desserts
    Fried Rice with Pineapple and Shrimp, 169
    Mango-Pineapple Salsa, 26
Pizza, Thai Chicken, 225
Plum Dipping Sauce, 25
poaching, xi
pork/pork dishes
    Bangkok-Style Roasted Pork Tenderloin, 92
    Barbecued Pork on Rice, 94
    Fried Won Tons, 51
    Grilling Rub, 19
    Lemongrass Marinade (for grilling), 16
    Lemongrass Pork, 95
    Omelet "Egg Rolls," 35
    Pork, Carrot, and Celery Spring Rolls, 34
    Pork and Eggplant Stir-Fry, 90
    Pork and Spinach Curry, 96
    Pork Medallions in a Clay Pot, 241
    Pork Tenderloin and Noodle Salad, 71
    Pork Toast Triangles, 41
    Pork with Garlic and Crushed Black
        Pepper, 91
    Pork with Tomatoes and Sticky Rice, 98
    Skewered Thai Pork, 50
    Spicy Egg Noodles with Sliced Pork, 161
    Spicy Ground Pork in Basil Leaves, 49
    Spicy Thai Dressing, 28
    Sweet Cambodian Broth with Pork and
        Eggs, 247
    Thai Marinade—1, 11
    Thai Noodles with Chicken and Pork, 160
    Thai-Style Grilled Pork Chops, 227
    Thai Vinegar Marinade, 15
    Vietnamese Pork Sticks, 254–255
potatoes
    about, 220
    Curried Beef and Potato Stew, 83
    Peanut-Potato Salad, 220
    Potato Samosas, 264–265
poultry/poultry dishes. *See also*
    chicken/chicken dishes
    about, 106, 113
    Grilled or Roasted Poultry with Banana,
        Tamarind, and Mint Salsa, 27
    Lemongrass Marinade, 16
    Malaysian Marinade, 14
    Roasted Duck (or Chicken), Melon, and
        Mango Salad, 238
    Southeast Asian Burgers, 228
    Spicy Rice Salad, 69
    Spicy Thai Dressing, 28
    Thai-Style Plum Dipping Sauce, 25
Prawns, Coconut Marinade for, 14
Pudding, Banana Brown Rice, 260

pumpkin. *See also* desserts; vegetables/vegetarian dishes
  Pumpkin Soup, 62–63
  Pumpkin with Peppercorns and Garlic, 140
Punjab Fish, 269

R

Ratatouille, 231
Red Chili Chicken, 107
Red Curry Cambogee, 250
Red Curry Pastes, 4–5
Redfish with Lime Vinaigrette, Baked, 120
Red Snapper, Steamed, 123
Rice Balls with 5-Minute Dipping Sauce, 26
rice noodles. *See* noodles/noodle dishes
Rice Paper Rolls, 32
rice/rice dishes. *See also* desserts; fried rice; stir-fries
  about, 166–168, 173, 175
  3-Flavor Rice Sticks, 44
  Barbecued Pork on Rice, 94
  Basic Sticky Rice, 167
  Basic White Rice, 166
  Chiang Mai Beef, 93
  Dill Rice, 178
  Flavorful Steamed Rice, 180
  Fragrant Brown Rice, 181
  Fragrant White Rice, 178
  Ginger Rice, 175
  Lemon Rice, 177
  Pork with Tomatoes and Sticky Rice, 98
  Shrimp Rice, 179
  Spicy Rice Salad, 69
  Vietnamese Oxtail Soup, 258
roasting, xii
  about, 122
  Chicken with Banana, Tamarind, and Mint Salsa, 27
  chilies, 105
  Fragrant Roast Chicken, 109
  Game with Banana, Tamarind, and Mint Salsa, 27
  Mint-Cilantro "Chutney" over Roasted Cauliflower, 30
  Roasted Asian Cauliflower, 143
  Siamese Roast Chicken, 102
rose water, 189
Royal Thai Kir, 210

S

safety tips
  food allergies, 22
  grilling, 89
  handling poultry, 106, 113
  hot chilies, 82, 151, 177
  hot ingredients in blenders, xiii

marinades, 10, 228
mussels, 127, 128
salad dressings
  Ginger-Lemongrass Vinaigrette, 29
  Jalapeño-Lime Vinaigrette, 29
salads
  about Thai salads, 75
  Asian 3-Bean Salad, 222
  Asian Couscous Salad, 221
  Asian Noodle and Vegetable Salad, 73
  Chicken Salads, 217–219
  Crunchy Coconut-Flavored Salad, 79
  Crunchy Sprout Salad, 222
  Cucumber Raita, 272
  Cucumber Salad with Lemongrass, 77
  Dinner Salad, 75
  Fiery Beef Salad, 68
  Grilled Calamari Salad, 74
  Jicama, Carrot, and Chinese Cabbage Salad, 219
  Mango-Cucumber Salsa, 27
  Many Peas Asian-Style Salad, 223
  Mee Krob, 42
  Papaya Salad, 78
  Peanut-Potato Salad, 220
  Roasted Duck (or Chicken), Melon and Mango Salad, 238
  Spicy Rice Salad, 69
  Spicy Shrimp, Mussel and/or Scallop Salad, 70
  Sweet-and-Sour Cucumber Salad, 76
  Thailand Bamboo Shoots, 80
  Thailand Seafood Salad, 72
  Thai Pasta Salad, 224
  Zesty Melon Salad, 79
Salmon with 5-Spice Lime Butter, Broiled, 121
salsas
  Banana, Tamarind, and Mint Salsa, 27
  Mango-Cucumber Salsa, 27
  Mango-Pineapple Salsa, 26
Salt-Cured Eggs, 44
sandwiches, Peanut Pesto for, 28
Satays, Chicken, Shrimp, and Beef, 38–39
sauces. *See also* peanuts/peanut sauces
  about, ix, 102
  5-Minute Dipping Sauce, 26
  Asian Marinara Sauce, 226
  Chilied Coconut Dipping Sauce, 262
  Lemongrass Curry Sauce, 250
  Macadamia Nut Sauce, 142
  Minty Dipping Sauce, 24
  Peanut Dipping Sauces, 22–23
  Quick Hot Dipping Sauce, 24
  Spicy Thai Dressing, 28
  Sweet-and-Sour Dipping Sauce, 25
  Tamarind Dipping Sauce, 273
  Thai-Style Plum Dipping Sauce, 25

Vietnamese Chili Sauce, 262
Yellow Bean Sauce, 9
scallops. *See also* seafood/seafood dishes
  about, 48, 130
  Basil Scallops, 132
  Coconut Marinade, 14
  Seared Coconut Scallops, 130
  Spicy Scallops, 48
seafood/seafood dishes. *See also* fish/fish dishes; mussels; scallops; shrimp
  about, 118
  Clams with Hot Basil, 129
  Coconut Marinade, 14
  Crab Spring Rolls, 33
  Cream of Coconut Crabmeat Dip, 214
  Grilled Calamari Salad, 74
  Grilled Lobster Tails with a Lemongrass Smoke, 229
  Seafood Stir-Fry, 126
  Shrimp (or Scallops) and Noodle Salad, 71
  Singapore Shellfish Soup, 236–237
  Spicy Seafood Soup, 61
  Spicy Shrimp, Mussel and/or Scallop Salad, 70
  Tamarind Marinade, 13
  Thailand Seafood Salad, 72
Sherbet, Pineapple-Mango, 196
shrimp. *See also* seafood/seafood dishes
  about, 131
  Basil and Shrimp Wedges, 36
  Clear Noodles with Baked Shrimp, 156
  Curried Shrimp with Peas, 131
  Fried Rice with Pineapple and Shrimp, 169
  Grilled Shrimp with Mango-Pineapple Salsa, 26
  Mee Krob (dried shrimp), 42
  Peanut Dipping Sauce—3, 23
  Rice Paper Rolls, 32
  Shrimp "Pâté," 253
  Shrimp Rice, 179
  Shrimp Satay, 38
  Shrimp Toast, 40
  Singapore Shrimp, 242
  Spicy Rice Salad, 69
  Spicy Shrimp Dip, 213
  Spicy Shrimp Salad, 70
  Stir-Fried Shrimp and Green Beans, 129
  Thai Noodles with Chicken and Pork, 160
  Tom Yum, 56
Siamese Roast Chicken, 102
simmering, xi
Singaporean dishes
  about, 240
  Shellfish Soup, 236–237
  Singapore Noodles, 246
  Singapore Shrimp, 242
Singapore Sling, Thai-Inspired (drink), 207

skewers, 50
Snapper Baked with Fish Sauce and Garlic, 118
Son-in-Law Eggs, 43
Soufflé for 2, Coconut-Pineapple (dessert), 194
soups
    Asian Chicken Noodle Soup, 59
    Asian-Inspired Chicken and Wild Rice Soup, 216
    Chicken Soup with Lemongrass, 58
    Chilled Mango Soup, 66
    Lemony Chicken Soup, 60
    Mulligatawny Soup, 267
    Oyster Mushroom Soup, 246
    Pumpkin Soup, 62–63
    Singapore Shellfish Soup, 236–237
    Spicy Seafood Soup, 61
    Sweet Cambodian Broth with Pork and Eggs, 247
    Thai-Spiced Beef Soup with Rice Noodles, 64
    Tom Ka Kai, 57
    Tom Yum, 56
    Vegetarian Lemongrass Soup, 65
    Vietnamese Oxtail Soup, 258–259
Southeast Asian Fish, Roasted, 122
Southeastern Vegetable Stew, 136
Southern (or Massaman) Curry Paste, 6
Spice-Poached Chicken, 239
spice rubs, 19
spinach. See vegetables/vegetarian dishes
spring rolls
    Crab Spring Rolls, 33
    Pork, Carrot, and Celery Spring Rolls, 34
Sprout Salad, Crunchy, 222
squash. See vegetables/vegetarian dishes
steaming, xi
stir-fries. See also fried rice; rice/rice dishes
    about, ix–x
    Basil Scallops, 132
    Black Mushrooms and Asparagus, 145
    Minty Stir-Fried Beef, 88
    Pork and Eggplant Stir-Fry, 90
    Seafood Stir-Fry, 126
    Shrimp and Green Beans, 129
    Spicy Stir-Fried Corn, 143
    Tamarind Stir-Fried Chicken with Mushrooms, 103
    Vegetarian Stir-Fry, 137
Sweet-and-Sour Chicken, 110
Sweet-and-Sour Cucumber Salad, 76
Sweet-and-Sour Dipping Sauce, 25
Sweet-and-Sour Vegetables, 251
sweet potatoes. See vegetables/vegetarian dishes

Sweet-Spiced Fried Rice, 168

T
Tamarind Concentrate, 18
Tamarind Dipping Sauce, 273
Tamarind Marinade, 13
Tandoori Chicken, 268
Taro Balls Poached in Coconut Milk, 199
Tea-Smoked Chicken, 240
Thai Fries, 45
Thailand, about, v–viii, 93, 125, 134, 140, 156, 171, 190
tofu/tofu dishes. See also vegetables/vegetarian dishes
    Curried Rice Noodles with Tofu and Egg, 162
    Fried Tofu with Dipping Sauces, 52
    Hot Noodles with Tofu, 245
    Japanese Eggplant with Tofu, 144
    Tofu with Sweet Ginger (dessert), 200
tomatoes, peeling, 70
Tom Ka Kai (soup), 57
Tom Yum (soup), 56
Tuscan herb grill, 229

V
vegetables/vegetarian dishes. See also asparagus; broccoli; cauliflower; eggplant; green beans; pumpkin; salads; tofu/tofu dishes
    about, ix, 65
    5-Spiced Vegetables, 243
    Asian Carrot Sticks, 212
    Asian Grilled Vegetables, 139
    Asian Ratatouille, 231
    crudités, Ginger-Lemongrass Vinaigrette for, 29
    Curried Rice, 176
    Dill Rice, 178
    Far East Fried Rice, 172
    Flavorful Steamed Rice, 180
    Fragrant Brown Rice, 181
    Fragrant White Rice, 178
    Fried Rice with Tomatoes, 173
    Jalapeño-Lime Vinaigrette over Grilled Vegetables, 29
    Minted Vegetables, 252
    Peninsula Sweet Potatoes, 244
    Pickled Chinese Cabbage, 232
    Sesame Noodles with Veggies, 157
    Southeastern Vegetable Stew, 136
    Spicy Stir-Fried Corn, 143
    Sweet-and-Sour Vegetables, 251
    Thai Fries, 45
    Thai Pickled Vegetables, 138
    Thai-Spiced Guacamole, 215
    Thai-Style Bean Sprouts and Snap Peas, 147

Thai-Style Fried Okra, 145
Thai Vegetable Curry, 134
Tropical Vegetables, 146
Vegetables Poached in Coconut Milk, 135
Vegetarian Fried Rice, 170
Vegetarian Lemongrass Soup, 65
Vegetarian Stir-Fry, 137
Vietnamese dishes
    Chilied Coconut Dipping Sauce, 262
    Chili Sauce, 262
    Happy Pancakes, 256
    Oxtail Soup, 258–259
    Pork Sticks, 254–255
    Vietnamese Bananas (dessert), 261
vinegars, 69
    Chili Vinegar, 18
    Lemon Chili Vinegar, 17
    Thai Vinegar Marinade, 15
Vongerichten, Jean-Georges, 112

W, Y
Watermelon Ice, 198
Wild Rice Soup, Asian-Inspired Chicken and, 216
wine, drinking, with Thai food, 210
woks, x, xiii
Won Tons, Fried, 51
    Yellow Bean Sauce, 9

The EVERYTHING Series!

BUSINESS & PERSONAL FINANCE

Everything® Accounting Book
Everything® Budgeting Book, 2nd Ed.
Everything® Business Planning Book
Everything® Coaching and Mentoring Book, 2nd Ed.
Everything® Fundraising Book
Everything® Get Out of Debt Book
Everything® Grant Writing Book, 2nd Ed.
Everything® Guide to Buying Foreclosures
Everything® Guide to Mortgages
Everything® Guide to Personal Finance for Single Mothers
Everything® Home-Based Business Book, 2nd Ed.
Everything® Homebuying Book, 2nd Ed.
Everything® Homeselling Book, 2nd Ed.
Everything® Human Resource Management Book
Everything® Improve Your Credit Book
Everything® Investing Book, 2nd Ed.
Everything® Landlording Book
Everything® Leadership Book, 2nd Ed.
Everything® Managing People Book, 2nd Ed.
Everything® Negotiating Book
Everything® Online Auctions Book
Everything® Online Business Book
Everything® Personal Finance Book
Everything® Personal Finance in Your 20s & 30s Book, 2nd Ed.
Everything® Project Management Book, 2nd Ed.
Everything® Real Estate Investing Book
Everything® Retirement Planning Book
Everything® Robert's Rules Book, $7.95
Everything® Selling Book
Everything® Start Your Own Business Book, 2nd Ed.
Everything® Wills & Estate Planning Book

COOKING

Everything® Barbecue Cookbook
Everything® Bartender's Book, 2nd Ed., $9.95
Everything® Calorie Counting Cookbook
Everything® Cheese Book
Everything® Chinese Cookbook
Everything® Classic Recipes Book
Everything® Cocktail Parties & Drinks Book
Everything® College Cookbook
Everything® Cooking for Baby and Toddler Book
Everything® Cooking for Two Cookbook
Everything® Diabetes Cookbook
Everything® Easy Gourmet Cookbook
Everything® Fondue Cookbook
Everything® Fondue Party Book
Everything® Gluten-Free Cookbook
Everything® Glycemic Index Cookbook
Everything® Grilling Cookbook
Everything® Healthy Meals in Minutes Cookbook
Everything® Holiday Cookbook
Everything® Indian Cookbook
Everything® Italian Cookbook

Everything® Lactose-Free Cookbook
Everything® Low-Carb Cookbook
Everything® Low-Cholesterol Cookbook
Everything® Low-Fat High-Flavor Cookbook
Everything® Low-Salt Cookbook
Everything® Meals for a Month Cookbook
Everything® Meals on a Budget Cookbook
Everything® Mediterranean Cookbook
Everything® Mexican Cookbook
Everything® No Trans Fat Cookbook
Everything® One-Pot Cookbook
Everything® Pizza Cookbook
Everything® Quick and Easy 30-Minute, 5-Ingredient Cookbook
Everything® Quick Meals Cookbook
Everything® Slow Cooker Cookbook
Everything® Slow Cooking for a Crowd Cookbook
Everything® Soup Cookbook
Everything® Stir-Fry Cookbook
Everything® Sugar-Free Cookbook
Everything® Tapas and Small Plates Cookbook
Everything® Tex-Mex Cookbook
Everything® Thai Cookbook
Everything® Vegetarian Cookbook
Everything® Whole-Grain, High-Fiber Cookbook
Everything® Wild Game Cookbook
Everything® Wine Book, 2nd Ed.

GAMES

Everything® 15-Minute Sudoku Book, $9.95
Everything® 30-Minute Sudoku Book, $9.95
Everything® Bible Crosswords Book, $9.95
Everything® Blackjack Strategy Book
Everything® Brain Strain Book, $9.95
Everything® Bridge Book
Everything® Card Games Book
Everything® Card Tricks Book, $9.95
Everything® Casino Gambling Book, 2nd Ed.
Everything® Chess Basics Book
Everything® Craps Strategy Book
Everything® Crossword and Puzzle Book
Everything® Crossword Challenge Book
Everything® Crosswords for the Beach Book, $9.95
Everything® Cryptic Crosswords Book, $9.95
Everything® Cryptograms Book, $9.95
Everything® Easy Crosswords Book
Everything® Easy Kakuro Book, $9.95
Everything® Easy Large-Print Crosswords Book
Everything® Games Book, 2nd Ed.
Everything® Giant Sudoku Book, $9.95
Everything® Giant Word Search Book
Everything® Kakuro Challenge Book, $9.95
Everything® Large-Print Crossword Challenge Book
Everything® Large-Print Crosswords Book
Everything® Lateral Thinking Puzzles Book, $9.95
Everything® Literary Crosswords Book, $9.95
Everything® Mazes Book
Everything® Memory Booster Puzzles Book, $9.95
Everything® Movie Crosswords Book, $9.95

Everything® Music Crosswords Book, $9.95
Everything® Online Poker Book
Everything® Pencil Puzzles Book, $9.95
Everything® Poker Strategy Book
Everything® Pool & Billiards Book
Everything® Puzzles for Commuters Book, $9.95
Everything® Puzzles for Dog Lovers Book, $9.95
Everything® Sports Crosswords Book, $9.95
Everything® Test Your IQ Book, $9.95
Everything® Texas Hold 'Em Book, $9.95
Everything® Travel Crosswords Book, $9.95
Everything® TV Crosswords Book, $9.95
Everything® Word Games Challenge Book
Everything® Word Scramble Book
Everything® Word Search Book

HEALTH

Everything® Alzheimer's Book
Everything® Diabetes Book
Everything® First Aid Book, $9.95
Everything® Health Guide to Adult Bipolar Disorder
Everything® Health Guide to Arthritis
Everything® Health Guide to Controlling Anxiety
Everything® Health Guide to Depression
Everything® Health Guide to Fibromyalgia
Everything® Health Guide to Menopause, 2nd Ed.
Everything® Health Guide to Migraines
Everything® Health Guide to OCD
Everything® Health Guide to PMS
Everything® Health Guide to Postpartum Care
Everything® Health Guide to Thyroid Disease
Everything® Hypnosis Book
Everything® Low Cholesterol Book
Everything® Menopause Book
Everything® Nutrition Book
Everything® Reflexology Book
Everything® Stress Management Book

HISTORY

Everything® American Government Book
Everything® American History Book, 2nd Ed.
Everything® Civil War Book
Everything® Freemasons Book
Everything® Irish History & Heritage Book
Everything® Middle East Book
Everything® World War II Book, 2nd Ed.

HOBBIES

Everything® Candlemaking Book
Everything® Cartooning Book
Everything® Coin Collecting Book
Everything® Digital Photography Book, 2nd Ed.
Everything® Drawing Book
Everything® Family Tree Book, 2nd Ed.
Everything® Knitting Book
Everything® Knots Book
Everything® Photography Book
Everything® Quilting Book

Everything® Sewing Book
Everything® Soapmaking Book, 2nd Ed.
Everything® Woodworking Book

HOME IMPROVEMENT

Everything® Feng Shui Book
Everything® Feng Shui Decluttering Book, $9.95
Everything® Fix-It Book
Everything® Green Living Book
Everything® Home Decorating Book
Everything® Home Storage Solutions Book
Everything® Homebuilding Book
Everything® Organize Your Home Book, 2nd Ed.

KIDS' BOOKS

All titles are $7.95
Everything® Fairy Tales Book, $14.95
Everything® Kids' Animal Puzzle & Activity Book
Everything® Kids' Astronomy Book
Everything® Kids' Baseball Book, 5th Ed.
Everything® Kids' Bible Trivia Book
Everything® Kids' Bugs Book
Everything® Kids' Cars and Trucks Puzzle and Activity Book
Everything® Kids' Christmas Puzzle & Activity Book
**Everything® Kids' Connect the Dots
Puzzle and Activity Book**
Everything® Kids' Cookbook
Everything® Kids' Crazy Puzzles Book
Everything® Kids' Dinosaurs Book
Everything® Kids' Environment Book
Everything® Kids' Fairies Puzzle and Activity Book
Everything® Kids' First Spanish Puzzle and Activity Book
Everything® Kids' Football Book
Everything® Kids' Gross Cookbook
Everything® Kids' Gross Hidden Pictures Book
Everything® Kids' Gross Jokes Book
Everything® Kids' Gross Mazes Book
Everything® Kids' Gross Puzzle & Activity Book
Everything® Kids' Halloween Puzzle & Activity Book
Everything® Kids' Hidden Pictures Book
Everything® Kids' Horses Book
Everything® Kids' Joke Book
Everything® Kids' Knock Knock Book
Everything® Kids' Learning French Book
Everything® Kids' Learning Spanish Book
Everything® Kids' Magical Science Experiments Book
Everything® Kids' Math Puzzles Book
Everything® Kids' Mazes Book
Everything® Kids' Money Book
Everything® Kids' Nature Book
Everything® Kids' Pirates Puzzle and Activity Book
Everything® Kids' Presidents Book
Everything® Kids' Princess Puzzle and Activity Book
Everything® Kids' Puzzle Book
Everything® Kids' Racecars Puzzle and Activity Book
Everything® Kids' Riddles & Brain Teasers Book
Everything® Kids' Science Experiments Book
Everything® Kids' Sharks Book
Everything® Kids' Soccer Book
Everything® Kids' Spies Puzzle and Activity Book
Everything® Kids' States Book
Everything® Kids' Travel Activity Book
Everything® Kids' Word Search Puzzle and Activity Book

LANGUAGE

Everything® Conversational Japanese Book with CD, $19.95
Everything® French Grammar Book
Everything® French Phrase Book, $9.95
Everything® French Verb Book, $9.95
Everything® German Practice Book with CD, $19.95
Everything® Inglés Book
Everything® Intermediate Spanish Book with CD, $19.95
Everything® Italian Practice Book with CD, $19.95
Everything® Learning Brazilian Portuguese Book with CD, $19.95
Everything® Learning French Book with CD, 2nd Ed., $19.95
Everything® Learning German Book
Everything® Learning Italian Book
Everything® Learning Latin Book
Everything® Learning Russian Book with CD, $19.95
Everything® Learning Spanish Book
Everything® Learning Spanish Book with CD, 2nd Ed., $19.95
Everything® Russian Practice Book with CD, $19.95
Everything® Sign Language Book
Everything® Spanish Grammar Book
Everything® Spanish Phrase Book, $9.95
Everything® Spanish Practice Book with CD, $19.95
Everything® Spanish Verb Book, $9.95
Everything® Speaking Mandarin Chinese Book with CD, $19.95

MUSIC

Everything® Bass Guitar Book with CD, $19.95
Everything® Drums Book with CD, $19.95
Everything® Guitar Book with CD, 2nd Ed., $19.95
Everything® Guitar Chords Book with CD, $19.95
Everything® Harmonica Book with CD, $15.95
Everything® Home Recording Book
Everything® Music Theory Book with CD, $19.95
Everything® Reading Music Book with CD, $19.95
Everything® Rock & Blues Guitar Book with CD, $19.95
Everything® Rock & Blues Piano Book with CD, $19.95
Everything® Songwriting Book

NEW AGE

Everything® Astrology Book, 2nd Ed.
Everything® Birthday Personology Book
Everything® Dreams Book, 2nd Ed.
Everything® Love Signs Book, $9.95
Everything® Love Spells Book, $9.95
Everything® Paganism Book
Everything® Palmistry Book
Everything® Psychic Book
Everything® Reiki Book
Everything® Sex Signs Book, $9.95
Everything® Spells & Charms Book, 2nd Ed.
Everything® Tarot Book, 2nd Ed.
Everything® Toltec Wisdom Book
Everything® Wicca & Witchcraft Book, 2nd Ed.

PARENTING

Everything® Baby Names Book, 2nd Ed.
Everything® Baby Shower Book, 2nd Ed.
Everything® Baby Sign Language Book with DVD
Everything® Baby's First Year Book
Everything® Birthing Book
Everything® Breastfeeding Book

Everything® Father-to-Be Book
Everything® Father's First Year Book
Everything® Get Ready for Baby Book, 2nd Ed.
Everything® Get Your Baby to Sleep Book, $9.95
Everything® Getting Pregnant Book
Everything® Guide to Pregnancy Over 35
Everything® Guide to Raising a One-Year-Old
Everything® Guide to Raising a Two-Year-Old
Everything® Guide to Raising Adolescent Boys
Everything® Guide to Raising Adolescent Girls
Everything® Mother's First Year Book
Everything® Parent's Guide to Childhood Illnesses
Everything® Parent's Guide to Children and Divorce
Everything® Parent's Guide to Children with ADD/ADHD
Everything® Parent's Guide to Children with Asperger's
Syndrome
Everything® Parent's Guide to Children with Asthma
Everything® Parent's Guide to Children with Autism
Everything® Parent's Guide to Children with Bipolar Disorder
Everything® Parent's Guide to Children with Depression
Everything® Parent's Guide to Children with Dyslexia
Everything® Parent's Guide to Children with Juvenile Diabetes
Everything® Parent's Guide to Positive Discipline
Everything® Parent's Guide to Raising a Successful Child
Everything® Parent's Guide to Raising Boys
Everything® Parent's Guide to Raising Girls
Everything® Parent's Guide to Raising Siblings
Everything® Parent's Guide to Sensory Integration Disorder
Everything® Parent's Guide to Tantrums
Everything® Parent's Guide to the Strong-Willed Child
Everything® Parenting a Teenager Book
Everything® Potty Training Book, $9.95
Everything® Pregnancy Book, 3rd Ed.
Everything® Pregnancy Fitness Book
Everything® Pregnancy Nutrition Book
Everything® Pregnancy Organizer, 2nd Ed., $16.95
Everything® Toddler Activities Book
Everything® Toddler Book
Everything® Tween Book
Everything® Twins, Triplets, and More Book

PETS

Everything® Aquarium Book
Everything® Boxer Book
Everything® Cat Book, 2nd Ed.
Everything® Chihuahua Book
Everything® Cooking for Dogs Book
Everything® Dachshund Book
Everything® Dog Book, 2nd Ed.
Everything® Dog Grooming Book
Everything® Dog Health Book
Everything® Dog Obedience Book
Everything® Dog Owner's Organizer, $16.95
Everything® Dog Training and Tricks Book
Everything® German Shepherd Book
Everything® Golden Retriever Book
Everything® Horse Book
Everything® Horse Care Book
Everything® Horseback Riding Book
Everything® Labrador Retriever Book
Everything® Poodle Book
Everything® Pug Book
Everything® Puppy Book

Everything® Rottweiler Book
Everything® Small Dogs Book
Everything® Tropical Fish Book
Everything® Yorkshire Terrier Book

REFERENCE

Everything® American Presidents Book
Everything® Blogging Book
Everything® Build Your Vocabulary Book, $9.95
Everything® Car Care Book
Everything® Classical Mythology Book
Everything® Da Vinci Book
Everything® Divorce Book
Everything® Einstein Book
Everything® Enneagram Book
Everything® Etiquette Book, 2nd Ed.
Everything® Guide to C. S. Lewis & Narnia
Everything® Guide to Edgar Allan Poe
Everything® Guide to Understanding Philosophy
Everything® Inventions and Patents Book
Everything® Jacqueline Kennedy Onassis Book
Everything® John F. Kennedy Book
Everything® Mafia Book
Everything® Martin Luther King Jr. Book
Everything® Philosophy Book
Everything® Pirates Book
Everything® Private Investigation Book
Everything® Psychology Book
Everything® Public Speaking Book, $9.95
Everything® Shakespeare Book, 2nd Ed.

RELIGION

Everything® Angels Book
Everything® Bible Book
Everything® Bible Study Book with CD, $19.95
Everything® Buddhism Book
Everything® Catholicism Book
Everything® Christianity Book
Everything® Gnostic Gospels Book
Everything® History of the Bible Book
Everything® Jesus Book
Everything® Jewish History & Heritage Book
Everything® Judaism Book
Everything® Kabbalah Book
Everything® Koran Book
Everything® Mary Book
Everything® Mary Magdalene Book
Everything® Prayer Book
Everything® Saints Book, 2nd Ed.
Everything® Torah Book
Everything® Understanding Islam Book
Everything® Women of the Bible Book
Everything® World's Religions Book

SCHOOL & CAREERS

Everything® Career Tests Book
Everything® College Major Test Book
Everything® College Survival Book, 2nd Ed.
Everything® Cover Letter Book, 2nd Ed.
Everything® Filmmaking Book
Everything® Get-a-Job Book, 2nd Ed.
Everything® Guide to Being a Paralegal
Everything® Guide to Being a Personal Trainer
Everything® Guide to Being a Real Estate Agent
Everything® Guide to Being a Sales Rep
Everything® Guide to Being an Event Planner
Everything® Guide to Careers in Health Care
Everything® Guide to Careers in Law Enforcement
Everything® Guide to Government Jobs
Everything® Guide to Starting and Running a Catering Business
Everything® Guide to Starting and Running a Restaurant
Everything® Job Interview Book, 2nd Ed.
Everything® New Nurse Book
Everything® New Teacher Book
Everything® Paying for College Book
Everything® Practice Interview Book
Everything® Resume Book, 3rd Ed.
Everything® Study Book

SELF-HELP

Everything® Body Language Book
Everything® Dating Book, 2nd Ed.
Everything® Great Sex Book
Everything® Self-Esteem Book
Everything® Tantric Sex Book

SPORTS & FITNESS

Everything® Easy Fitness Book
Everything® Fishing Book
Everything® Krav Maga for Fitness Book
Everything® Running Book, 2nd Ed.

TRAVEL

Everything® Family Guide to Coastal Florida
Everything® Family Guide to Cruise Vacations
Everything® Family Guide to Hawaii
Everything® Family Guide to Las Vegas, 2nd Ed.
Everything® Family Guide to Mexico
Everything® Family Guide to New England, 2nd Ed.
Everything® Family Guide to New York City, 3rd Ed.
Everything® Family Guide to RV Travel & Campgrounds
Everything® Family Guide to the Caribbean
Everything® Family Guide to the Disneyland® Resort, California Adventure®, Universal Studios®, and the Anaheim Area, 2nd Ed.
Everything® Family Guide to the Walt Disney World Resort®, Universal Studios®, and Greater Orlando, 5th Ed.
Everything® Family Guide to Timeshares
Everything® Family Guide to Washington D.C., 2nd Ed.

WEDDINGS

Everything® Bachelorette Party Book, $9.95
Everything® Bridesmaid Book, $9.95
Everything® Destination Wedding Book
Everything® Father of the Bride Book, $9.95
Everything® Groom Book, $9.95
Everything® Mother of the Bride Book, $9.95
Everything® Outdoor Wedding Book
Everything® Wedding Book, 3rd Ed.
Everything® Wedding Checklist, $9.95
Everything® Wedding Etiquette Book, $9.95
Everything® Wedding Organizer, 2nd Ed., $16.95
Everything® Wedding Shower Book, $9.95
Everything® Wedding Vows Book, $9.95
Everything® Wedding Workout Book
Everything® Weddings on a Budget Book, 2nd Ed., $9.95

WRITING

Everything® Creative Writing Book
Everything® Get Published Book, 2nd Ed.
Everything® Grammar and Style Book, 2nd Ed.
Everything® Guide to Magazine Writing
Everything® Guide to Writing a Book Proposal
Everything® Guide to Writing a Novel
Everything® Guide to Writing Children's Books
Everything® Guide to Writing Copy
Everything® Guide to Writing Graphic Novels
Everything® Guide to Writing Research Papers
Everything® Improve Your Writing Book, 2nd Ed.
Everything® Writing Poetry Book